Philip Howard Colomb, Sir John Frederick Maurice

The great War of 189-

A Forecast. Second Edition

Philip Howard Colomb, Sir John Frederick Maurice

The great War of 189-
A Forecast. Second Edition

ISBN/EAN: 9783337114688

Printed in Europe, USA, Canada, Australia, Japan

Cover: Foto ©ninafisch / pixelio.de

More available books at **www.hansebooks.com**

THE GREAT WAR OF 189—

THE BOMBARDMENT OF VARNA.

'A black mass of some kind was seen to drop from the Russian balloon; as it reached the level of tallest buildings it suddenly exploded, its course being marked by crashing buildings and falling ruins.'

Frontispiece.

THE
GREAT WAR OF 189—

A FORECAST

BY

REAR-ADMIRAL P. COLOMB
COLONEL J. F. MAURICE, R.A., CAPTAIN F. N. MAUDE
ARCHIBALD FORBES, CHARLES LOWE
D. CHRISTIE MURRAY AND F. SCUDAMORE

WITH NUMEROUS ILLUSTRATIONS FROM SKETCHES
SPECIALLY MADE FOR 'BLACK AND WHITE'
BY F. VILLIERS

LONDON
WILLIAM HEINEMANN
1895

NOTE.

The following narrative appeared originally in the pages of *Black and White*, the work being the outcome of consultations between some of the most eminent authorities upon modern warfare and international politics. The story has been carefully revised, and is now reprinted in response to a general wish that it should be available in a convenient form.

CONTENTS

	PAGE
Attempted Assassination of Prince Ferdinand of Bulgaria,	1
Russian Movement upon the Austrian Frontier,	26
Interview between General Caprivi and the French Ambassador,	30
Departure of Troops to the East,	32
Banquet in the Schloss,	33
Ill-treatment of a War-correspondent by the German Hussars,	37
The Austrian Plan of Campaign,	40
First Collision of Russian and German Troops,	43
Warlike Excitement in Paris,	44
Declaration of War by France,	52
The German Plan of Campaign,	61
The French Plan of Campaign,	65
Public Feeling of England,	66
Battle at Alexandrovo,	71
Occupation of Alexandrovo by the Germans,	74
Capture of Czenstochau by Prince George of Saxony,	76
Night Attack by the Russians,	78
Repulse of the German Army,	85
Excitement in Brussels,	86
The Meeting of the Four Fleets,	92
Retreat of French Cruisers,	96
On Board the Flagship,	99
Preparations for the Landing of British Troops at Trebizonde,	102
Repulse of the Russians,	106
The Russo-German Campaign—Great Battle at Skierniwice,	110
Italy mobilises her Army, and takes the Field against France,	121
The Council of War,	124
Italian Route—Through the Riviera,	126
Battle of Costebelle,	129
The Landing at Trebizonde,	132
Mobilisation of the First Army Corps,	138
Russia declares War against England,	147
Declaration of War in London,	148

Contents.

	PAGE
The Position of Affairs,	158
Preparations in the Mediterranean Fleet,	160
The Battle of Sardinia,	165
The Franco-German Campaign—Cavalry Engagement near Ligny,	171
Engagement at Vaux Champagne,	178
The Battle of Machault,	184
The War in the far East—The Capture of Vladivostock,	193
Events in the East of Europe,	199
Arrival of British Troops in the Sea of Marmora,	201
Feeling in Australia,	206
Instructions from the Admiralty,	211
The Franco-German Campaign—The German Advance,	213
Advance of the Second and Third Armies on Paris,	221
The March upon the French Capital,	223
British Campaign in Bulgaria,	225
The Bombardment of Varna,	228
Rout of the Russian Army,	234
The Battle of Kosluji,	236
Enthusiasm in Cairo,	241
French Intrigues in Egypt,	248
Fierce Battle near Wady Halfa,	252
The Franco-German Campaign—Rescue of Paris,	258
Advance of General de Galliffet,	262
Brisk Cavalry Engagement,	265
Great Victory of the French,	267
The General Situation,	274
Capture of Sierra Leone by the French,	279
Siege of Herat,	281
Dispatch of Troops by the Canadian Pacific Railway to India,	282
Cessation of Hostilities—France and Germany,	287
England and Russia,	289
The Services of England,	293
General Effects of the War,	295

APPENDIX.

Sir Charles Tupper on Imperial Defence,	299
An Interview with the Right Hon. Sir Charles Dilke,	303

LIST OF ILLUSTRATIONS

	PAGE
The Bombardment of Varna, ... *Frontispiece*	
The Attempted Assassination of Prince Ferdinand of Bulgaria, . .	11
M. Stambuloff, Prime Minister of Bulgaria, appointed Regent after the attempted Assassination of Prince Ferdinand, . . .	13
The Bulgarian Mobilisation—Troops marching through the streets of Philippopolis, ...	15
The Servo-Bulgarian Campaign—Through Pirot to the Front, . . .	17
An Affair of Outpost—The First Shot in the Servo-Bulgarian Campaign,	19
The Occupation of Belgrade—'Here at Last!'	21
With the Turks: Admiral Woods Pacha's Fleet of Torpedo Boats steaming through the Bosphorus, ...	24
Russian Infantry Landing at Varna, ...	25
The Knights of Malta at Ambulance Work, ...	41
Extraordinary Scene in the Place de la Concorde: The Mob tearing the Mourning Emblems from the Statue of Strasburg, . . .	47
The Naval Battle off Dantzig—The Sinking of a Russian Torpedo Boat and Rescue of the Crew by an English Yacht, ...	58
The Naval Battle off Dantzig—Wounded Russians on Board the English Yacht, ...	60
A Scene in the House of Commons—Sir William Harcourt questions the Government, ...	68
British Troops in the Place Verte, Antwerp, ...	88
Sinking of the Yacht 'Elaine,'	97
British Troops landing at Trebizonde, ...	103
The Storming of Skierniwiçe, ...	119
Italian Artillery crossing the Mont Cenis, ...	128
Lord Salisbury addressing the House of Lords on the Question of Peace and War, ...	134

List of Illustrations

	PAGE
The Mobilisation of the English Army—Troops marching through the Dock Gates, Portsmouth,	139
Reserve Men served with the New Magazine-Rifle, and off to the front to-morrow,	143
Reading the Mobilisation Order,	145
Declaration of War against Russia from the Steps of the Royal Exchange,	149
Calling Out the Volunteers—Parade of the Signallers of the St. Martin's Le Grand Corps,	155
Our Correspondent at the Battle of Vaux Champagne,	180
The Battle of Machault: The German Cavalry charging the Rallying Squares of the French,	186
The Taking of Vladivostock: Goorkas Protecting the Guns,	197
British Transports passing the Dardanelles: Fort Chanak saluting the English Ships,	202
The Sultan, Lord Wolseley, and Sir Clare Ford watching the Passage of the British Fleet through the Bosphorus from the Steps of the Dolma Baghtche Palace,	205
German Cavalry Attack by Night on the French Bivouacs,	220
Scene in the Streets of Rheims: German Troops clearing the Streets of French Rioters,	222
The Battle of Kosluji: Sir Evelyn Wood's Attack on the Russian Forces,	238
Map of the Fight near Varna,	239
Scene outside Shepheard's Hotel, Cairo: Tommy Atkins about to quit Egypt,	243
Soudanese Attack upon a Reconnoitring Party,	254
French Cavalry charging the Prussian Infantry,	270
Our New Route to India: A Sleeping-Car on the Canadian Pacific Railway,	283
Tommy Atkins bargaining with the Indians on the Canadian Pacific Railway,	285
Our New Route to India: Rations on the Canadian and Pacific Railway,	286
Sir Charles Tupper in his Private Office in Victoria Street, Westminster,	300
The Right Hon. Sir Charles Dilke,	304

THE GREAT WAR OF 189—

THE GREAT WAR OF 189—

A FORECAST.

In the following narrative an attempt is made to forecast the course of events preliminary and incidental to the Great War which, in the opinion of military and political experts, will probably occur in the immediate future. The writers, who are well-known authorities on international politics and strategy, have striven to derive material for their description of the conflict from the best sources, to conceive the most probable campaigns and acts of policy, and generally to give to their work the verisimilitude and actuality of real warfare.

ATTEMPTED ASSASSINATION OF PRINCE FERDINAND OF BULGARIA.

FULL ACCOUNT OF THE MURDEROUS ASSAULT; CRITICAL CONDITION OF THE WOUNDED PRINCE.

(*By Telegraph from our Own Correspondent, Mr. Francis Scudamore.*)

CONSTANTINOPLE, *Sunday, April* 3 (*viâ* VARNA).
Noon.

A REPORT has been current here since a late hour last evening, to the effect that an attempt has been made to assassinate Prince Ferdinand of Bulgaria, at a mining town named Samakoff, about forty miles south of Sofia. It is said that the Prince, who had been shooting in the Balabancha Balkans, was driving into Samakoff towards evening yesterday, when his carriage was stopped, and he was attacked by a number of men armed with knives and pistols. The Prince's attendants succeeded in saving their master's life and in beating off some and capturing others of his assailants, but not before His Highness had been severely wounded.

Prince Ferdinand was carried into the house of an American missionary resident in Samakoff, where he now lies. His Highness's condition is serious, and is rendered the more critical from the fact that there is no very adequate surgical aid obtainable in Samakoff, and it was necessary to telegraph for doctors to Sofia and Philippopolis.

The greatest excitement reigns in Constantinople since the receipt of this intelligence, and very grave anxiety is expressed in diplomatic circles as to the possible consequences of this terrible misfortune.

Editorial Comments.

It is impossible to overrate the grave significance of this attempted assassination at Samakoff, which in the light of our Correspondent's telegrams would seem to be the prelude to very serious complications in the East. It is, of course, too early to estimate its influence upon general European politics, but we are quite within reason in saying that the dramatic incident may prove to have endangered the peace of Europe. We have long familiarised ourselves with the thought that the Great War of which the world has been in constant dread for some years back, and which is to re-adjust the balance of the Continent, is much more likely to break out in the region of the Danube than on the banks of the Rhine, and the incident at Samakoff may well precipitate the catastrophe. The situation is most perilous, and it is to be hoped that strenuous endeavours will be made by the Powers to chain up the 'dogs of war,' and spare this dying century, at least, the spectacle of their release. Since the Treaty of Berlin patched up the last serious disturbance in Europe, there has been peace; peace, it is true; but a peace subject to perpetual menace, and weighty matter for the consideration of statesmen. Europe has lived, as it were, in armed camps, neutral and watchful; and all the time the nations have prepared against war as though war were at their doors. The dastardly outrage at Samakoff comes at a sorry time.

For we repeat our firm conviction, based on long and close attention to the political motives at work among the nations, that it is on the Danube and not on the Rhine that the torch of war will first be kindled. To a pessimist, indeed, if not to an unbiassed observer, we may well seem of late to have been drawing nearer and nearer to a general war. The world has never been afflicted with more persistent rumours of war. No single day has passed without bringing us its perturbing crop of tremors and apprehensions about the stability of the European peace. From week to week the Jewish speculators on all the Bourses of Christendom have been robbed of their sleep, and, worse still, of their dividends, by telegrams as to the secret massing of troops on this or that frontier, and of ruinous uprisings in various subject and down-trodden countries. Now it is the Black Sea Treaty that is going to be forcibly robbed of its entire Dardanelles clauses, and again the Bargain of Berlin is about to be perforated, for the sixth time, by the sword-point of the Czar. Then the Roumanians wake up to find the Russians beginning to hem them in on three sides; while, again, newspaper readers are horrified by a revelation of the rapacious passions which some dignify by the title of 'principle of nationality,' and others denounce as criminal 'lust of land,' that are on the verge of outbreak at Athens and Sofia, at St. Petersburg, at Belgrade, at Vienna, at Paris, and even at Rome.

Where is the wisdom of highly-placed men like the German Emperor and his new Chancellor assuring the world, in addresses from the throne and after-dinner speeches, that the peace of Europe was never more assured than at present, and that the political horizon is without a cloud even of the size of Elijah's ominous and initial speck of vapour? What is the truth or the wisdom of such assurances, when the thorn of Alsace-Lorraine is still sticking in the flesh of the unforgiving and revengeful French; when Italy still has some territory 'unredeemed;' when Denmark still harbours a deep grudge against her truculent despoiler; when even the peaceful Swedes, who are still animated by the spirit of the Great Gustavus, long to free their former subjects, the Finns, from the tyrannical mastery of the Russians; when the Spaniards would gladly profit by a European complication—even if they shrank from the thought of an audacious *coup de main*—to repossess themselves of Gibraltar; when the Portuguese, following suit, would never hesitate to kick their British rival in Africa, if they deemed him to be down; when the Cretans, egged on by the Greeks, are firmly resolved to throw off the galling yoke of the Turks; when ex-ministers like M. Tricoupis stump about the Balkan Peninsula, openly preaching Pan-hellenism and Balkan Federation against the advocates of disunited nationalities; when the Servians secretly vow to settle up old scores with their Bulgarian vanquishers, and when these Bulgarian victors themselves, with their Prime Minister more than their Prince at their head, are sternly determined to be free and independent alike of Sultan and of Czar; when Austria continues to cast longing eyes in the direction of Salonica; and when, above all things, the Colossus of the North, with his head pillowed on snow, and his feet swathed in flowers of the sunny South, has sworn by the soul of his assassinated and sainted father that he will ever remain true to the intention of his sire in exacting a solid equivalent of power, prestige, and territorial foothold on the Balkan Peninsula for all the blood and treasure spent by Russia in the task of 'liberating' the Bulgarians; when all these things, all these slumbering passions and meditated schemes of aggression and revenge are duly considered, how is it possible for any one, be he sovereign or subject, to lull the world asleep by false assurances of peace which is sooner or later doomed to be broken?

The Triple Alliance will no more succeed in terrorising the souls of all these secret plotters and designers, and in giving them pause, than three inter-locked mountain oaks or firs could stay the downward course of an extended series of separate avalanches, which rend away with them pines, and oaks, and all, in their resistless rush. But has the avalanche, which we thus dread, really and truly at last begun to move? We sincerely trust not, but for the present at least, the omens in the East have an exceedingly ugly and alarming look, and we shall await the arrival of further telegrams with the greatest anxiety. The Triple Alliance is not an embankment that can bar the advancing flood of war, but rather a detached fortress which must itself soon incur the danger of being surrounded and even submerged by the rushing, whirling waters of European strife. Though the parties to this three-cornered pact have agreed to place their fire-engines, so to speak, at each other's disposal in the event of external danger from fire to their respective domiciles, it is beyond the reach of these Powers to prevent the outbreak of a conflagration, from accident or arson, among the rickety, wind-swept, and thatch-roofed mansions of their neighbours; nor is there any fact better established in connection with fires than that they are used by thieves and anarchists for the purpose of sudden plunder and disorder, at once upon the persons and property of the victims and beholders of such catastrophes.

Let us suppose, for example, that as a consequence of this most alarming incident at Samakoff, hostilities should ensue between Russia and Austria, the former being the aggressor. In that case Germany—in virtue of her published Treaty with the Hapsburg Monarchy—would almost immediately have to take the field. Now, in such a contingency, is there not a grave danger that France, seizing the golden opportunity for which she has so long been waiting, would at once mobilise her army, and march the greater part of it towards the Rhine? And is it not certain that the immediate result of such a revengeful step on her part would be that Italy, true likewise to her Treaty engagement with Germany, would make haste to spring upon the flank of the Republic?

It is not well to forecast evils, but at the same time it is well to look clearly ahead. We know surely enough the real nature of the feelings with which the Bulgarians are regarded by their 'Liberators,' just as we are equally cognisant of the true character of those who profess to be the Sultan's 'friends,' and who, with the privilege of most intimate amity, have repeatedly helped themselves to disintegrating slices of his dominions. We need not remind our readers of the bitterness which still rankles in the breasts of the Roumanians at the memory of the manner in which they were 'rewarded' for services rendered at the Gravitza Redoubt and elsewhere during the war against the Turks; a bitterness which was only equalled by the rage of the Russians when they recognised the supreme folly of their conduct in forcing Roumania to accept the Dobrudja in exchange for Bessarabia, and thus depriving themselves of a *pied à terre* and strategical base of operations south of the Danube, in the direction of the grand goal of their ultimate ambition—the Golden Horn. It is as much the desire of Russia to undo this unfortunate bargain as it is to shake herself free from the intolerable shackles that restrain her liberty of action in the Black Sea, and seal up the outlets thereof against her ships of war. Russia is only awaiting a proper opportunity for accomplishing these two other stages in what she deems to be her destiny (and does not everything come to him who can wait?) just as she continues to pursue her anti-English policy in Central Asia with steady, disdainful, unresisted strides, ever lessening the distance between her own frontiers and those of India, and thus paving the way for the execution of her policy of preventing the forces of England from being thrown into the balance should any complication arise in the East of Europe. 'And ever,' as Tennyson sang, 'upon the topmost roof the banner of England blew;' but that proud banner has now, at last, been blown away by Cossack colonels from the topmost roof of all—the 'Roof of the World' itself, thus enabling Russia to overpeer our very Indian plains, and thence despatch her Calebs and her Joshuas to spy out this other land of promise.

It may be quite true—and, indeed, from all we know of the character of the Czar, we think it is quite true—that Alexander III. has a holy horror of war, into which he is determined not to plunge his people; and we have been assured by the greatest master of modern war, the late Count Moltke, that the period of dynastic conflicts, or struggles resulting from the personal passions and petulance of rulers, has come to an end, and been succeeded by wars between peoples and nations. This is also quite true; but it is precisely herein that the greatest danger lurks. For a ruler —as witness the case of the present Czar's own father—may prove too weak to restrain or deflect the set of the popular tide, and be plunged into a war against his own will. It is also conceivable that the French Government might find it impossible to resist the clamours of the Chamber to embrace the first opportunity—and what could be a better one than a general European conflagration? for ousting the English from Egypt—an object which all good Frenchmen deeply have at heart. But it is on the Balkan Peninsula, where there are no rulers or restraining influences to speak of, that popular passions and aspirations must enjoy most unbridled sway; and therefore it is that we look with anxiety for the further development of this tragic event at Samakoff, which has already thrown the Balkan countries into a state of wild excitement, and all Europe into a fit of ever-increasing alarm.

(*By Telegraph from our Special Correspondent, Mr. Francis Scudamore.*)

PHILIPPOPOLIS, *April* 4.

(*Sunday Night.*) I date this message from Philippopolis, whence indeed it will be despatched on our arrival there tomorrow; but, as a matter of fact, it is written in the sleeping car of a special train by which I am travelling to Ichtiman *en route* for Samakoff, in company with Drs. Patterson, Stekoulis, and Lelongt, who have been invited by telegraph to meet their Bulgarian colleagues in consultation at the bedside of the wounded Prince. It is to these gentlemen's courtesy that I owe the privilege of my passage.

I am enabled, by the kindness of my friends at the United States Legation, which, as is natural in the circumstances, has received minute information as to the occurrence, to give you a fuller and more authentic account of the Samakoff tragedy of yesterday by which Prince Ferdinand of Bulgaria so nearly lost his life, than is likely to have been transmitted as yet, and of which no doubt garbled first reports have already thrown consternation into every European capital. I have already stated that it is in the house of an American missionary that Prince Ferdinand is at present lying. I must now explain that Samakoff, which is nestled in the heart of a picturesque valley formed by the rough triangle of the Kilo Dagh, the Kadir Téré, and the De mir Kapou Dagh at the head of the Balabancha range of Balkans, is not only one of the wealthiest towns in the principality,—thanks to the iron mines by which it is surrounded,—but is also famous and dear to Bulgarians by reason of the presence there of the American Mission School, whose principals rendered such devoted and signal service to the oppressed Christians throughout the terrible time of the massacres of 1876 and the war of 1877. At that time, when, as will be remembered, to be a Bulgarian was all-sufficient reason for being summarily hanged (if a man), or foully outraged (if a woman), the principal of the school and his courageous wife snatched many victims from the gallows, and rescued from a terrible fate, by harbouring in the mission-house, numerous young girls and children, fugitives from the devastated villages of the Balkan slopes. And when brighter days dawned for Bulgaria, and it became a principality, the services of the American Mission at Samakoff were not forgotten. It became a custom, inaugurated by Prince Alexander and studiously maintained by his successor, for the Ruler of Bulgaria to visit Samakoff in an informal manner once or twice a year, for the purpose of inspecting the mission school and complimenting its directors.

The snows which have held Samakoff isolated from the rest of the world throughout the past four months, are now just melted, and thus it chanced that Prince Ferdinand, who for a week past had been shooting in the hills around Philippopolis, decided to pay his first visit of the year to the missionaries of Samakoff, and had, unfortunately as it turns out, announced his intention of so doing.

The Prince, with this purpose in view, left Philippopolis on Friday evening, passing the night in his sleeping-car, and yesterday morning started in a *calèche* from Ichtiman-i-Vakarel, formerly the boundary between Bulgaria and the province of Eastern Roumelia, to drive to the little township in the mountains.

His Highness has usually been accompanied on these visits by one or other of the ministers, but on this occasion, owing partly, no doubt, to his hurriedly-formed plans, he had with him only one of the aides-de-camp who had been of the shooting-party. The Prince's carriage was preceded by half-a-dozen mounted guards, and followed by a like number, as an escort. This is a precaution which Prince Ferdinand's advisers have prevailed with him, much against his will, to adopt of late, in view of the renewed activity of Russian agents and sedition-mongers throughout the Principality and the neighbouring States, where, indeed, a great anti-Bulgarian and anti-Turkish propaganda has been actively carried on for the past year; and in view also of the growing apprehension of his advisers that the recent success in this city of assassins in Russian pay, coupled with the immunity from punishment which the Czar's representatives have shown their ability and readiness to secure for them, would prompt the conspirators, soon or late, to fly at higher game than either M. Stambuloff or the late Dr. Vulkovitch. That his Highness's advisers were in the right has been proved by the attempt of yesterday. The event, however, may be said to offer encouragement at once to would-be regicides and to their intended victims, inasmuch as it has been shown yet once again to the former, how useless as a protection against assassins is the presence of an armed escort, and to the latter, how apt is a well-matured plot to be frustrated by a commonplace accident.

The Prince's carriage was expected to reach Samakoff about noon, and shortly before that hour a considerable number of persons had collected in the main street, while small crowds had gathered round the gates of the Prefecture and about the door of the American Mission-house, which is situated in a side street leading off the high road, and where the usual modest preparations had been made for the princely visit.

His Highness, on arrival, after halting for a moment or two at the gate of the Prefecture where he did not alight, drove on through the town towards the Mission-house. At the moment when the carriage turned the corner into the narrower street, a man wearing the long black gown and brimless stovepipe hat of a priest of the orthodox church stood forward from the crowd, in which were several other persons dressed as he was, and, raising a revolver, took deliberate aim at his Highness. And then occurred the accident to which, in all probability, Prince Ferdinand owes his life. The cartridge did not explode. The sham priest lowered his weapon slightly, raised it once more, and again pulled the trigger; but as he did so the pistol barrel was struck up—the ball burying itself in the wall of a house across the street—and the assassin was seized and firmly held by many willing hands.

The whole occurrence had taken but a moment. The Prince, when he saw the pistol levelled at him, had leapt to his feet, with the evident intention of thowing himself upon his murderer. As it was, his Highness's intervention seemed very necessary on behalf of the baffled assassin, who stood in no small danger of being lynched incontinently by his furious captors.

The carriage had stopped; the escort was hastily dismounting, and the Prince, shouting orders to the people to spare their prisoner's life, had alighted, and turning, was in the act of throwing his heavy pelisse to his companion, when sudden as thought a second ruffian sprang from amid the vociferating mob, hurled himself upon the Prince, and thrusting a great, broad-bladed Circassian *khanga* into his bosom, was away and out of sight almost before any of the bystanders had recovered from this second shock of horror and surprise.

His Highness, who had sunk to the ground under the blow, though he did not lose consciousness, was at once carried into the Mission-house, distant a few yards only, and very speedily all the best medical advice obtainable in Samakoff was at hand, while telegrams for further assistance were at once despatched to Sofia and to Philippópolis, the latter place being perhaps more rapidly accessible than the capital. The first examination of the wound showed that the broad knife had turned on the point of a rib—very fortunately—and had therefore missed, by a hair's-breadtht the envelope of the heart. It was not till to-day that a persisten, recurrence of internal hæmorrhage aroused the gravest fears of the Prince's surgeons, and prompted them to appeal to Constantinople for further advice.

The pretended priest, when searched, was found to be costumed beneath his robes in the ordinary dress of the petty trader of the

THE ATTEMPTED ASSASSINATION OF PRINCE FERDINAND OF BULGARIA.

towns here. His long flowing locks proved a wig, and his thick unkempt beard was also false. Upon him, among other papers said to be of great importance, but as to which I know nothing, was found a passport issued by the Russian Consulate at Odessa no less recently than last month, and bearing the *visé* of the Russian Chancellor at Sofia. The passport is made out in the name of Ivan Bendukdjieff, and belongs, the fellow avows, to a man, a stranger to him, who left it with him by mistake a week ago. But the authorities entertain few doubts as to the scoundrel's identity with one of the men implicated with Shishmanoff in the recent murder of Dr. Vulkovitch.

I have said that the news of this dastardly attempt on Prince Ferdinand's life caused the greatest excitement in Constantinople. There is indeed no doubt that both the Palace and the Porte are very seriously alarmed, as, in view of the Sultan's disgraceful action in the Vulkovitch affair, it is only just they should be. It is significant of his Majesty's state of mind that, when early this (Sunday) morning, first the French and then the Russian Ambassador drove to the residence of the Grand Vizier, they were unable to see him, orders having been sent from Yildiz ordering the Pasha not to receive them. Sir Clare Ford, on the other hand, had a long interview with the Sultan this morning.

PHILIPPOPOLIS, *April* 4.

When the train steamed into the station here, I learned in the restaurant, where every one was eagerly discussing the events of the past two days, that the second assassin was captured yesterday afternoon at Banja, as the result of an order widely circulated by both telegraph and horse messengers throughout the country, calling upon all Tchorbadjis, or headmen of villages, to detain any stranger found within their jurisdiction, and at once communicate with the nearest central authority. The man has been identified as one Nicholi Nāoum, a very well-known character who, besides being suspected of participation in the murder, last spring, of M. Beltcheff, is known to have been acting for the past six months as a revolutionary agent on the Macedonian frontier. Nāoum, who, as leader of a gang of border brigands, has gained a bloody notoriety in connection with various dastardly outrages against society, is believed to have been recently engaged in distributing arms and ammunition among Macedonian villages, and in inciting the Macedonians to molest the Bulgarians dwelling among them. Nāoum, when arrested, was found to be provided, like his accomplice, with a Russian passport executed in regular form. He was immediately carried back to Samakoff and confronted with Bendukdjieff, against whom he at once began to rail as a bungler, making no attempt to exonerate himself, or to deny his share in the tragedy. In this course, perhaps, he was guided by the knowledge that his life was already forfeited for many atrocious crimes before he set his hand against Prince Ferdinand. As a consequence of his last

M. STAMBULOFF
Prime Minister of Bulgaria, appointed Regent after the attempted assassination of Prince Ferdinand.

admission of guilt, a very brief trial was necessary, and the two wretches were hanged this morning outside the house in which they had lodged on Friday night in Samakoff.

The Prince is apparently doing well. M. Stambuloff, who, on receipt of news of the disaster, hurried to his master's bedside, remained but one hour in Samakoff, during which time, despite the doctors, the Prince insisted on seeing him, and **returned direct to Sofia**. **Late on** Saturday **night**, at a meeting attended by most of the Ministers, hurriedly convened, he was declared Regent during the serious illness of **the Prince, and for such time** as might be necessary, and the formal **proclamation in** accordance with this decision was issued yesterday **morning.**

Sofia, *April* 6.

Instead of accompanying Dr. Patterson and his colleagues on a, to me, fruitless expedition to Samakoff, I bid them good-bye at Ichtiman, where they left the train, and came on here. As might be expected, I have found this city boiling with tumultuous emotions, and not only—though that were sufficient cause—on account of the outrageous attempt on Prince Ferdinand's life.

It appears that the Cabinet has received news of the greatest importance from the Macedonian frontier. The assiduous efforts of Russian agents, who have been actively engaged for the past six months or more not only in the provinces itself, but also in the Greek and Montenegrin borders, in fomenting an anti-Bulgarian rising, are now on the eve of being crowned with success. Already reports have reached the capital of disturbances, caused apparently by raids made across the border at Petrovich and Melnik. That there is a great shifting of troops at present in progress as a result of this intelligence, is not denied. It is said, indeed, though I cannot as yet tell with what truth, that a half division has been ordered to Petrovich, and another like force to Strumnitza. The latest rumour here is to the effect that the movement in Macedonia is as much anti-Turkish as anti-Bulgarian, and that Turkey is also despatching a large military force to Salonika. If this report be true, it is surely an instance of the irony of fate. In this country it is a matter of common talk that any anti-Bulgarian movement in Macedonia is mainly due to the attitude of Zuknir Pasha, the Vali of Salonika, towards the large Bulgarian element of the population of the province under his control. This functionary's persistent ill-treatment of Bulgarians has been very frequently re-

THE BULGARIAN MOBILISATION—TROOPS MARCHING THROUGH THE STREETS OF PHILIPPOPOLIS.

presented to the Porte in notes from this capital as being contrary at once to the interests of Turkey and of Bulgaria. The Principality, it has been said, has consistently refused to take side with those who seek the dismemberment of Turkey, and has claimed a right to expect that the development of the Bulgarian element in Macedonia would not be crushed by Pashas who, by their arbitrary actions, paralyse the intentions of the central government, and prepare the way for events which had better, in the common interest, be avoided. It is needless to say these sensible warnings have been altogether disregarded by the Porte, with the present inevitable result.

It is further rumoured here—for the place is full of suspicion—that in view of certain movements of Servian troops, a large Bulgarian force has been hurriedly thrown forward to strengthen the troops at Radomir, Trn, and Zaribrod.

SOFIA, *April* 8.

The latest reports as to Prince Ferdinand are more favourable than could have been hoped for. The dangerous symptoms have subsided. Internal hæmorrhage has been checked. The Prince sleeps and takes nourishment, and his pulse and temperature are satisfactory. Hopes are held out that in a week's time His Highness may be moved from Samakoff. Meanwhile, during the past few days, events have marched so rapidly that people here are prepared for almost any eventuality. There is no longer any attempt to conceal the movements of Servian troops. Great numbers of men are already massed at Nisch and Vranja, and at points on the line of railway between Nisch and Pirot. The main body of the Servian army has its headquarters at Knuzevatz. From Belgrade, we learn of the steady despatch of war material and siege-train to Negotin on the frontier against Widdin, and a telegram from the same source announces the arrival at Nisch of a train of the Red Cross Society, consisting of eighteen carriages furnished with all the necessary equipment for active service.

News from Constantinople is to the effect that the Porte, alarmed at the aspect of affairs in Macedonia, has, in addition to the calling out of the last class of rediffs, decided on the formation of five new Army Corps. Fresh levies are to be made in order to form a strong reserve. The transport of rediffs, mainly from Smyrna, Skanderoun, and the Tripolitaine, is being carried on on a large scale. Over 27,000 reservists have already passed through Smyrna. Many of the Austrian Lloyd vessels being engaged in the transport of troops to Salonika to guard the frontier line and to reinforce the Bitolia garrison, the Seraskierate is negotiating with

THE SERVO-BULGARIAN CAMPAIGN—THROUGH PIROT TO THE FRONT.

some English shipping companies for additional transport. More than fifty thousand troops are to be employed on the Macedonian border in a line stretching from Mitrovitza on the north, all round to Raslok on the south-east. Their chief stations will be Palanka, with Uskub as base, and Djuma and Neurokoy with Strumdja as base. No further disturbances are reported from the frontier.

M. Stambuloff left here last night to inspect the troops on the frontier. I am, of course, unable to give any information as to their numbers or disposition, but it may be said that Bulgaria is well prepared to resist any attack. It is infringing no rule to say that the Prince's army possesses no fewer than 400 pieces of ordnance of all calibres. The report that his appointment as Regent has met with disapprobation among a large section of the community here is absolutely without foundation.

A trusted agent of the Government has also left here for Berlin, for the purpose, it is understood, of raising a loan in that capital.

SOFIA, *April* 10.

We are now at war, and fighting is going forward even as I write. This morning rifle-shots were exchanged between Servian and Bulgarian patrolling parties on the frontier, near Trn, without result on either side. A body of some 300 Servians then crossed the frontier and advanced about a mile, seeking to cut off a party of fifty Bulgarians, who, however, retreated and escaped. Later on heavy fighting was reported in the neighbourhood of Vlassina. How it originated is immaterial. The Bulgarians lost 17 men killed and 54 wounded. This set fire to the torch all along the frontier line. Some time before the official declaration of war, which, though it announced that hostilities would begin at noon to-day, did not reach the Minister for Foreign Affairs here until nine o'clock this evening, reports had been posted up in the cafés announcing fighting in the vicinity of Planinitza, Beuskedol, Miloslawtzi, Zelene, and Gard, in the Trn district. The Servian Minister, who had twice telegraphed to his Government for instructions during the afternoon, demanded a special train as soon as he had presented the declaration of war, and left half an hour later, under escort, for the frontier.

A solemn *Te Deum* was sung this evening in the Cathedral, M. Stambuloff and the Ministers being present. The streets are crowded—no one shows any intention of going to bed; the popular enthusiasm and confidence are immense, and there is apparently a general sensation of relief at the relaxation of the strain of the past few days, and a feeling of satisfaction that the dastardly attack on the Prince will be promptly avenged. I am, by the way, authorised to state that, by order of Prince Ferdinand's physicians, all news of these exciting events is rigidly withheld from his Highness.

Fresh troops are hourly leaving Sofia and Philippopolis for the front.

At the moment of closing this despatch, news comes of an

AN AFFAIR OF OUTPOSTS—THE FIRST SHOT IN THE SERVO-BULGARIAN CAMPAIGN.

important action near Dragoman, with reported defeat of the Servians with heavy losses.

Sofia *April* 11.

There is to be no more fighting. The brilliant and most sanguinary engagement at Dragoman, which I reported in progress last night, in the course of which the Bulgarians, who were completely successful, drove the enemy back from all their positions on the heights above the pass : an incessant artillery duel, maintained ever since the commencement of hostilities between the heavy Servian batteries before Negotin and the Bulgarian forces garrisoning Widelin, and a very successful unopposed advance along the Vranja road as far as the Morava river by a Bulgarian force, composed of three brigades from Sofia, from Trn, and from Radomir, make up all there is to report of the campaign. For when hostilities were about to be opened this morning near Kumareno, which was evidently held by a large Servian force, an officer bearing a white towel, with a pink fringe, tied to a hedge stake, as a flag of truce, rode out from the Servian lines and demanded a *pourparler*. It then transpired that the Servians found themselves in a terrible quandary, and were at their wits' end what to do.

Late last night a large Austrian force had, without warning, crossed the Save into Belgrade, which city they had taken so completely by surprise that it was not until the morning that the populace was made aware of the presence of the strangers in their midst by the sight of the troops bivouacking in the squares, and the officers quietly breakfasting outside the principal cafés. An Austrian force, said the parlementaire, had also crossed the Danube to Semendria, and there were rumours that another force had crossed the same river at Orsova. In these circumstances, with their capital cut off from them, and their young king and government in a manner locked up, the Servian generals considered they had no alternative but to demand a suspension of hostilities, at least for forty-eight hours. An armistice was therefore granted, much to the Bulgarian leaders' annoyance and disgust.

We learn that Austria has notified the Powers that she has occupied Semendria and Belgrade as a precautionary measure, in view of the wanton aggression of Servia.

It is here considered unlikely that Bulgaria will have any more trouble from this quarter. On the other hand, however, grave rumours reach us from Constantinople, where apparently there is very great anxiety as to certain mysterious and as yet undefined threats by Russia. The Turkish capital is, as matters

THE OCCUPATION OF BELGRADE—'HERE AT LAST!'

stand at present, likely to be the chief centre of interest for some time to come, and I shall therefore return there to-morrow morning.

All through the day long trains of Bulgarian and Servian wounded have crept one after another into Sofia. It is noteworthy that a considerable percentage of the sufferers are bright and lively and make light of their injuries. These are men who have been struck by the small nickel bullets of the new rifle, which has been used in pretty equal proportions on both sides.

CONSTANTINOPLE, *April* 15.

There is no doubt good cause for the grave fears at present agitating Porte and Palace. By his foolishly near-sighted policy of pandering to the wishes of whatsoever Power bullies him with most brutal persistency, at the risk though it be of injuring a friendly State, the Sultan has, as he is beginning to realise, succeeded in alienating, for the moment at least, the sympathies of all his legitimate friends. By his attitude—wilfully perverse and undignified—throughout the varying phases of the Vulkovitch episode, his Majesty has aroused throughout Bulgaria deep distrust of himself, and fierce indignation against his ministers and his methods. The inane and futile strivings of the Porte to throw difficulties in the path of the young Khedive, and to cheat him, if possible, of rights clearly accorded and amply paid for, have produced similar sentiments in Egypt and in England. And having, at the cost of much labour and intrigue, achieved this wholly unsatisfactory position of being an object of contempt, suspicion, and obloquy, the Sultan finds himself suddenly but decidedly thrown over by the very Powers with whom he had sought to curry favour. The Russian Ambassador is now too thoroughly pre-occupied with the immediate policy of his own Government to have any further care to wear gloves in his dealings with the Porte, and his mood has so affected M. Cambon, the French Ambassador, that that astute personage, unable to find those sweet professions and gracious persuasion—half unmeaning promise, half veiled threat with which he has been wont to *dorloter* the

Ministers at Bab Aali—come readily to his tongue, has ceased for a fortnight past to hold any other than mere chancellerie communication with the Turkish Government.

Let it be said at once that, despite very natural indignation, Bulgaria shows every disposition to behave well towards the Suzerain Power. Officially, indeed, her attitude has been in every way admirable. When the Servians opened hostilities, when they declared war, when they asked for an armistice—in every phase, in short, of the quarrel, M. Stambuloff apprised, and asked counsel and aid of, the Sultan. To be sure he got nothing for his pains, but it must have been a satisfaction to the Sultan to receive proof that, in one quarter at any rate, he is not regarded as a European Power of merely sentimental importance.

CONSTANTINOPLE, *April* 16.

Fresh alarm was caused here this morning by the discovery that our telegraphic communication has been interrupted at once with Odessa and with Batoum. All inquiries as to the cause of the rupture made by other routes failed to elicit any explanation. Later in the day a vessel of the Cunard line arrived in the Bosphorus, and her captain has stated that the Russian harbour-master at Odessa is detaining all ships, of whatever nationality, in that port. His own vessel, he says, was the last to leave Odessa, and only got away by a chance, the order having reached him when he had already got under way. He states that there were several Russian ironclads, and quite a fleet of torpedo boats at Odessa, all with steam up, and says that when he was on shore there the day before yesterday the town was full of soldiers, and the approaches to the dockyards crowded with a constantly-increasing mass of guns, horses, ammunition, and other war material.

CONSTANTINOPLE, *April* 18.

I have received a telegram from my correspondent in Sofia, who tells me that the Bulgarian Government understands that the Russians are preparing an expedition for sea at Odessa, and intend to occupy some portion of Bulgarian territory. The Princely Government has reason to expect the attack will be directed against Varna, and has called upon the Sultan to aid Bulgarian arms by sending his fleet to guard the Varna roads. The Sultan has as yet made no reply to this request, says my correspondent, but it is not difficult to guess what His Majesty's action will be, inasmuch as Turkey has no single ship of war in condition to be got to sea under a month at the least, and it is more than questionable whether even then any of the ironclads could be completely manned or provided with serviceable ammunition. There are, indeed, some torpedo boats—unprovided, I understand, with torpedoes—and a

WITH THE TURKS: ADMIRAL WOODS PACHA'S FLEET OF TORPEDO BOATS STEAMING THROUGH THE BOSPHORUS.

couple of the monitors that did some service in the Danube in the last war. If the Admiralty should elect to place these vessels at the service of the Bulgarian Government, they might be of some use as scouts. But that is about all that Turkey can hope to do for her vassal.

Here there is terrible anxiety lest the Russian expedition be directed, not against Varna or Bourgas, but against the Kavaks, and the Seraskierate is busily taking precautions to meet such a contingency with all the forces available.

Despite the recent draining of the Stamboul camp by the despatch of a large force to Salonika, there are still some 45,000 men in and around the capital. These, with the exception of the Sultan's guard of about 15,000 men, have been distributed along the chain of forts extending from Roumelie Kavak to the Golden Horn. The telegraph is kept busily at work summoning troops from all parts of the Empire. 15,000 men from the Adrianople garrison are expected to arrive here to-night.

The Russian Ambassador is said to be ill. He has not left the Embassy in the Grand Rue de Pera for now almost a week, and refuses to receive any one. Even his French colleague found the door closed to him yesterday.

RUSSIAN INFANTRY LANDING AT VARNA.

Constantinople, *April* 19.

A Russian force, variously computed at from 50,000 to 70,000 men, occupied Varna this morning. There was some smart resistance, but the comparatively small Bulgarian force was powerless against the heavy metal of the Russian fleet, and after an hour's fighting was compelled to abandon the position.

Coincident with the receipt of this news is the delivery of a note by the Russian Ambassador—suddenly restored to health—to the Minister for Foreign Affairs, setting forth that, as a result of the extraordinary and uncalled-for position taken up by Austria, the Czar's Government feels the necessity of acquiring a material guarantee for the maintenance of **peace**, and will therefore effect a peaceful occupation of Bourgas and **Varna with that** end in view.

RUSSIAN MOVEMENT UPON THE AUSTRIAN FRONTIER.

MOBILISATION OF GERMAN ARMY CORPS—WILD EXCITEMENT IN BERLIN.

(By Telegraph from our Special Correspondent, Mr. Charles Lowe.)

BERLIN, *April* 21 (8.50 P.M.).

NEVER since the fateful days of **July 1870 has** so much excitement been caused here as by the news—which now seems to be beyond all doubt—that Russia, having received an evasive, **or, as** other telegrams put it, a flatly negative reply to her peremptory demand for **the immediate evacuation of** Belgrade by the Austrians, has already begun to move down immense **masses of** troops towards her south-western frontier; **and** it is even rumoured that a division of cavalry has suddenly made **its** appearance near the border, on the Warsaw-Cracow **road, at a place** called Xiaswielki. This is a grave situation, indeed, **as alarming as** it is sudden. The Unter den Linden, which is a perfect Babel with the bawling voices of the newsvendors, is rapidly filling with crowds rushing hither, as to the main channel of intelligence, from all parts of the city, and the Foreign Office in the Wilhelm-Strasse is besieged by a huge throng clamouring to hear the truth.

For on **this depends the issue** of peace or war for Germany. Let but Russia **lay one** single finger of aggression **on** Austria, and Germany must at once unsheath **her** sword and spring to her ally's aid. Pray let there be no mistake as to the terms of the Austro-German Treaty of 1879, which was published a year or two ago, for it has often been misinterpreted. Under this instrument a *casus fœderis* does not arise for Germany in all and any circumstances of a war between Russia and Austria, but only in the event of the former being the aggressor; and it looks very much as though Russia were now seriously bent on taking the offensive. Does she really mean to do this? is the question on every one's lips here, and the excitement of people is equal to their suspense. It is known that an active correspondence by wire is proceeding between here and Vienna, but the authorities are very reticent, and only beg the crowds to keep calm and hope for the best.

9 P.M.

I have just returned from the Schloss, whither the multitude, which was unable to gratify its curiosity at the Foreign Office, had surged along to pursue its eager inquiries, but only to find that the Emperor was closeted with his Chancellor, General Count von Caprivi, and his Chief of the Staff, Count von Schlieffen. It was remarked that when both these magnates emerged from their interview with His Majesty, and drove off at a rapid rate, they looked very serious and pre-occupied, paying but little heed to the cheering which greeted their appearance. This only tended to deepen the apprehension of the vast crowd in front of the Schloss, whose fears were further augmented by a rumour (a true one, as I found on tracing it to its source), which spread like lightning, that the Emperor had telegraphed for the King of Saxony, Prince Albrecht of Prussia, Prince-Regent of Brunswick—both Field-Marshals—as also for Count Waldersee, Commander of the Ninth Army Corps in Schleswig-Holstein, whom the Emperor, it may be remembered, when parting with this distinguished officer, as Chief of the General Staff, publicly designated as the Commander of a whole army in the event of war.

10 P.M.

After despatching my last message, which I had the utmost difficulty in doing owing to the frantic mass of newspaper correspondents of all nationalities struggling desperately into and out of the Telegraph Office, I had the good fortune to meet Baron von Marschall, the amiable and accomplished Foreign Secretary, who favoured me with a brief conversation on the momentous subject of the hour. Yes, he said, it was unfortunately quite true that the Russians were rapidly concentrating their forces towards the Austro-German frontier, and that a sotnia of prying Cossacks, coming from Tarnogrod, had even pushed forward on the Austrian side of the border towards Jaroslav, an important railway junction point in Galicia. He had just received intelligence to this effect from Prince Reuss, the German Ambassador in Vienna, who added that things indeed looked their very worst. 'But this,' I remarked, 'is an act of invasion on the part of Russia, is it not, and means war?' The Baron shook his head ominously, and, with a kindly 'come and see me again to-morrow morning,' squeezed my hand and hurried off to see Count Syéchényi at the Austrian Embassy, which stands over against the former home of M. Benedetti, with all its associations connected with the beginning of Germany's last great war.

On my way back to the Telegraph Office, where I write this, I encountered, just at the entrance to the Russian Embassy, Unter den Linden, its genial and honest occupant, Count Schouvaloff, who was good enough to return my greeting by motioning me to stop, and telling me that he had just been to see Count Caprivi, and assure him, on the part of his Imperial master, that all these warlike preparations in Western Poland implied no menace whatever to Germany, with whom Russia had not the least cause of quarrel, but that, nevertheless, so long as Austria threatened to derange the balance of power in the Balkan Peninsula for her own selfish ends, Russia would be incriminating herself in the eyes of history if she stood by with folded hands and sought not to safeguard her most vital interests by all the means at her disposal. And as Pitt had created a new world to redress the balance of the old, so Russia was now compelled to re-establish equilibrium in one part of the Eastern Continent of

Europe by giving the would-be disturber of this equilibrium work enough to engross all his attention in another. 'These were not, of course, the very words,' added the Count, 'which I used to the Chancellor, but they express the exact sense of my communication.'

MIDNIGHT.

Berlin, which has poured all its teeming million-and-a-half into the streets, is at this hour a scene of the wildest excitement, owing to a rumour (and a friend of mine in the General Staff, whom I chanced to meet, confirmed the truth of the rumour), that the awful and electrifying words '*Krieg, mobil!*' had (as in 1870) been already flashed again to no fewer than seven of the twenty Army Corps constituting the Imperial host—viz., to the 1st, or East Prussian; the 17th, West Prussian; the 3d, Brandenburg; the 4th, Province of Prussian Saxony; the 5th, Posen; the 6th, Silesian; and the 12th, Kingdom of Saxony.

Loud and long was the cheering in front of the Schloss—which is thronged by an ever-increasing and excited multitude—when this intelligence oozed out, and with one accord (for your Germans are a most wonderful people of trained choral-singers) the whole mighty assemblage burst forth with a battle-ballad, in which some deft patriotic poet had been quick to embody the fears and determinations of the last few days under the title of '*Die Weichsel-Wacht*,' or the 'Watch on the Vistula'—a war-song which promises to fill as large and luminous a page among the lyric gems of the Fatherland as Schneckenburger's immortal '*Wacht am Rhein.*' When the frantic cheering which followed the chanting of this stirring battle-anthem had subsided, the Emperor (who has now completely recovered from the accident to his knee) came out to bow his acknowledgments from the front balcony of the castle; and on his arm was the Empress holding the hand of the pretty little flaxen-haired Crown Prince, who had been routed out of his warm bed at this late and chilly hour to add one crowning touch of spectacular effect to the *tableau* which, amid another frenzied outburst of 'hochs' and 'hurrahs,' thus closed the drama of a most exciting and momentous day.

INTERVIEW BETWEEN GENERAL CAPRIVI AND THE FRENCH AMBASSADOR.

DISPOSITION OF THE GERMAN TROOPS.

(*By Telegraph from* our *Special Correspondent, Mr. Charles Lowe.*)

BERLIN, *April* 23.

THE excitement of the last few days has now calmed down into the serious and stolid determination, which is the most striking characteristic of the German race, and though it is known that, since the order to mobilise seven Army Corps was issued, M. Herbette, the French Ambassador, has had repeated interviews with General Caprivi, the nation is meanwhile content to suppress its suspicion with regard to the possible—nay, probable—policy of its western neighbour, and devote all its attention to the development of events on its eastern border.

Certain official telegrams which I have been allowed to peruse leave little doubt that, while the Russians are making a show of massing troops in the direction of Cracow, the real line of their strategic advance is towards the Lemberg side, whence a railway leads across the Carpathians to Buda-Pesth. It is argued here that, had the Russians merely to deal with Austria alone, the likeliest line of their advance would be by way of Cracow and its fortress, which they would endeavour to turn, and then strike for Vienna by the route which has been deemed, on the whole, the easier for them, namely, that which leads to the valley of the Danube across Austrian Silesia, and through the gap between the Bohemian and Carpathian mountains. But with a German army massed in Silesia, and menacing their right flank, the advantages of this route would be more than countervailed, and so the

Russians seem to have chosen an invading route as remote as possible from the German base of attack, namely, *viâ* Lemberg and Stryj.

Meanwhile the mobilisation of the seven German Army Corps, enumerated by me in a previous despatch, is in full swing, the reserve men hastening to the colours with great alacrity; and as the railways are working night and day, all public traffic being suspended, the troops will soon be in the various positions assigned them. The 12th, or Royal Saxon Corps, it seems, is to be sent over to strengthen the Austrians, which will appear a wise and tactful disposition, when it is remembered how the Saxons fought shoulder to shoulder with the Austrians at Königgrätz; while Field-Marshal Prince George (brother of the King of Saxony) has been intrusted by the Emperor with the command of what is to be called the Army of Silesia, consisting of the 5th and 6th Corps, now swiftly concentrating between Breslau (which, being at present an open town, is undergoing rapid circumvallation by a ring of earthwork forts armed with Schumann gun-turrets) and Neisse, the Prussian Crown Prince's point of departure for Bohemia in 1866. On the other hand, a Second Army, consisting of the 3d and 4th Corps, to be called 'of the Vistula,' and to be commanded by the King of Saxony, is swiftly massing round Thorn, that Metz of the East; while a Third Army, compounded of the 1st and 17th Corps (East and West Prussia), and denominated 'of the Baltic,' has been assigned to Count Waldersee, and is fast taking position on the line flanked by the fortresses of Königsberg and Lötzen, the task assigned to it being evidently an invasion of the Baltic Provinces and the consequent splitting up and diversion of the Russian forces from their southern objective. As to the First and Second German Armies (those of Silesia and the Vistula), a glance at the map will show that, roughly speaking, they form the base ends of a triangle whereof Warsaw is the apex, and that a well-aimed advance by road or rail, for both are available, would enable them to effect a junction (on Moltke's principle of marching separately and fighting combined, as applied with such brilliant success at Sadowa), and give decisive battle to the Russians somewhere near Warsaw.

But I may not indulge at present in a more detailed forecast of the impending campaign and its incidents. Suffice to say that the Germans promise to keep General Gourko, commanding the Russian forces in Poland, quite as busy as General Dragomiroff, commander at Kieff, and chief director of the operations against Galicia, will be kept by the Austrians themselves on their particular side of the seat of war.

DEPARTURE OF TROOPS TO THE EAST.

'THE WATCH ON THE VISTULA.'

BERLIN, *April* 24.

I HEAR that the Guard Corps is also about to be mobilised as a precautionary measure. This will, of course, be followed by similar orders to all the rest of the German Army should France assume a threatening attitude, and the signs that she means to do this are increasingly ominous.

Meanwhile, the armies of the East are pouring towards the frontier with machine-like order and rapidity. All night and all day long, heavily-laden trains conveying the troops of the 4th Corps have been passing through Berlin, one at the tail of the other, towards Thorn; and there was tremendous cheering this afternoon at the Central Station, which is littered about with beer barrels and piles of edibles offered by the citizens for the refreshment and encouragement of the '*tapfere Krieger*' who are going at last to measure their strength with the Muscovites, when the Bismarck Cuirassiers from Halberstadt steamed slowly up to the platform for a stoppage just long enough to let the couple of powerful engines water. Rolls and sausages were showered into the carriages containing these splendid heavy troopers (in whose ranks, by the way, Lieutenant Campbell of Craignish, a young Argyllshire laird—now Rittmeister, like Dugald Dalgetty, and *aide-de-camp* to the Grand Duke of Coburg-Gotha—had captured a French eagle at Mars-la-Tour); and when their heavy train again began to move away there arose another ringing cheer mingled with 'Hochs' for Bismarck (and I wonder how the exile of Friedrichsruh feels at the contemplation of all this!)—cheers and 'hochs' that were responded to by these big, deep-chested fellows roaring out the 'Watch on the Vistula,' which has already spread like wildfire throughout the nation, and kindled its heart into a fine warlike glow.

BANQUET IN THE SCHLOSS.

OMINOUS SPEECH BY THE EMPEROR.

(By Telegraph from our Special Correspondent, Mr. Charles Lowe.)

BERLIN, *April* 25.

TO-NIGHT the Emperor gave a grand military banquet in the White Saloon of the Schloss previous to his starting for Thorn—that tremendous bulwark on the Vistula over against the Russian frontier, where the work of concentrating the German troops is proceeding rapidly. At this banquet I was favoured with a seat in the gallery, from which I have witnessed so many pomps and pageants at this Court; and when the third course had been reached, His Majesty (who wore the gala uniform of the Gardes du Corps) rose, and, amid a silence in which you might have even heard the fall of a hair, addressed his guests as follows, in a most resolute and rasping voice:—

'*Meine Herren*, God has willed it that Germany should draw her sword in defence of her ally, and to God's high, holy will we all must bow. German loyalty ('*Deutsche Treue*') has ever been one of the most conspicuous virtues of our race, and, if we now failed to prove true to our treaty engagements, we should justly deserve to become a mockery and a byeword among the nations. Remembering, as I do, the very last words almost which were addressed to me by my beloved grandfather, now resting in God, who conjured me to be considerate towards and cultivate the friendship of Russia, it is with a heart full of exceeding heaviness that I look forward to the events that are ahead of us. Nevertheless, it shall be in the power of no one to say that the German Government was ever wanting in fidelity, or the German army deficient in courage.

'Gentlemen, that courage has been displayed on a thousand glorious battle-fields, and never more so than in those stupendous and heroic encounters which made of us a great and united nation —a nation whereof the safety and integrity would be gravely imperilled by disaster, involving, perhaps, disruption to the dual monarchy of our allies. Such a result, gentlemen, we cannot endure; and it is to obviate the bare possibility of such a thing that we are now about to respond to the solemn call of treaty obligations, by placing some of our heroic troops side by side with the brave army of my august friend and ally, His Majesty the Emperor Francis-Joseph; nor is it to be doubted that this companionship-in-arms, among other things, will have the blessed effect of wiping out all memory of our past conflicts and estrangements, and of re-uniting, in the bonds of fraternal love and loyalty, the two greatest sections of the mighty and invincible German race.

'*Meine Herren*, God is above us, but uncertainty, to some extent, is before us. Within the last few years the science of war has been completely revolutionised, and we are all now about to grapple with military problems which never taxed the powers of our predecessors. As the Supreme War-Lord ('*oberste Kriegs-Herr*') of our armies, I mean to make inspection of such of our forces as are now marshalling themselves on our Eastern marches and also to remain at their head unless—which God forfend!—the course of events should call me elsewhere. (Sensation.)

'But, gentlemen, I do not require to tell you that the duties and functions of a commander are very different now from what they were at the beginning of this century, not to speak of the time of my invincible and immortal ancestor, Frederick the Great, who inspired his troops by his very presence and directed them *in* battle; whereas now all that is nearly left to the modern commander-in-chief is to lead his forces up *to* battle and then leave them to the charge of his subordinates—an era in the science of warfare which was inaugurated by that great scientific soldier, lately, alas! taken from us, who has written his deathless name in indelible letters of gold on the tablets of his country's history.

'Forbidden by the nature and necessities of warfare, as now practised, to be a tactician—such as Cæsar, or Frederick, or Napoleon, or Wellington—the modern commander-in-chief must restrict himself to the task of strategy, and intrust his colonels and his captains with the duty of beating the enemy in detail. And as a modern battle must necessarily stretch over a vast extent of front, it really resolves itself into a hundred separate combats, in which even company leaders become independent commanders; and thus, gentlemen, to all of you there is opened up a glorious prospect of doing your duty to your country and achieving a distinction which was reserved to the generalissimos of yore. But though thus every colonel and every captain among you is now a commander-in-chief, it behoves you to remember that, what with smokeless powder, magazine rifles of vast range, and other innovations, the conditions of fighting have altered immensely even since Germany last took the field; but I doubt not that you will all prove true to our highest traditions, and that our brave army, with God's blessing, will once more show the stuff of which it is made.

'Gentlemen, this is a solemn moment, and it is not in a spirit of festive mirth, but rather under the influence of the serious feelings which dominate us all, that I ask you to drain your glasses to the health of my august ally, His Majesty Francis-Joseph, Emperor of Austria-Hungary. Hurrah, hurrah, hurrah!'

To-morrow the Emperor will leave for the frontier, and I have been graciously permitted by His Majesty to attach myself to his Headquarter-Staff.

DEPARTURE OF THE EMPEROR FOR THE EAST.

BERLIN, *April* 26.

It is long since the Linden Avenue witnessed such a scene of crowding and excitement as it presented to-day, when the Emperor (who wore the drill uniform of his Silesian Bodyguard Cuirassiers, named of the Great Elector), drove from the Schloss to the Central Station to take train for Thorn. His Majesty was accompanied by the Empress, who looked very sad, where her august husband only wore a serious mien. The fine sunny weather, balmy already with the fragrance of the budding spring, had lured thousands and thousands into the streets to see the away-going of the Emperor on his first campaign; and it was only with great difficulty that the demi-squadron of cavalry (Gardes du Corps) escorting the Imperial victoria could advance through the packed and cheering masses of people who thronged every inch of standing-space in Unter den Linden, and reached up to the very house-tops.

At one point of its route, just opposite Café Bauer, the Emperor's carriage was even brought to a stop; and it was then that a very excited gentleman (who turned out to be an American admirer of His Majesty) profited by the opportunity to throw a laurel wreath into the Imperial equipage. Quick as thought, the Emperor placed the wreath on the point of his sword-scabbard and tossed it back to his adulator, saying with a smile, 'Wait a little, my friend; let us earn this first'—a sally that was the signal for a perfect storm of cheers on the part of the witnesses of this charming incident, which furnished them with additional reason for lauding the Emperor's modesty and good sense.

There was much cheering, hat-waving and fluttering of handkerchiefs as their Imperial Majesties—who never ceased bowing their acknowledgments—threaded their way to the station, on the platform of which was assembled Headquarter-Staff, with the great Household officers and Ministers of State (who looked very grave indeed), and others whom duty or curiosity had brought to see the Emperor off. After conversing for a few minutes with Count Caprivi (who, unlike his predecessor in office, is not to go to the front in the meantime, pending the development of French schemes), His Majesty turned to his sad-eyed consort, whom he embraced with great warmth, and then entered his travelling saloon carriage. In another moment, amid three parting 'hochs,' the train had glided away, carrying with it the first German Emperor who has unsheathed his sword against the Czar of all the Russias.

ILL-TREATMENT OF A WAR-CORRESPONDENT BY THE GERMAN HUSSARS.

THE BIVOUAC AT THORN.

SIGNIFICANT REMARK OF THE EMPEROR.

(By Post from our Special Correspondent, Mr. Charles Lowe.)

THORN, *April* 27.

FOLLOWING the route taken by the Emperor, I arrived here this morning, thanks to the courtesy of Baron von Tauchnitz (a son of the great Leipzig publisher of the well-known Continental edition of our English classics), who kindly allowed me a place (it was only a standing one) in the train conveying to the front the Magdeburg Artillery Regiment of his command, as well as the Train, or Army Service, Battalion of the 4th Corps.

While crossing the bridge from the railway station to claim the quarters that had been assigned me at the 'Black Bear,' my eye and ear were suddenly struck by a strange hubbub going on below. A troop of red-tunic'd Zieten Hussars ('Duke of Connaught's') were watering their horses in the Vistula, which has here a broad, placid, and majestic course; and while these thirsty animals were revelling in delicious draughts of the first water they had tasted since leaving Rathenow (their garrison townlet, near Bismarck's native place), their riders were amusing themselves by roaring and laughing at the frantic efforts of what seemed to me to be a big Newfoundland dog to extricate himself from the stream. Presently the poor brute, which to my great astonishment gradually assumed human shape, struggled, spluttering and gasping, on to the shelving bank; and then it was that I recognised in this buffeted and bedraggled creature, Solomon Hirsch, the well-known correspondent of the *Berliner Tageblatt*, whose shock head of hair, all touzled and dishevelled, had given him the semblance of canine form and feature alluded to. It appears that poor Hirsch, fulfilling his functions with more zeal than discretion, had already made himself an object of universal execration at the front by communicating to his paper most minute details as to the massing and position of the German troops towards the Russian frontier, and that being recognised by these rollicking and resentful Zieten Hussar fellows, to whom he had, in an evil moment for himself, appealed for information as to their ultimate destination, this 'curse of modern armies' was at once set upon, hilariously tossed in a horse-rug, and then contemptuously heaved into the Vistula. I have made a point of dwelling on this serio-comic incident, which I myself was quick to take to heart, as it will serve to explain the absence from my telegrams of all but the most meagre and general references to the positions and movements of the German troops; and, indeed, I should be worthy the fate of my hapless colleague did I abuse the hospitality which has been so graciously extended to me by revealing unexecuted plans.

Indeed, I have only been promised the use of the field and other telegraph wires on the strict condition that my messages never exceed a limited number of words, which will necessarily restrict my reports to the briefest and barest, yet, I trust, sufficient summaries.

The Emperor (who was accompanied by the King of Saxony

and other high general officers) has just returned from a rapid ride round the circle of the outer forts, within which the troops are all lying under canvas; and from the top of the Garrison Church Steeple, the highest point in this mighty fortressed town, nothing can be seen but endless vistas of tented bivouacs. Never before has the German soldier been allowed any other night covering in the field but the canopy of heaven, though, indeed, in a country like France, which is, in truth, a land flowing with milk, wine, and honey, and teeming with villages and other opportunities of cantonment, he had comparatively little need of tents. But it is quite a different thing in Russia, with its raw and rigid climate, its vast, uncultivated, and uninhabited spaces; and it was in view of the probable contingency of a campaign in such a foodless and roofless wilderness that the General Staff, with that remarkable foresight and wisdom which has always distinguished it, resolved to equip all the Army Corps lying nearest the Eastern frontier with the very best tents procurable—namely, such as were at once waterproof, windproof, and even fireproof. For otherwise what ruin might not a spark from a bivouac fire entail upon the tented fields which stretch away in every direction towards the horizon, both here and at Posen, at Neisse, and at Königsberg, reminding one of the hosts, countless as the sands on the sea-shore, of the five kings who encamped over against Gibeon.

But I must not omit to record a curious incident which happened as the Emperor was riding past the statue of Copernicus, whose birthplace was Thorn. Just when abreast the monument of that immortal astronomer, His Majesty remarked to his suite: '*Ja, meine Herren*, there you see the man who first opened the eyes of the world to the true nature of the solar system; and I think that with God's help we shall equally be able to assign Russia her proper place in the system of nations.'

THE AUSTRIAN PLAN OF CAMPAIGN.

DETAILS OF PREPARATION.

(*By Telegraph from our Special Correspondent, Mr. Charles Lowe.*)

THORN, *April* 29.

TO-NIGHT the Emperor (who continues to display wonderfully good spirits and energy) gave a banquet in the hastily furbished-up rooms of the gloomy old Schloss, in honour of Feldzeugmeister Baron Beck, the Chief of the Austrian Staff, who, pending the progress of his well-thought-out mobilisation and massing scheme, which he had set a-going by a simple order from Vienna, had hastily run up here by rail to concert united action with his German colleague, Count von Schlieffen, the present occupier of Moltke's high and responsible office. From a trustworthy source I gather that this was the substance of Baron von Beck's communication :—

It had been discovered, beyond all doubt, that the main objective of the Russian invasion was Lemberg, in the direction of which Dragomiroff was concentrating immense masses of troops, drawn from the 4th, 8th, 9th, 10th, 11th, 12th Army Corps, in the rear of whom other forces, furnished by the remoter 13th, 16th, 17th and other Corps, were pushing up as fast as the defective railway system of the country would allow them. Austria, on her part, had resolved to combine her defensive forces into three armies—one of about 300,000 strong, in East Galicia, on the Dniester; another, about as half as strong (150,000), on the San, with its back on Przemysl, that tremendous bulwark of Middle Galicia; and a third, of about 120,000, near Cracow, that almost equally formidable *place d'armes*, and key of Western Galicia on the Upper Vistula.

But these numbers do not include a force of eight independent Cavalry Divisions, each of four Brigades, or four regiments, which are to be ranked along the Galician frontier at the likeliest points of danger from the mass-raidings of Russian horsemen.

THE KNIGHTS OF MALTA AT AMBULANCE WORK.

Such were meanwhile the relative dispositions and prospects on either side of the Austro-Russian border, while, on the other hand, General Gourko, the hero of the Balkans, was concentrating at Warsaw an army consisting of the 5th, 6th, 14th, 15th Corps, and other troops, for the double purpose of holding the Germans in check, and of operating towards Cracow, on the Austrian left flank. Moreover, the 2nd Russian Corps from Wilna, and the 3rd from Riga, seemed to be marshalling on the lower Niemen with the view of looking over into Königsberg; and of these Muscovite troops in the Baltic Provinces, no less than in Western Poland, Baron Beck trusted that the Germans would give a good and satisfactory account.

As a token of his complete satisfaction with the Baron's lucid and hopeful exposition of the military situation, the Emperor, at parting, which was very cordial on His Majesty's part, conferred on the distinguished Chief of the Austrian Staff the Red Eagle of the first class (with swords), and, at the same time, intrusted him with an autograph missive for his august master at Vienna.

(By Telegraph from our Special Correspondent, Mr. Charles Lowe.)

THORN, LATER.

From my correspondent with the Army of the Baltic at Königsberg I learn that its mobilisation is now complete, and that Count Waldersee (who has had a bad fall from his horse, but is better again) is burning to make a dash across the frontier and pluck a leaf from the laurel-wreath of General Gourko.

The 2nd, or Pomeranian Corps, has meanwhile been appointed to cope with any descent from the Russian Fleet on the Baltic shore; while the 9th Corps has been similarly left in Schleswig-Holstein for the double purpose of frustrating any attempted landing in that quarter, and also of keeping an eye on Denmark, whose hearts are practically with the Russians, and who have not yet forgotten the Redoubts of Düppel.

On the other hand, the fortification of Breslau is proceeding at a rapid rate, Prince Pless and the Duke of Ratibor having lent a little army of their miners to do the necessary pick and spade work; while the Army of Silesia (under Prince George of Saxony) is now echeloned along the railway line, parallel to the Russian border, between Kreuzburg and Tarnowitz—*in utrumque paratus*—that is to say, ready either for a front march across the frontier on Czenstochau, on the Warsaw railway, or for a flanking movement of support in the direction of Cracow, as occasion may demand.

The Austrians, we know, are well forward with their concentration; but owing to the fact that the telegraph wires of the Russians have now ceased to speak to the outer world, and that travellers are neither allowed into nor out of Russia, we are still very much in the dark with regard to their massings and their movements. To-morrow, however, we mean, if possible, to try and penetrate a little the veil of this mystery.

FIRST COLLISION OF RUSSIAN AND GERMAN TROOPS.

SKIRMISH AT ALEXANDROVO.

(*By Telegraph from our* **Special** *Correspondent, Mr. Charles Lowe.*)

THORN, *April* 30.

I HAVE just returned from a reconnoitring ride with two squadrons of the Zieten Hussars, who pushed across the Russian frontier to within sight of Alexandrovo, the scene of the meeting (of which I had the good fortune to be an eye-witness) between the old German Emperor and the late Czar Alexander II., in September 1879, shortly before the signature of the Austro-German Treaty of Alliance.

It is a curious coincidence that the first blood in the present campaign should have been drawn within view of the spot to which the old Emperor—greatly against the advice of his irate Chancellor, Bismarck—then hastened to conjure the Czar to desist from his warlike operations, and assure him, on the other hand, of his own unalterable determination to keep the peace.

When we had advanced by the road skirting the railway to within about a mile of Alexandrovo, a gun attached to a body of Cossacks (they were of the Don, as I could make out through my glass, from their blue tunics faced with red) opened fire on us; and the shell, bursting right in front of our leading troop, killed two horses and seriously wounded one man (a Wachtmeister). So having thus caused the enemy to give tongue, we turned bridle and trotted back, carrying with us the intelligence—the rich fruit of our reconnaissance—that Alexandrovo was strongly occupied by troops of all arms. Four sotnias of Cossacks came pelting after us, but we were quick to outrun these rampaging gentry, to whom a gun from one of our horse-batteries sent hurtling over a few shells as a parting souvenir of our hasty yet successful visit.

WARLIKE EXCITEMENT IN PARIS.

(By Telegraph from our Special Correspondent, Mr. D. Christie Murray.)

PARIS, *April* 30.

PARIS to-night is in a state of the maddest ferment. For some days past the public have followed with breathless interest the rapid development of events on the Russo-German frontier, and the news of the first skirmish at Alexandrovo, which was printed in *Le Soir* this evening, has roused the wildest enthusiasm. Long and anxious consultations of Ministers have been held daily, and the Press, with hardly an exception, have been urging on the Government an immediate declaration of war. Many of the better-class Germans have been hurrying from Paris—a precaution which, in the issue, has been shown to be judicious. When to-day's news became known, every trade and artifice was instantly abandoned, and the streets since three o'clock till now have been thronged by vast crowds, pulsating to a more and more impassioned excitement. By four o'clock there were literally fifty thousand people standing in the street with newspapers in their hands, and every reader was the centre of an excited throng. I was standing opposite the Vaudeville when a man, bearing a prodigious bundle of newspapers wet from the press, came staggering swiftly towards the kiosque. The mob fell upon him, despoiled him of his burden, and tore open his parcel. There was such a wild hurry to learn the news, and everybody was so eager to be first with it, that scores of the journals were torn to ribbons, and hundreds more were trampled into the mud of the pavement. The proprietress of the kiosque wrung her hands and wept over the spectacle, and a gentleman who, by pressure of the crowd, was forced half-way through one of the windows, vociferously demanded to know the value of the lost journals. The woman instantly became business-like, and appraised them roughly at a hundred francs. The gentleman produced a pocket-book and paid her twice over, shouting noisily, 'I present this glorious news to Paris! *Vive la Russie! A bas la Prusse!*' That was the first signal I heard, and in one minute the whole boulevard rang with frenzied roar on roar. Omnibuses, public carriages, and vehicles of every description were wedged immovably in the crowd which thronged the horse-road. The drivers rose from their seats, the passengers and occupants of the carriages stood up in their places and roared and gesticulated with the rest. Hundreds of people at once strove to make speeches, and the combined result was such a *charivari* as can scarcely have been heard since the great day of the Confusion of Tongues.

I, myself, had occasion to be thankful for that inconquerable English accent which has always disfigured my French. A blond beard and spectacles have always helped me to something of a German look, and to-day has given the few Germans who happen to be left in Paris such a scare as the bravest of them is not likely to forget. At one moment I was surrounded by a wild section of the mob, whose yells of 'Down with Prussia!' were far too obviously intended to be personal to me. There was nothing for it but to join in the shouting, and I cried '*Vive la France!*' and '*A bas la Prusse!*' as lustily as any of them. There was an instantaneous laugh at the English accent, and I was left alone; but I could not help thinking what would have happened had I chanced to learn my French mainly in Berlin rather than in London. One unfortunate German is reported fatally injured by the violence of a mob at the Gare du Nord. He had booked for London, and is said to have carried with him only a small handbag, and to have left all the rest of his belongings at the hotel, in his hurry to catch the train for Calais. The director of the Opera came near to paying with his life for his artistic allegiance to Wagner. Happily for him he was able to take refuge in the house of a friend, and the mob contented itself by keeping up a ceaseless boo-hooing for an hour or more.

EXTRAORDINARY SCENE IN THE PLACE DE LA CONCORDE.

The wildest manifestation of the afternoon was in the Place de la Concorde, where an immense mob fell to dancing about the statue of Strasburg. Everybody knows the sullen threat with which that statue has been placarded for so many years. It runs 'L. D. P. (the initials standing for "Ligue de Patriotes") Qui Vive? La France. 1870—18—.' When the prodigious noise created by the mob seemed at its highest, it was cloven, as it were, by a din still greater, and a solid phalanx of men forced a way into the already crowded square. In the centre of this phalanx twenty or thirty men marched, bearing a long ladder, the heads of many of them being thrust between the rungs. In the middle of the ladder was seated a working painter in a blue blouse. The man was literally wild with excitement, and was roaring 'Quatre vingt douze' to a sort of mad, improvised tune, in which the packed marchers about him joined with the fell stress of their lungs. In one hand the man flourished aloft a pot of red paint, with the contents of which he occasionally bedewed his unheeding companions, some of whom had playfully bedaubed their own and others' features, so that they looked as if they had just come fresh from some scene of massacre. In the other hand

EXTRAORDINARY SCENE IN THE PLACE DE LA CONCORDE:
THE MOB TEARING THE MOURNING EMBLEMS FROM THE STATUE OF STRASBURG.

the man held aloft a sheaf of brushes, and in an instant the vast crowd seized the motive of his presence there, and the meaning of the rhythmic repetition of 'Quatre vingt douze!"

A way was cleared for the advancing cohort as if by magic. The ladder, still supporting the painter, was drawn up lengthwise before the statue, and the workman knelt to his task. At first it was impossible for him to work, for the bearers of the ladder were jigging to the tune they sang; but by and by they were persuaded to quiet, and a very striking and impressive silence fell upon the crowd. The man, with great deliberation, and with a much firmer hand than he might have been supposed to own at a time of such excitement, drew the outline of the figures 9 and 2 in white chalk, at as great a size as the space of the placard admitted. His movements were watched with an actually breathless interest, and when, after the completion of his drawing, he rose and clasped the knees of the statue in his arms with a joyful and affectionate cry, two or three people in my neighbourhood sobbed aloud. The man knelt down again and filled in with red paint the outline he had drawn. One grim personage, with a squint and a pock-marked face, who held a short, well-blacked clay between his teeth, shouldered me at this moment, and said, '*C'est le sang de la France, ça.*' He thought so well of this that he moved away among the crowd repeating it, nudging his neighbours to call attention to the saying, and pointing a dirty forefinger at the red paint of the figures to indicate its meaning. I was waiting for an outburst of enthusiasm when the figures were completed, but to my amazement the mob accepted the proclamation they conveyed with a grave silence, as if it had been in some way authentic and official, and as if for the first time they recognised the terrible significance of the hour. Their quiet did not endure long, for one of their number, having contrived to scramble on to the ladder, clambered up the statue, and amid great cheers tore from it the ragged emblems of mourning which have so long disfigured it.

Then came an episode, the like of which would be possible nowhere but in Paris. The whole thing might have been arranged for scenic effect, and the distinguished artist who made the *coup* had never, brilliant as his triumphs have been, arrived on the stage at so opportune a moment, or encountered so overwhelming a reception. The new-comer was no other than M. Jean de Reszke, who was on his way to dine with a friend before appearing as Faust in Gounod's masterpiece this evening. His coachman was slowly making way along the crowded road when the great singer was recognised. He was greeted with a roar of applause, and a dozen members of the crowd threw open the closed landau he sat in, while a thousand voices clamoured for the *Marseillaise*. The statue had, at that instant, been denuded of its last rag of mourning, and M. de Reszke, who had risen bareheaded in the carriage, was whipped out of it in a trice, and borne, *nolens volens*, to the figure, and placed aloft on the pedestal. His companion, a lady attired with much distinction, was at first evidently alarmed, but soon gathered the peaceful intention of the crowd, and seizing the meaning of the moment, she stripped from her own shoulders a handsome scarlet cloak, and threw it towards M. de Reszke. It was immediately passed on to him, and he, with considerable difficulty, and at the risk of a tumble on the heads of the people below him, succeeded in casting the cloak over the shoulders of the statue. At this, all the previous noises which cleft the air of Paris this afternoon seemed as nothing. The cheering was simply deafening and maddening, and lasted for full three minutes. At length perfect silence was restored, and M. de Reszke began to sing the *Marseillaise*. He was pale at first, and obviously unstrung at the spectacle of this prodigious audience, and for the first few notes his voice was broken and ineffective. He gathered confidence, however, before he had completed the singing of the first line, and gave the rest of the song with an inspiring vigour and *élan*.

From the beginning of the whole extraordinary scene people had been flocking in from every quarter, and I believe that I am well within bounds when I say that the singer had an audience of a hundred and twenty thousand. The chorus was one of the most stupendous and moving things which can ever have been heard by human ears. It rose from the densely-packed mass of humanity in one amazing roll and roar of sound, and its echoes came straggling faintly from the Rue de Rivoli and the Tuileries Gardens, from the Avénue des Champs Elysées, from the Rue Royale, from the Pont de la Concorde, and the embankment on the further side of the river. When the whole song was finished it was redemanded, and was sung through again with undiminished relish both by the soloist and the chorus. Finally, the singer was permitted to descend from the pedestal, and was escorted to his carriage. The crowd had taken out the horses, and M. de Reszke and his companion were drawn away by some hundreds of volunteers. The great singer's nationality has made him the idol of Paris during all the late days of strained expectation. Every night the Opera-house has been thronged, and every song from his lips has been received with literal thunders of applause.

THE PRESIDENT SPEAKS—'A BERLIN!'

LATER.

The crowd had already begun to thin when the news passed round that the Ministers were in conclave at the Elysée. I acted immediately on the first hint I received, and with great difficulty made my way across the Place. I found myself almost at once wedged in anew, this time in a streaming current which set steadily owards the Elysée. The crowd grew vaster every moment, for by this time all Paris seemed to have been drawn to that quarter of the town. For a long time there was silence, or what seemed like it after the torrent of noise which had roared so long in all ears, but at last the babble of excited tongues began again, and was intermixed with occasional cries of impatience. These grew in a steady crescendo, until no single voice was audible. But before things reached that point I had heard a hundred excited conjectures as to the course which would be adopted by England at this crisis. By seven o'clock the patience of the mob was quite outworn. The building, so far as could be seen from the outside, was in complete darkness, and the rumour of the meeting of the Ministers seemed likely to be practically denied. At length, however, a sudden swell in the storm of sound greeted the appearance of light at three windows, and certain ill-defined shadows were seen moving on the blinds. One profile was distinct and stationary for a moment, and there was a roar of 'Ribot!' A minute later the blind of the centre window was drawn up, the window itself was thrown open, and the figure of M. Ribot, Minister of Foreign Affairs, was seen. This apparition was the signal for a new outburst in which only the name of the President of the Republic could be distinguished. The air rang with shouts of 'Carnot! Carnot!' and M. Ribot having braved this incredible tempest for a few seconds only, bowed and retired. A minute later the President himself appeared. From where I stood his features were invisible, but his attitude was erect, and he stretched out his right hand with an impressive gesture to command silence. It was some time before this injunction was obeyed, but when he was allowed to speak his voice was firm and unusually clear. His words were few and to the point. 'Citizens! Germany has declared war upon the ally of France. Those gentlemen whom you have appointed as the guardians of the national honour have debated the serious intelligence which has to-day awakened the heart of Paris. It is my duty to tell you that there is no dissentient voice amongst them. France will fulfil her pledges!' At this point M. Carnot was interrupted by a unanimous outburst of applause, which made speech impossible for a space of at least five minutes. Again and again, when it seemed about to quiet down, it was taken up from distant quarters, and came rolling along like a wave, again to subside and again to be renewed. When order was once more restored the President continued: 'France speaks to-night, and demands of her neighbour that the menace against her ally shall be withdrawn. She couples with that a demand for the surrender of those provinces which were torn from her twenty years ago!'

There was at this more cheering, and yet more. The President retired, and a great deluge of rain which had been threatening to fall all day speedily cleared the streets. The latest and most important of the day's events is yet hardly an hour old, but we seem now to be living in a city of the dumb. Everybody is hoarse with four hours' almost continuous shouting, but the popular excitement is as great as ever.

The house of M. Ferry has been guarded by the military, and only the *entente cordiale* existing between the troops and the populace has saved it from attack. At the moment of writing the Boulevards are again crowded. The reply of Germany is, of course, a foregone conclusion, but it is awaited with intense eagerness.

DECLARATION OF WAR BY FRANCE.

DRAMATIC RECEPTION OF THE NEWS BY THE GERMAN EMPEROR.

(By Telegraph from our Special Correspondent, Mr. Charles Lowe.)

THORN, *May* 1.

FOR this morning the Emperor had ordered a review of all the troops, amounting to about 60,000 men concentrated hereabouts—the scene of the parade being a long sweep of meadow-land, not unlike the Champ de Mars at Paris, on the right bank of the Vistula. His Majesty and his Staff took their stand on a convenient knoll commanding all the ground, and scarcely had the serried battalions of the 3d Corps, with their bristling bayonets glittering in the bright sun, begun to stride along in all their martial and magnificent array, when the march past was interrupted by a most dramatic and thrilling incident.

I was standing on the outside fringe of the brilliant circle of His Majesty's suite, quietly chatting to Dr. von Leuthold, the Emperor's body physician, when suddenly we saw an orderly officer dash up to his Majesty and deliver a message, which we could discern from the colour of the envelope to be a telegram.

The Emperor tore it open, glanced through the contents, then looked up, and let his eye wander all round the circle of his suite, as if to note the impression produced upon their minds by the news which His Majesty felt had already been intuitively divined by those about him. '*Ja, meine Herren,*' he at last said; 'it is just as we all expected. This is a telegram from General von Caprivi; France has declared war against us ' (*Frankreich hat Uns den Krieg erklärt.*) There was a moment's pause, each man looking at his neighbour to study the effect of this terrible announcement, and then all eyes were again turned on the Emperor, who looked a shade paler than before, but not a whit less calm and resolute.

'Gentlemen,' he said at last, 'this is a serious moment for us all, but the news dismays just as little as it surprises us. Yet I must now leave you, for the danger to the Fatherland is much greater on its western than on its eastern frontier; and where the danger to the Fatherland is greatest, there also must Germany's Kaiser be.

'*Meine Herren,* my place as Commander-in-Chief of our armies here will now be taken by that tried and gallant soldier, my dear friend and brother, the King of Saxony, who will, I am sure, bring honour and victory to our arms. One foe at a time is quite enough, and the sooner we can help our allies to dispose of their invader, the sooner shall we be able to concentrate all our forces and inflict a crushing blow on our hereditary enemy (*Erbfeind*), who has again, in the most wanton manner, broken loose against us.

'Gentlemen, this is no time for words, when the call to action is tingling through all our veins, so I will only invoke the blessing of God upon the course of our arms in this quarter, and hasten myself to where the peril of our Fatherland is sorest. Adieu, and may each and all of us do his duty throughout the coming period of grievous trial and tribulation!'

So saying, the Emperor put spurs to his steed and, accompanied only by his immediate suite, galloped off back to Thorn, receiving as he went three enthusiastic 'hochs.'

Just as I am closing this despatch information reaches us from

Berlin of a naval engagement in the Baltic between our fleet and some Russian ships; but you, in London, will probably hear all the details before they reach us here.

WITH THE GERMAN FLEET IN THE BALTIC.

We have been favoured with the following letter, under date April 30, from Rear-Admiral Philip Colomb, who has been an eye-witness of the naval operations in the Baltic:—

I was at Kiel with my yacht when the news of the attempt on Prince Ferdinand's life reached us. The successive telegrams and published news created the greatest excitement among all classes, but especially amongst those connected with the navy. Simultaneously with the news that Russia had crossed the Austrian frontier, several German cruisers went to sea, and in a day or two a regular fleet began to assemble in the port. I don't understand German, but my wife does, and she told me whenever we met an eager crowd discussing, that it was all about whether the fleet would not be kept to defend the place, and the danger of an attack by the Russian Fleet if the German Fleet did not remain.

I thought I had better get out of it, as if such an attack were made it might be awkward for me. I think my wife was so excited about it that she wanted to stay where we were and see it all; but I thought we might see all there was to be seen in greater safety from the seaside. And then from the conversation of some German naval officers which my wife overheard, I gathered that the navy, at least, believe that it would try to carry war into the enemy's country. There were, however, great discussions about some German coast defence vessels that had not coal supply enough to go up the Baltic, and great arguments as to what ships would go and what would stay. As every day more heavy ships arrived and stayed, while only small ones came and went, I began to think that after all it was most likely that the Germans would not stay quiet to let the Russians ravage their coasts. Then, by the time that nine or ten large turret-ships and others, besides several smaller ones, had assembled, I understood that the German armies were about attacking Russia by way of Königsberg, as well as to the south. I thereupon made sure that the German fleet would go up in support, even if they were not ready to do more.

So the end of it was that I waited till ten big ships and five or six smaller ones got under way, and then I did ditto, and steamed out with them. I was afraid I might be left behind, as my coal supply did not allow me to go at any speed; but I found the Germans, after putting their big ships into two lines a good distance apart, with some of the smaller ones close at hand on each side, and two or three others a long way in front, steamed quite slowly along, not more than five or six knots. I went in-shore of them, and kept them in sight a couple of miles off.

We passed close to Rügen Island the afternoon succeeding our departure, and the south end of Bornholm in the night. I made out that we were steering straight for Libau, which is about 450 miles from Kiel. We scarcely had seen anything in the shape of a ship except a couple of homeward-bound English trading steamers; but on the second morning at daybreak I noticed all the German ships had been stoking up, and were making an immense amount of smoke. There was a good deal of signalling going on between the German flagships—there were two of these yesterday, one at the head of each line—and one or two of the cruisers, which sped away nearly out of sight, and then came slowly back, signalling as they came. The same sort of thing went on on the third morning, when we had got beyond Dantzig, with the difference that two German cruisers were seen steaming up, one from the southward, and one from the south-westward. The fleet stopped, and a boat from each of these went to the flagship and returned, after which there was more signalling, and a boat from every ship went on board the flagship. I suppose the other Admiral and the captains were in them, but I was too far off to make certain.

After a couple of hours we all went on again slowly as before, but electric and other lights were flashing about all night, so that we were very excited, and made sure that something was in the wind. As a consequence, long before daylight on the fourth morning we were on deck looking out in all directions, and with a good head of steam so as to get out of the way in case of accidents. Sure enough at daybreak there was a great bank of smoke to the northward, and presently I could make out a mast or two sticking up. The two German cruisers, which were five or six miles in front, at once became very busy with their signals, and soon afterwards the whole fleet formed into a single line and turned to the westward, not steaming any faster, but making such clouds of black smoke that they almost hid themselves from me. It did not seem that the Russian Fleet—I was not sure whether it was or not—was closing much, but one or two ships appeared to draw more in front as if to close the two German cruisers. Presently the other cruisers that had kept closer to the fleet also drew out in front, but none of them seemed more inclined to close the strangers than the strangers were to close them.

I could not make it out at all. I had always understood that in a modern naval battle, everybody would immediately run at everybody else, and this looked so little like the sort of thing that I was inclined to think that what I saw was only an advance guard of the Russian Fleet. Yet it looked too large a mass for that, and my doubts were presently set at rest.

Signals were made to one of the German cruisers that had come to us the day before, and she presently turned and slowly steamed to the southward. She passed us so very close that I took heart of grace to call out—

'Is that the Russian Fleet?'

And the answer came back—

'Oh! ye-es, zat is ze Russians—ve sall fight zem! So!' and the steamer went on her way.

I began to have some sort of an idea that, perhaps, neither fleet was able to make out the force of the other, and was, therefore, not in a hurry to bring it to action. And this might easily be so. Though the sky was clear overhead and the water quite smooth, it was misty round the horizon, and so far as the Russian Fleet was concerned, it seemed to me very likely that even the advanced German cruisers were not able to discover more than I could, between the mist and the smoke.

But as I puzzled myself over this, I also thought that, perhaps, as the main attack of Germany was going on by land, it might be her game merely to watch the Russian Fleet. For if the Germans were badly beaten at sea, Russia might be left free to land and cut their communications. I had never thought of this kind of thing before, and I quite woke up with a new sort of idea, for I saw quite well that the Russian Fleet could not do anything unless they first thoroughly beat the Germans.

ENGAGEMENT OFF DANTZIG—SINKING OF A RUSSIAN TORPEDO-BOAT.

I was so keen on my new ideas that I wanted to know more about it, and so steamed well to the N.E. to see what the Russian Fleet was like. Just as I did so, I saw a very small Russian steaming away to the south-eastward as if to get the look at the German Fleet which I was going to get at the Russian. She was stoking up tremendously, and evidently going at great speed. Two of the German cruisers in front immediately turned to the eastward to cut her off, but the plucky little Russian did not seem to mind; they closed one another very rapidly, and some puffs of smoke, followed by distant bangs, showed a little game of long balls. The Russian had evidently much greater speed than the others, and was drawing them astern, but quite away from her own fleet or supports of any kind. All of a sudden I saw she was blowing off steam furiously, and that her speed had slackened, if not dropped altogether. She began to fire more rapidly, and so did the Germans. All three were hidden by the cloud of smoke they raised. My engineer was frightfully excited; he said, 'It was one of them new boilers a-priming,' and that it was all up with the Russian. Sure enough it was, for all three ships pre-

sently came out of the smoke, the little Russian with the German flag flying over her own.

I had got far enough now to see that the Russian Fleet was much more numerous than the German, but I could only make out six or seven really big ships. But there were a crowd of small ones, and behind, eight or nine little things like those we had seen taking the *Excellent's* men for training. I thought it might be dangerous to get mixed up with such a crowd, so I returned to the southward and eastward of the German Fleet. I had noticed that the Russians were steering slowly parallel to the position of the Germans, and night closed, leaving all things in this position. Both sides never left off flashing their electric lights up into the sky and all over the sea, and it really seemed to me as if they must all be a good deal confused by such things.

So matters went on till eleven o'clock, when I made my wife go below, while I lay down for a sleep on deck. I was awoke at one o'clock by such a row as never was, the whole German Fleet was a blaze and a roar of artillery. I supposed, of course, a Russian torpedo-boat attack, but it was impossible to tell what had happened,—all one knew was that an attack of some kind had been made. After a very few minutes the fire began to slacken, and some of it I noticed, with an unpleasant sensation, was coming my way. But that, too, soon came to an end. My wife was at that moment beside me again, and she suddenly cried out, 'Hark! what's that?' I could hear a rushing and a panting sound drawing close to us, and then the ball of white foam that I had seen one night from a torpedo boat. The panting suddenly stopped, and the rushing became fainter and fainter until out of the dark came a torpedo-boat evidently making for the yacht, but very slowly. Just as she was coming alongside there was a sort of wild cry, and I saw she had suddenly gone to the bottom. Our little boat was down in an instant, and I got hold of somebody floating at once, while the men helped in two Russian sailors. I found I had hold of a Russian officer, but he was evidently unable to help himself. I could not get him in but we drew him alongside and the men carried him up. I then saw that the poor chap was badly wounded in the shoulder. No one on board could speak Russian, but we laid him down on the deck, and my wife threw herself down beside him with her scissors and began to cut away his dress, while she cried to her maid to bring her water and linen. It was of no use, however. The poor fellow was quite unconscious and bleeding to death. It was all over in ten minutes, and we could do nothing but reverently commit the body to the deep. Our other two Russians were

THE NAVAL BATTLE OFF DANTZIG—WOUNDED RUSSIANS ON BOARD THE ENGLISH YACHT.

unwounded, but could not make us understand anything. We put them next day into an English vessel bound to Revel.

We were eager enough in the morning to see what had happened, but there seemed to be no ships absent. One of the battleships was, however, evidently very much down by the head, and in the course of the morning we saw her quit the fleet for the southward. Everything else was, in fact, in the same position on both sides, and it was evident that a regular battle was no nearer.

I presently saw a vessel—I think it must have been one of the German Emperor's yachts, from the look of her—coming up fast from the southward, and as soon as she got near enough, she began making a long signal. Almost directly, the German ships all turned towards her. They stopped when she reached them, and after she had sent a boat to the flagship, the whole fleet put on good speed, and stood nearly due west, as if for Kiel again. I could not keep up with them, so I am going to Colberg to post this and hear the news.

P.S.—I have learnt at Colberg that the Emperor's yacht brought news of the declaration of war by France, and orders for the whole German fleet to return to the Jahde at full speed, to avoid being caught between the Russian and French fleets. The Germans say they sank several of the Russian torpedo-boats, and that they had their broadside nets out. Only the *Oldenburg* was struck by a torpedo, the one I saw. She got into Kiel all right, but was badly damaged. It is said that the Russians are spread along the whole German Baltic coast, and descents are expected.

THE GERMAN PLAN OF CAMPAIGN.

PROPOSED LINE OF INVASION THROUGH BELGIUM.

LONDON, *May* 3.

THE declaration of war by France was the inevitable result of the action of Germany in regard to Russia. Events, indeed, have marched with a ruthless and tragical directness ever since the day, barely four weeks since, when Prince Ferdinand narrowly escaped death from Russian intrigue. In Germany, least of all, can there have been any doubt as to the course France would take. The experience of 1870 must have made abundantly clear to her what would be the outcome of the scenes on the Paris boulevards which our Correspondent has so graphically described. With powerful enemies on either flank, Germany cannot afford to adhere to punctilio. With the double contest on her hands she cannot now hope to bring into the battle-fields superior numbers, as in the wars of 1866 and 1870-71 ; prospects of success, as her chiefs well know, lie for her in promptitude of action, in blows struck in unexpected places, in carefully planned efforts to bewilder and divide the forces opposed to her.

To strike anywhere at the eastern frontier of the French adversary, barred as it is with almost continuous fortresses from Verdun to Belfort, must necessarily involve prolonged delay, even if the heavy siege-work which is inevitable should be ultimately successful. True, Germany will no doubt be able to foil any offensive on the part of France from the base of the fortified eastern frontier, but merely to do this would be to confine herself to that defensive which is intensely repugnant to her military character. Yet her only opening for the offensive, unless she were to force or obtain by diplomacy a right of way for her armies through neutral territory, of necessity must be by that eastern frontier of France which is coterminous with her own territory, and through or over the chain of fortresses which loom out sullenly from behind that frontier line.

The ideal line of invasion of France by Germany obviously lies through Belgium. It would turn and negative the chain of French fortresses on the eastern frontier, and give the shortest route through hostile territory to the French capital. Belgium is neutral ground ; her neutrality guaranteed by the Great Powers ; but how vain a pretence is this guarantee is already proved by the latest news from our Berlin Correspondent. It is believed (he states on credible authority), that Germany has been successful in exacting or obtaining from Belgium a secret Convention, whereby the armies of the Empire shall be free to traverse the former State, and to utilise for their purposes the Belgian railway system. The advantages of this arrangement may be said to fairly compensate Germany for the numerical superiority of the French forces over those which she herself is able to bring into the field.

The German plan of campaign, as explained by our Berlin Correspondent, is as follows:—Seven of the twenty Army Corps are engaged on the Russian frontier under the King of Saxony. To cope with France there remain thirteen corps, with a proportionate number of independent cavalry brigades. The First Army, under the command of Prince Albrecht of Prussia, is to advance through Belgium by Verviers, Liege, Namur, and Charleroi, and cross the northern frontier of France between Maubeuge and Rocroy, at and about Hirson. The fortresses on the French northern frontier east of Maubeuge are of little account, and there are none on the section specified. The Ardennes and Eifel districts are regarded as affording considerable protection to the line of communication as far as the frontier, and a further protection will presently be mentioned. It is unfortunate that between Aix and Liége there is available but one line of railway, but the accommodation is copious on either side of this section, several lines being serviceable right to the frontier.

This First Army is to consist of six Army Corps, the Guards, 7th, 8th, 10th, 11th, and 16th being those whose respective provinces are nearest to the region of concentration west of Cologne. Among its Corps-commanders are such men as Generals Meerscheidt-Hüllessem, Von der Burg, Von Versen, Albedyll, Von Loë, all distinguished names in the war of 1870-71. The Emperor himself, who of course is Commander-in-Chief of all the German forces in both fields of operations, accompanies this army, after leaving the eastern frontier with General von Schlieffen, the Chief of the great General Staff, and a number of the German princes. The cavalry commander is General the Grand Duke Frederick of Baden.

The Second Army is to consist of the 9th, 14th, and 15th Army Corps. The course of action prescribed for this is to advance from Trèves through Luxembourg, with the consent of the Grand Duke, following the Trèves-Brussels railway as far as Arlon, whence it is to approach the French frontier between the fortress of Montmedy and Sedan, and in this vicinity, while covering the communications of the main army, draw on itself the attention of the French field army presumably lying behind the northern section of the French frontier fortresses from about Verdun southward, so hindering it from marching westward to swell the forces opposing themselves to the main German army moving by Namur and Charleroi. Having accomplished this 'holding' operation, whether with or without a battle, it is to disengage, move westward below Mézières, and approach that army after it has crossed the frontier. In performing this arduous task the Second Army will have to encounter the physical difficulties of the Eastern Ardennes, and protect its line of communication running perilously near the frontier. To aid in this work, severe at once, and delicate, it is to be furnished with a strong cavalry force, under the command of Lieutenant-General von Kleist.

If from behind the curtain of their eastern frontier fortresses the French are bent on taking the offensive, German strategists, says our Correspondent, freely recognise the impossibility, owing to the diversion through Belgium of the bulk of the German force, of hindering them from over-running Alsace and Lorraine up toward the left bank of the Upper Rhine, where the German fortresses would give them halt. Yet such an advance, if attempted, they will not find quite an unchequered promenade. In Lorraine, Metz, for instance, will somewhat interfere with free transport by rail. In the chain of frontier forts the French engineers have designedly left between Toul and Epinal an undefended gap or *trouée* of considerable breadth. Because of the fortifications of the second line of defence this specious interval is greatly in the nature of a trap, but its debouche toward France nevertheless needs to be watched by a strong field force on either flank.

Confronting this gap, on the plateau behind the Meurthe, between Luneville and St. Die, with advanced posts about Ramberville, and a strong wide-stretching cordon of cavalry still further forward, the Third German Army, consisting of the 13th Würtemberg, and 1st and 2d Bavarian Army Corps, under the command of Leopold, Prince Regent of Bavaria, is to take up its position. The Prince is to make demonstrations from time to time to hold in position the French field-forces on its flanks and rear. If threatened in palpably overwhelming strength, the army has a line of retreat across the Middle Vosges open, striking back in the passes as it retires. Should the gap be judged practical by-and-by because of the withdrawal of the French field-forces to participate in the *mêlée* in the interior of France, instructions how to act will, of course, be sent from the Imperial Headquarters. As soon as the mobilisation of the active army is complete, the Landwehr is to be mobilised with all speed to the last man, and got into readiness to reinforce the armies already in the field, for the Fatherland will be contending against heavy odds, and will need the devotion of all its sons. It should be said that the 2d (Pomeranian) Army Corps is retained in Germany for the protection of the northern coast.

THE FRENCH PLAN OF CAMPAIGN.

WHILE these preparations have been made by Germany, France has not been idle. According to the latest telegrams from Paris, the original plan of campaign devised by the French Etat-major has undergone modification, now that it has become virtually certain that the main German advance is to be made through Belgium. The contingency that a contributory stroke may be made in that direction had, indeed, been in a measure provided for originally. To meet it four Army Corps were to take up an initial position in the fortress-bound triangle, La Fere-Soissons-Laon. Two were to be on the Meuse between Mouzon and Dun to confront a possible German entrance between Montmedy and Longwy. Three were allotted to the frontier on the extreme south-east, since Italy is a member of the Triple Alliance. The garrison of the Government of Paris was not to move. The remaining ten corps were destined for the eastern frontier from Verdun to Belfort.

But these arrangements have been dislocated now that it has become apparent that a great German army is gathering on the eastern frontier of Belgium, with plain intent to strike for Northern France through that State. General Saussier, who holds the high position of Commander-in-Chief of all the French armies, and the chief of staff, General Miribel, have had the sudden task of planning other dispositions. No fewer than seven Army Corps, the 1st, 2d, 3d, 4th, 9th, 10th, and 11th, all furnished by the most adjacent territorial military 'regions,' are now to constitute the army to be massed in and beyond the La Fere-Soissons-Laon triangle, and beyond toward the northern frontier west of the Givet salient, and this army Saussier himself is to command. An army of two corps, the 5th and 6th, commanded by General Carre de Bellemar, is to line the Meuse on the north-east, as in the original disposition. Seven corps, the 7th, 8th, 12th, 13th, 17th, and 18th, are to constitute the field forces and garrisons of the eastern frontier, divided into two armies, the northern army of three corps commanded by General de Gallifet, the southern of four by the Duc de Auerstädt (Davoust). Three corps, the 14th, 15th, and 16th, all of south-eastern domicile, are to watch the Italian frontier from Albertville to Mentone, under the chief command of General Thomassin. The French mobilisation was set about appreciably later than the German; but once begun, no time has been lost, and the rapidity with which it has progressed and is being completed has surprised even those who were most strongly convinced of the regeneration of military France.

PUBLIC FEELING IN ENGLAND.

DEBATE IN THE HOUSE.

LONDON, *May* 3.

WHILE, thus armed and fortified, France and Germany stand watching each other across the Rhine, we in England remain in a suspense profounder than we have experienced any time this side of the Napoleonic wars. The political excitement during the last few days has been intense, and at the prospect now imminent of the violation of the neutrality of Belgium has set the country by the ears. The people, the Press, and the politicians of England are deeply stirred, and the crowded public meeting, called at a few hours' notice, which was held yesterday in London is a proof, if proof were needed, that the Government will be compelled by popular feeling to strain every nerve to avert from 'gallant little Belgium' the violation of that neutrality, to the maintenance of which Britain stands pledged. The opposition press, ablaze with zeal for the honour of England now that there seems an opening for the charge of supineness against the Government, shrieks in scathing leaders that the voice of the nation should enforce on the *fainéant* Ministry its imperative duty of addressing vehement remonstrances to the Great Teuton power. The journals favourable to the Government cannot refrain from addressing strong representations to the Cabinet regarding the uncertain future of Antwerp if Belgium is again to become the cockpit of Europe, and the standing menace to Britain which that great fortress will become if it pass into other hands than those of the Belgians. The House, too, appears equally moved, and not a day has passed but at the question hour a rattle of shrewish interpellations has been shot across the House at the target of the Treasury Bench. The inexplicable composure of Her Majesty's Ministers has, however, at length, broken down before the insistance of the Opposition.

On Tuesday, when the German mobilisation over against the eastern frontier of Belgium was well forward, and when there remained no longer any doubt that the army gathering there would traverse that State, Sir William Harcourt rose in his place, every eye in the House centred on him, and with portentous earnestness of aspect and manner, demanded that the Leader of the House should name an early day for a debate on 'the grave international questions and eventualities connected with the imminent violation of the neutrality of Belgium, and the attitude of the ministry in relation to those questions and eventualities.' Sir William re-seated himself with, indeed, a brow of care and gravity, as beseemed a statesman dealing with a momentous crisis; but the

A SCENE IN THE HOUSE OF COMMONS—SIR WILLIAM HARCOURT
QUESTIONS THE GOVERNMENT.

lower section of his expressive visage mantled with a conscious complacency which seemed to indicate a conviction that he had propounded something in the nature of a 'settler' for this apparently inertest of Governments. 'Take to-morrow, if you like,' drawled the Leader of the House without rising, and then he actually and visibly yawned. The smirk faded out of Sir William's face at the roar of laughter, irrepressible on the part of the Liberals and Conservatives alike, which followed Mr. Balfour's drawl and yawn.

The Opposition papers have vied in vituperation of Mr. Balfour's *insouciance*, which they described as 'insolence,' 'impertinence,' and 'insult.' One provincial journal congratulates Sir William Harcourt on his self-restraint in having refrained from pulling Mr. Balfour's nose, and another, with startling novelty, compares the latter to Nero fiddling while Rome was burning. But yesterday's scene in the House has shown, at least, that the Government, though composed, has not been indifferent. It must have been galling to many of the hot-brained to have observed that when in the afternoon Mr. Balfour lounged into the crowded House, he showed no symptoms of being crushed, or even perturbed, by this avalanche of invective. In opening the debate, the ordinarily bland and gentle Sir William Harcourt displayed a truculent aggressiveness which startled all listeners, so foreign was it to his previously disclosed nature. When he had finished, and the dust had settled a little, Mr. Balfour slowly rose. He spoke as follows:

'Her Majesty's Government were confidentially informed a year ago, both by Germany and Belgium, that those two States had concluded a secret convention, in terms of which, in case of war between Germany and France, Belgium was to permit German troops to pass through her territory and to utilise her railways. It no doubt is a question whether Belgium has any right thus to permit the violation of her neutrality guaranteed by the Great Powers, but the question in the circumstances is an abstract one. Who is to intervene to hinder her? Not Germany, who has made a bargain with her for the right of violation. Not France, who violated Belgian neutrality with impunity in 1870, and who, if she now is ready in time, will, in her anxiety to fight the Germans outside the French frontier, assuredly violate it again—if, indeed, the act can be termed violation when the neutrality is virtually dead already by Belgium's own act. In eastern Europe there is other business on hand just now, than solicitude for the protection of Belgian neutrality. Does the right hon. baronet propose that England should undertake this task single-handed, and, *inter alia*, force Belgium against her will to co-operate with us in retrieving the neutrality she has already surrendered? We should, and in hostility to Belgium, stand alone, in an attempt to make good the guarantee we entered into conjointly with other Powers; and I say frankly that this is not a Quixotic Government. But when we were informed, in strict confidence, of this convention, we took measures for the interest and protection of Great Britain. Those measures may give umbrage in certain quarters; that we cannot help. We claimed and obtained from Belgium the right to occupy and garrison the great fortress of Antwerp if the convention alluded to should become operative, and to hold that fortress pending the solution of the momentous events now clearly impending on the Continent of Europe. We recognised the impossibility of enduring in Antwerp a possibly hostile neighbour so close to our own street-door, and we resolved and have secured the right to be our own neighbour over the way in the troublous times approaching. During the past week we have been quietly and unostentatiously making some needful preparations. These are now so forward that I may inform the House that a complete division of British infantry and artillerymen 15,000 strong will be embarked at sundry of our ports on the day after to-morrow, and will land at Antwerp on the following morning, being conveyed swiftly in steam transports under the convoy of the Channel Squadron. The division will sail fully equipped with an adequate supply of stores. Its commander will be a soldier whose name and fame are familiar to us all; I refer to that distinguished officer, Sir Evelyn Wood. The Belgians hand us over Antwerp as it stands, with fortress, artillery, ammunition, and all appliances for defensive operations which we fervently pray and trust that there shall be no occasion to engage in.'

The cheering throughout Mr. Balfour's short but pregnant speech had been frequent and hearty; when he sat down it swelled in volume and force that seemed to shake the roof. Sir William Harcourt, with the best grace he could assume, professed himself satisfied, and the debate collapsed.

Late last night it was reported that the Government asked and received powers to enlist 20,000 men, and to call out for duty a large number of militia battalions.

BATTLE AT ALEXANDROVO.

DEFEAT OF THE RUSSIANS.

(By Telegraph from our Special Correspondent, Mr. Charles Lowe.)

ALEXANDROVO (IN RUSSIAN POLAND), May 2.

As a result of the scouting ride undertaken by a squadron of Zieten Hussars from this place, as mentioned in a late telegram of mine, it was resolved at Headquarters here (and the decision was sanctioned by the Emperor before his return to Berlin *en route* for the Rhine) to make another reconnaissance, this time in force with the view, if possible, of ousting the Russians from Alexandrovo and possessing ourselves of that important frontier position; for that the best defensive is an energetic offensive is a maxim which still forms the chief guiding principle of German warfare.

To-day, accordingly, a force consisting of the 6th Infantry Division, under Lieutenant-General Von Schnabeltitz, a combined Cavalry Brigade (Zieten Hussars and 3d, or Kaiser Alexander II. von Russland, Uhlans), under Major-General von Säbelschlucker; and two sections (comprising six batteries each, of six guns) under Major Count von Donnerkeil; to-day, I say, this force, starting at dawn, made a rapid march eastward, and was soon across the little stream forming the frontier, where the Russian outposts—who seemed to be singularly supine—were quickly driven in by a few shots from our advance guard. From a wounded Muscovite, who was shot in the thigh and had to be left behind by his comrades, we learned that Alexandrovo was, after all, not quite so strongly held as our late reconnaissance had led us to suppose, its entire defending force consisting of only one Infantry Brigade, under Major-General Grodnovodsky, with several guns, a few sotnias of Cossacks, and two squadrons of Dragoons. Perceiving, therefore, that we were considerably stronger in all our arms—especially our infantry and artillery—we made haste to push on towards our objective, and managed, by advancing at the double, to gain the rising ground on our side of Alexandrovo before the enemy could anticipate our design. But it was a close race; nor was it won by us without a sharp brush, involving several casualties on either side, between one of our Hussar squadrons, under Rittmeister Von Rummelsburg, and a sotnia of Don Cossacks, who were very bravely led, whoever was their commander.

Von Rummelsburg, who was sent forward with his Hussars to feel the ground in front of our infantry, had just gained the brow of the acclivity in question when he perceived the Cossacks making for the same vantage-ground from the opposite side, and at once charged down upon them in the gallantest style, emptying a few Russian saddles even before the shock, for his regiment was one of those that had been experimentally armed with the new combination lance-rifle—the invention of an ingenious locksmith at Potsdam—of which the Emperor became enamoured last year, and several of the brave Cossacks had thus succumbed to the impact of lead before they could come within stabbing distance of the equally fatal German spear—a notable feature this in *fin de siècle* warfare, and one that is likely to impress itself still more vividly in the course of the present campaign.

The Cossacks being thus flung back on their infantry, whose movements were of an unaccountably slow and confused kind, our guns dashed up to the top of the bluff, which had formed the bone of contention between us and the Muscovites, and, unlimbering like lightning, began to blaze away at the retreating horsemen with shrapnel which seemed to do further execution amongst them. Then, laying their pieces at long range and loading with percussion-fuse shells, Donnerkeil's gunners hastened to rain a terrific torrent of destructive projectiles on the railway station of Alexandrovo, behind which Grodnovodsky's infantry had retired for temporary shelter. His guns planted on a rising bit of orchard ground on his left, were energetically enough worked against our batteries, but did us little or no harm, as the Prussian artillerists, always very careful in their selection of a firing position even in the tumult of action, showed little more than the mere muzzles of their guns over the crest of the land-wave, in the rear dip of which the infantry of the 6th Division were lying prone and scatheless in eager readiness to rush on as soon as the cannon of the Russians should be reduced to silence.

Nor had they long to wait for this result, for the furious artillery duel had barely lasted an hour when Grodnovodsky's guns were seen to limber up—such of them as had escaped dismounting—and lumber off; and then our impatient battalions, throwing out their first fighting line, fanlike, in skirmishing order, with supports behind and reserves following, all in as machine-like and magnificent order as at a field-day on the Tempelhof Common, began to push forward, the guns firing over their heads all the while as they swarmed down the Russian-ward slope of our eminence and across the rye and potato fields, still rather wet and cloggy from last night's rain, in front of Alexandrovo. The Russian infantry attempted to debouch from their shell-shattered position behind the railway station and other adjacent buildings, and deploy in line of purpose to stem our steadily advancing tide; but our guns, which were still able to pound away over the heads of our own battalions, played dreadful havoc with their shrapnel charges among Grodnovodsky's out-manœuvred troops, who were also mown down in great numbers by the fearful fire of our magazine-rifles, of which the murderous volleys appeared to inspire our opponents with a feeling of panic as unfamiliar to them as the effects of smokeless powder; and, for the first time probably in all the military history of Russia, the soldiers of the Czar positively turned tail and fled before superior numbers and unaccustomed terrors.

Yet the dead and wounded whom they left behind amply attested the tenacious bravery with which they had fought; and the losses on our side were not insignificant, including, as they did, the death of Colonel von Degenzieher and Lieutenant Prince Zu Sonnenwalde-Drachenfels-Schinckenstein, a young man as brave as he was handsome, both of the 8th Brandenburg (Prince Frederick Charles's) Infantry Regiment.

Still, the loss of these two gallant officers, and other brave men on our side, was more than compensated for by the capture of Alexandrovo (into which we marched, or rather rushed, with colours flying, and drums beating) with its rich accumulation of railway rolling stock, which will be far more precious to us than acres upon acres of military stores.

How in the Heaven's name the Russians could ever have failed to concentrate, at the very outset of this war, a more formidable defending force around so very important a strategic point as Alexandrovo, is a bewildering puzzle even to those who have busied themselves with the systematic study of the Russian character; but, at any rate, there *they* were and here *we* are, thanks to the incredible supineness of our foes, their contemptible outpost service, the audacity and sudden swiftness of our movements, and the disastrous surprise which we then sprung upon them.

My courier returns with this despatch to Thorn, where I trust he will be able to commit it to the wires.

OCCUPATION OF ALEXANDROVO BY THE GERMANS.

ALEXANDROVO, *May* 3.

It is not yet twenty-four hours since the victorious 6th Division of the German Army occupied this place, and already it is bristling on the Warsaw, or south-eastern side, with a most formidable line of earthworks, thanks chiefly to the marvellous exertions of the Engineer Battalion of the 3d Corps, which was quick to arrive here by rail yesterday, within an hour of our triumph—the first of the campaign. But, indeed, the spades of all our infantry have also been incessantly at work since they piled their rifles here, it being thought certain that the Russians will endeavour to get a double amount of work out of their cranky, creaking mobilisation machine, and hasten to deliver a desperate counter-attack, with the view of repairing the disastrous error they have committed— an error that has placed us in possession of a railway base of operations of incalculable price. Among other spoils we captured 123 railway waggons of various kinds, and nine locomotives, which, added to the rolling stock that is hourly pouring in from the direction of Thorn, with the remainder of the German Army of the Vistula, now rapidly massing here, render us certain of the means of transport in the event of our deciding to carry the torch of invasion deeper into the heart of Russia.

It is true that the railway from here to Warsaw consists of only a single track, but the gauge, unlike that of all Russian lines on the right bank of the Vistula, is of the ordinary European size, and that in itself is a tremendous advantage for us. Our Army of the Baltic, under Count Waldersee, will be hampered in its forward movements into Russia, if it decides to push across the frontier also, by the fact that the line from Eydtkuhnen is a broad-gauge one, though, indeed, it is understood that the General Staff— prescient in all things—has also made provision for adapting the axles of German lines to the broader gauge of Russian; but, on the other hand, the Army of Silesia, under Prince George of Saxony, will enjoy the same transport facilities as ourselves, if it can only manage to effect, like us, a *pied à terre* on the Warsaw and Vienna line, and we are anxiously awaiting news of its movements.

CAPTURE OF CZENSTOCHAU BY PRINCE GEORGE OF SAXONY.

PRINCE ALEXANDER OF BATTENBERG A PRISONER.

(By Telegraph from our Special Correspondent, Mr. Charles Lowe.)

ALEXANDROVO, *May* 4.

THERE is great jubilation among the troops here, for, following hard on the telegram announcing the Emperor's departure from Berlin to the Rhine amid an unparalleled scene of excitement and enthusiasm, came a despatch reporting that Prince George of Saxony, by dint of forced marches of immense difficulty through the devious moors and marsh-grounds east of Rosenberg and Tarnowitz on the Kreuzburg-Tarnowitz line, had also succeeded in surprising the Russians at Czenstochau, on the Warsaw-Vienna Railway, and, capturing that important place, after a desperate but unavailing resistance on the part of its defenders, who, incredible to relate, consisted of not much more than its usual garrison—a brigade of infantry and two brigades of cavalry. But the German losses here were much more serious than with us yesterday, one infantry regiment in particular—the 22d Silesian—being more than decimated in its desperate, yet successful, endeavours to drive the enemy from a clump of wood, surmounted by a battery—a proof that it still continues to be animated by the heroic spirit of its name-chief, Field-Marshal James Keith, whilom of Inverugie and Dunnottar, in the Kingdom of Scotland, who, at its head, met his own death, under the eye of Frederick the Great, when saving the surprised right flank of the Prussian Army from utter annihilation by the Austrians at Hochkirch in the Lausitz.

These two engagements, then, though on a smaller scale, have been the Wörth and Spichern of the present war; and it now only remains to be seen whether we shall be able to improve upon these initial successes—which were due to a great extent, I repeat, to the exceeding swiftness and daring of our own movements, as compared with the incredible slowness of our foes, and the faultiness of their mobilisation process, no less than to the fact that the Russians, imagining the Germans would never dare invade Poland, but remain upon their guard and form a flanking reserve support in Silesia to their Austrian allies, directed the main stream of their mobilisation further to the east, towards Dragomiroff's line of hostile advance upon Lemberg and the Carpathian Passes to the south thereof at Stryj.

How Gourko, who is known to be still at Warsaw, though the bulk of his forces must now be well in front of him, will endeavour to cope with the situation thus so suddenly created for him, is naturally the question which occupies all minds here, and it cannot be very long before his intentions are made manifest.

Meanwhile the telegrams from Galicia, where our Austrian allies have concentrated the bulk of their forces, are not quite so encouraging, indicating, as they do, less initiative and promptitude of action on their part, as well as considerable difference of opinion in the minds of the Corps and Army Commanders as to whether they ought to remain on the defensive, or espouse an audacious policy of invasion like ourselves, and essay to beard the lion, or rather the bear, in his den.

Count von Schlieffen, who proves to be as amiable a man as he is an able Chief of the Staff, tells me that news reached the German Headquarters this afternoon of a tremendous conflict between no fewer than five Cavalry Divisions, three on the Russian side and two on the Austrian, somewhere near Brod, on the Volhynian frontier—a conflict which resulted, as it could scarcely otherwise have done from the relative proportion of numbers, in the total defeat of the Austro-Hungarian horsemen. The latter, it seems, were covering the movements of the 3d Austrian Corps, which had been appointed to head an advance in the direction of Dubno; and when they had been overthrown in a *mêlée* which, in its colossal magnitude, recalled the mounted conflicts of the Crusaders, the victorious Russians, rallying and reforming line, swept down upon a detached portion of the Austrian infantry, regardless of the smokeless volleys from the

Mannlicher repeating rifle, and made awful havoc among the sturdy men from the Steiermark, taking one whole battalion prisoners, including, it is rumoured, the colonel of the regiment, the 27th, who is none other than Count Hartenau, better known as Prince Alexander of Battenberg, ex-Prince of Bulgaria—a wonderful piece of luck, indeed, for the Russians, if the rumour proves true.

LATER.

Later despatches confirm the rumour of Prince Alexander's capture by the Russians, and add that, when the news became known at Dragomiroff's headquarters—which are said to be at Dubno—there was almost as much jubilation as when the intelligence of Napoleon's surrender flew like wildfire around the German lines at Sedan.

The ex-Bulgarian Prince is to be sent to St. Petersburg, where rooms are being already prepared for him at the Katherinenhof, and meanwhile he has been allowed to retain his sword in order that his unforgiving and exultant cousin, the Czar, may have the satisfaction of receiving it from the humiliated captive's own hands—a picture that will eclipse in interest all the romantic incidents which have already marked the Prince's strangely chequered career.

NIGHT ATTACK BY THE RUSSIANS.

FIGHTING BY THE ELECTRIC LIGHT—ROUT OF GENERAL GOURKO—
RETREAT UPON WARSAW.

(By Telegraph from our Special Correspondent, Mr. Charles Lowe.)

ALEXANDROVO, *May* 7, 5 A.M.

THE German Army of the Vistula has just inflicted on the Russians another Plevna, and they are now in full retreat towards Warsaw. Such, in brief, is the result of the sanguinary night battle of which I have just been a witness. The Russians were the first to practise night attacks as a means of obviating the dreadful losses certain to result from magazine-rifle fire during the day, but they will long have cause to remember their first serious application of the nocturnal principle of modern warfare.

By seven o'clock last night the 3d and 4th German Corps had completed their concentration at and near this place, and, after extending the lines of entrenchment begun by the 6th Division on capturing Alexandrovo, had gone into fireless bivouac on both sides of the railway line, their tents extending for about a couple of miles in either direction. Several reconnaissances executed by us during the day had elicited that the Russians were marshalling in great force at a place called Waganiek, and were receiving reinforcements from the right bank of the Vistula, by means of a pontoon bridge which had been thrown across the stream a little higher up, at Dobrowniki; but, owing to the dense masses of cavalry which hovered on their front, concealing their movements as a stage curtain hides from view the shifting of the scenes in a theatre, it was impossible for our scouts to bring back more definite information. One item, however, of their intelligence, gathered from a captured Cossack, had a special interest for us, to wit, that the Russian forces immediately in front of us consisted mainly of the 5th and 6th Corps, with part of the 4th (including the relics of Grodnovodsky's Brigade), and were under the personal command of General Gourko, the hero of the Balkans. On the strength of this information it was decided to attack Gourko before he got his preparations complete, and for this purpose to break bivouac, and start in quest of him at the dawn of day, as Prince Frederick Charles had done with Benedek at Sadowa.

I had spent the evening with a particular friend of mine, Captain von Jagdkönig, of Stülpnagel's Brandenburg Infantry Regiment, and was just on the point of setting out with him on a visit of inspection among the foreposts, when a Uhlan dashed up with the intelligence that there were signs of a mysterious commotion in front, and that something was audible in the otherwise noiseless night like the distant rumbling of waggon and cannon wheels. Anon other messengers from the front came spurring in with similar news, and as the general purport of all these 'Meldungen' could no longer be doubted, the bugles were at once set to work, and presently all the silent bivouacs, taking up the shrilling war-note one after the other, like the multiplication of a distant echo, were resonant with the thrilling call to arms; and thanks to the severe training in the discipline of 'alarms' which the German army has been put through by the present Emperor since his accession to the throne, the army of the Vistula had all started from its sleep and was standing in perfect battle array, with its face to the suspected foe, within ten minutes of the first trumpet summons.

The night was intensely dark, the moon having just gone down behind an impenetrable bank of pitchy clouds, and all fighting seemed to be utterly out of the question. Presently, however, the inky darkness all around us was pierced, one may almost say scattered, by a sudden blaze of light, which, appearing to possess all the illuminating power of the mid-day sun, flashed lightning-like upon us its blinding beams from the murky forehead of the midnight sky. 'The electric light!' ran from mouth to mouth, after a moment's bewildered pause, while every one instinctively shaded his eyes from the glare of this all-irradiating and all-penetrating lamp which modern Science had thus hung up to facilitate the work of slaughter, as if the very sun refused to look any longer upon human carnage. For some moments the more than mile-long rays of this blinding ball of light, this detective bull's-eye of modern science, swept round the horizon in front of it, as if uncertain where to fix its focus—now shooting beyond, now falling short of us, and anon settling on us and suffusing us with a sea of dazzling light. Presently another, and yet another such luminary burst forth from elevations of pretty equal distances in front of us, and the process of their groping about for our lines revealed to us dense masses of grey and darkgreen coated battalions picking their cautious way down the distant slopes in front of us. For the electric light has this disadvantage, that in flinging its beams about to discover the locality of foes, it frequently at the same time unveils the whereabouts of friends. This was the case here, but our gunners were on the alert, and next time the focus of the light, in its jerky search-movement, fell on the Russian troops in the course of their stealthy advance towards us, we opened the concert with a screaming chorus of shells, accompanied by a rattling orchestration of small-arms. Nor had we long to wait for the antiphone; for next time the search-light managed to flood us with its blinding effulgence, the Russian batteries, which had been planted on the same elevations, gave lusty voice, and bellowed away at us in most leonine fashion, though their projectiles, being aimed at much too long a range, flew high over our heads and left us scatheless. Not so, however, the rifle-rain of our enemies, which, first in intermittent showers, and then in a steady downpour, began to fall among our ranks with deadly effect; and the word was passed from flank to flank for all the infantry to lie down and court the shelter of our field intrenchments, which crested the ridge of our line of battle.

Between us and the Russian infantry there intervened a depression in the ground, a little deeper than that which separates Mont St. Jean from Belle Alliance; but what enhanced the value of this ground to our foes was the fact that their batteries in the rear, planted as they were on the electric light elevations overlooking the terrain, could fire over the heads of their infantry till the latter was pretty well within storming distance of our position, much in the same way as the guns of the 6th Division had been able to do the other day on the occasion of our first engagement, which resulted in the capture of Alexandrovo.

The Russians advanced against us with a steady, stolid courage worthy of the men who had essayed to capture the Sand Bag Battery and storm the redoubts of Plevna; and as the fitful flashes of the electric light revealed to us, for a few moments at a time, their dense battalions advancing and deploying into the fighting-

F

lines demanded by modern tactics and the rules of fire-discipline, I could not help thinking of that cold and dark November morning when, without the aid of the electric light, they crowded to their doom, with the same dreadnought and devoted bravery, up the slippery slopes of Inkerman.

It was not long before the roar of the cannon on both sides became outvoiced almost by the reverberating rattle of musketry, which was all the more bewildering, as only the very faintest flashes of flame from the smokeless powder of both sides served to indicate the exact position of the opposing lines of infantry fire; and it was only when a new turn of the electric light (which, by-the-bye, might have changed the course of Egyptian history, had Arabi enjoyed the advantage of it at Tel-el-Kebir) registered the progress of the Russian advance, that we could make out the development of a battle in which unity of command was simply impossible, and each captain had to be his own general officer. The development of a modern battle is a very slow process, and this one was doubly so from the fact, due to the utter darkness in which each side was occasionally enveloped, that there was much random and ineffective firing on both parts. But there came a point of time in the Russian advance when the manipulators of their electric lights found it impossible to illumine our lines without also including the Russians within the Asmodean sweep of their rays, and then it was that our men, seizing their opportunity, plied their magazine rifles with infernal industry and effect.

But this opportunity did not last long, for suddenly the four midnight suns of Science, of far more dazzling splendour than the tourist orbs of the North Cape, which had been rendering possible the work of slaughter, disappeared from our firmament as completely as if they had been blazing torches plunged into a pool of ink; and their disappearance was followed by a brief period of almost painful silence which overspread the broad and lengthy field of battle.

We never doubted that this pall of pitchy darkness had thus been suddenly thrown around the battle-field to enable our foes to make another rush towards us, unimpeded by the accurate aim of shell and bullet; and a curious thrill, half of pleasure, half of undefined dread, went shooting through our veins when, as we were listening intently, peering into the impenetrable darkness beyond, our ears were struck by a faint peculiar tinkling as if of jangled metal rods, and the meaning thereof at once became clear to us. The Russians were fixing bayonets, preparatory to a charge on our position; and the sound was quickly answered by the loud and stern command: '*Aufpflanzen!*' which ran all along our lines, and was likewise followed by a repetition, on our side, of the clinking and sharp clicking above alluded to.

Scarcely had silence in the ranks been again restored when another order: 'Load for magazine-fire!' rang out in stentorian tones, and at the same time, almost, the electric lights were again flashed full upon us, converting darkness into open day, and showing us the Russians striding swiftly towards us in successive irregular waves of ever-increasing volume, the nearest to us being hardly more than a hundred and fifty yards off. On they came firing all the way, equally regardless of the awful volcanoes of shrapnel which our batteries belched forth against them and of the terrific torrent of our small-bore bullets, aimed from behind the comparative shelter of field-trench parapets, which incessantly tore through their stolid ranks, mowing them down and massacring them by thousands. It was impossible for them to preserve anything like their proper formation under these trying circumstances, and disorder was spreading rapidly among their irregular ranks; but the swaying, struggling masses of the grey and green-coated soldiery of the Czar still came surging stubbornly up the slope, ever lessening the distance between them and our entrenchments, till the moment at last seemed come when they should hurl themselves upon us and try conclusions with the cold steel. And then, as if by instinct more than pre-concert, the whole surging masses raised a tremendous shout, and rushed full upon us with the bayonet.

But when only about twenty paces in front of us, their onward career was suddenly stopped short by some invisible barrier, which made them crowd upon each other like penned cattle, passive targets for the bullets of our repeating rifles that rained upon them thick and fast as hail, knocking them over like so many rabbits in a ride. This barrier, which thus strangely stemmed the rush of their storming tide, was composed of fencing wire of several coils, strongly stretched and impaled, which had been run along all the front of our entrenched lines as an additional measure of defence against the contingency of such an attack, and formed one of the most recent innovations in the field warfare of the Germans—an innovation which had commended itself to the Emperor, who himself put it to a practical and approved test at the autumn manœuvres of last year.

A yell of savage fury rose from the storming columns of the Russians, who had thus been stopped in their career and baulked of their objective in this most bloody and calamitous manner; and though the impact of succeeding waves of assailants soon levelled all the wire fencing with the ground, still the mass momentum of their charge had been diminished, their dogged courage had also been shaken by the busy doings of Death among their huddled ranks during their temporary check; but worst of all, before the Russians could recover the force of their forward rush, the Germans were out of their entrenchments and upon them with the bayonet.

A few moments of grim and ghastly hand-to-hand fighting then ensued—and let it never after this be said that the bayonet has been entirely supplanted by the bullet; but I had only time to observe that Gourko's brave,—I was almost going to say indomitable,—troops were beginning to waver, to go down, to yield before the forceful push of the Teutonic pike, when suddenly again the electric lights of the Russians were turned off, and the dark curtain of night, in mercy to the vanquished, fell upon the bloody drama.

Pursuit by the Germans in such circumstances was quite impossible, but, recovering their ranks with singular precision, they sent salvo after salvo of artillery and musketry in the direction of the retreating foe, until the 'Cease firing' was sounded all along our victorious line as the faint and startled dawn began to blush—as if for very shame at such infernal work; and the bugle-sounds were supplemented by the shrill whistles of the company commanders, reminding me of the days when I loved to listen to the clear piping of the darting water-ousel among the rocky streams of the Grampians, amid scenes unsullied by the bloody hand of war.

When the day broke the results of the nocturnal battle revealed themselves in all their ghastly horrors; but, beyond saying that about 10,000 dead and wounded Russians lay in front of our extended lines, and nearly a third of that number of Germans in and about our own entrenchments, I will not disgust your readers with a realistic description of the ghastliness of the battlefield—the first of its kind, and one which has resulted from an endeavour to neutralise, or at least minimise, the destructive effects of the murderous magazine-rifle.

REPULSE OF THE GERMAN ARMY.

(By Telegraph from our Special Correspondent, Mr. Charles Lowe.)

ALEXANDROVO, *May* 5, 7 P.M.

This first great victory of ours over the Russians has been somewhat damped by the news, just received, that our army of Silesia, which had begun to marshal around Czenstochau preparatory to a further push forward, has suffered a rather serious reverse at the hands of the Grand Duke Vladimir, commanding the 14th and 15th Russian Corps d'Armée, who fell upon Prince George of Saxony before he had completed his concentration, and compelled him to fall back.

On hearing, however, of Gourko's crushing defeat by us, and his retreat towards Warsaw, the Grand Duke Vladimir, like the victorious Wellington at Quatre-Bras (who desired to effect a junction with Blücher, **on the latter being worsted by** the French at Ligny), resolved to forego **the immediate fruits of** his triumph and retire **to a point that would** enable him **to** join hands with the retreating Gourko, and thus give **combined** battle to the Germans. **This point will** probably be Skierniwiçe, the junction-point of the railway lines from Alexandrovo and Czenstochau to Warsaw, famous in modern history as the pacific meeting-place of the three Emperors and their Chancellors several years ago.

Skierniwiçe, therefore, will probably be the Waterloo of the Russo-German portion of the campaign, whoever proves **its** Wellington; but Skierniwiçe **is very** much further from Alexandrovo and Czenstochau than Quatre-Bras and Ligny were from **Mont St. Jean, and some little time, therefore,** must necessarily yet **elapse before I shall have it in my** power to chronicle the Waterloo **of the present war.**

EXCITEMENT IN BRUSSELS.

(*By Telegraph from our Special Correspondent.*)

BRUSSELS, *May* 5.

BRUSSELS **to-day is rent** by **conflicting emotions.** Frenzied rage, poignant anxiety, and boiling excitement are struggling not so much for mastery as for satisfactory expression. The news of the forthcoming occupation of Antwerp by a British Army Corps has not been received here with expressions of unmixed **satisfaction. The very fact that the negotiations were** kept wholly **secret, with the result** that the announcement of so important a **decision first reached us through the public** report of the debate in **the House of Commons, has, whether justly or otherwise** matters not, set **a vast number of well meaning people by the ears.** When the news **reached Brussels yesterday it produced an** extravagant sensation which **grew as the** night **advanced. By tacit** consent people refused to go **to bed—clubs** and cafés were **kept** open till morning, and all through the principal thoroughfares the noise of heated discussions might be heard in full blast round the tables outside the cafés and at every street corner. A large section of the population, in which ranked many of the better classes, were greatly incensed against the King's Government. 'It is not astonishing,' they said, 'that the measure was kept secret; otherwise the people would never have permitted so infamous a traffic!' All the old arguments of 1859 and the half dozen succeeding years were revived, and in every group of angry disputants the name of Adelson Castiau continually recurrent, was flung passionately on the night with every varied accent of which the human voice is capable. '*Il l'a bien dit, Castiau.* He knew, he foresaw what must happen, and idiots that we were, we would not listen.' This was the prevailing cry.

It must be explained that M. Adelson Castiau—who is just at present given posthumous rank as a hero and patriot—was an eminent lawyer and ex-deputy, who, from the first, vehemently opposed the fortification of Antwerp. From the day when in 1859 a committee of twenty-seven officers were appointed to discuss the subject until the completion of the immense work some six years later, M. Castiau waged war against the scheme. He spoke, wrote, organised committees, and headed deputations protesting against the plan. His argument was that, from a military point of view, the project involved in principle the abandonment of the country, and a shameful flight by the army towards the 'Polders de l'Escaut,' where certainly no one would ever come to molest it, but would be quite content to leave it to be destroyed by marsh fevers. The fortification of Antwerp, he said later, meant the destruction of our neutrality. Antwerp offers to-day, with her forty kilometres of heavily-armed works, her citadel and her dozen attached forts, a standing invitation to invasion. It was handing over the country to the first comer, and building up one of the finest military and commercial positions in the world, only for the benefit of England, which had coveted it for over a century.

And to-day the good people of Brussels, and, I fear of Belgium generally, are regretfully recalling his words and indorsing his opinion. Hence the frenzied rage of which I have spoken leaping flame-like all the length of the Boulevards.

BRUSSELS, *May* 7, 10 A.M.

I have just heard that the British Army Corps, under Sir Evelyn Wood, has reached Antwerp, and that disembarkation is rapidly going forward. Until the transports with their escort of cruisers and torpedo boats actually steamed up the river, people

BRITISH TROOPS IN THE PLACE VERTE, ANTWERP.

here affected to believe that they would not come. Chatterers in the clubs boasted loudly that the wind of popular opinion would drive the English vessels back from the shores of the Scheldt. The obvious absurdity of this anticipation is but emphasised by the fact that the worthy Antwerpers have received the invaders, if not with enthusiasm, at any rate with a demeanour at once friendly and business-like. Telegrams in the clubs here comment rather bitterly on the fact, that instead of visiting them with haughty resentment, the townsfolk are doing a lively trade with the alien soldiers in light beers and other cheap beverages, which the troops are freely purchasing beneath the Rubens Statue in the Place Verte, where they are being rendezvoused before proceeding to their billets.

The fear has now grown into dread certainty that what we have always expected is about to happen. France intends to invade Belgium, and we have before us the prospect of another Waterloo. Why have the German troops delayed? It has been set forth again and again by strategists that Germany's most obvious plan would be to concentrate her Army Corps of the North upon the Belgian frontier of France, that it would therefore be to her advantage either to make use of the two railway lines which, from Cologne and Aix-la-Chapelle, run to Luxembourg, Thionville, and Virton—one by way of Trèves and the other by Verviers—or, and by this even more important results might be obtained, she might combine with this movement the seizure of the line of the Meuse, when, by debouching a part of her forces by Chimay into the Entre-Sambre-et-Meuse, she would be able to attack in flank the French forces engaged in preventing the Northern Army Corps forcing the passage of the Meuse between Dun and Mezières.

It was always considered as certain, therefore, that instead of violating Swiss territory to attack France, Germany would certainly, immediately on the declaration of war, throw an Army Corps into Belgium. It was supposed that a German First Army Corps could be concentrated at Aix-la-Chapelle on the eleventh day of mobilisation, and that it would be established on the Meuse and on the Sambre to the south of Namur at latest by the evening of the fifteenth day—that is to say, twenty-four hours after the Second German Army Corps had deployed before the position on the Othain.

This has no doubt been Germany's intention. A huge army is being concentrated on the Eastern frontier. But France is likely to forestall the movement, and to reach Namur before her adversary.

The extraordinary rapidity of her mobilisation may be said to be due in great measure to the perfection of her railway system on the Belgian frontier. She has established between Dunkerque and Mezières no less than seven lines of railway, of which four are double lines, which place her in direct and immediate communication with Belgium. These roads are linked and tapped by a transversal line that follows the whole length of the frontier as far as Longwy. Then she has, moreover, on this frontier four huge entrenched camps capable of serving as manœuvre pivots for her army, and as supports to her base of operations. These camps are Dunkerque (with its annexes—Bergues and Gravelines), Lille, Valenciennes (centre of a system of defence which comprises Condé, Bouchain, and Le Quesnoy), and Maubeuge. To ensure the retreat of her army in case of failure, she has created a first line of defence, formed by Valenciennes, Maubeuge, Landrecies, Hirson, and Mezières. For her second line she has the town of Reims, surrounded by forts commanding the valleys of the Aisne and the Marne, and the iron-bound triangle La Fère, Laon, and Soissons which defends the valley of the Oise, and with the support of Peronne, the valley of the Somme.

Thus encouraged by the rapidity of mobilisation—a rapidity certainly never anticipated by Germany, and probably a little unexpected by her own officers—France has decided to attack Germany by Belgium. The seven natural obstacles in her path are not in themselves formidable. She has, indeed, to cross the Meuse, the Lower Rhine, the Teutoburgerwald, the Weser, the Hartz, and the Elbe. The Teutoburgerwald checked, it is true, the Legions of Varus, but to-day the great roads pierce it in several broad cuttings, and it is, moreover, traversed by two railway lines, running from Hamm to Hanover and Magdeburg. The Hartz also is traversed by good roads and girdled by two railway lines running to Berlin, one of which is the line which places the German capital in communication with Coblentz and Metz. Thus her advance should unquestionably be more rapid than by the inter-Moselle and the Rhine. If, moreover, she can make good her footing in Belgium before the German army, she will undoubtedly find there better roads, better cantonments, and far greater resources of every kind than she would find in Lorraine and Oldenburg and the Palatinate.

With this object, we hear that the 1st and 2d French Army Corps are being concentrated at Maubeuge, the 3d and 10th at Hirson, the 4th and 9th at Givet, and it is expected that all these forces will be united in the neighbourhood of Namur in the course of the next four days—that is to say, sooner by five days than any military authorities have believed possible.

The entire interest in this country is, therefore, centred in Namur, for which place I start at once.

NAMUR, *May* 8.

The wildest excitement animates this place. Garrison and townsfolk alike are filled with generous enthusiasm for the French cause, a rapid change of feeling which may be attributed in some degree to the Antwerp episode. The most extravagant rumours are abroad. Belgian co-operation with the French forces is talked of openly, and with a grandiloquent disregard of consequences that would be almost amusing if it were not so grave. It is loudly proclaimed that Chartreuse and the old citadel of Liége are determined to resist the German advance, and here at Namur itself the populace (not the army) declare their intention of holding the 'Key of Belgium,' if need be, until their French allies can support them. As for Namur, its strategical position might well entitle it to be considered as one of the keys of Belgium. Till lately, however, the fortifications were in no condition to resist modern artillery. Thanks, however, to the wisdom of the Belgium Government in adopting the plans of General Briamont all this has been changed. Within the year 1892 the fortifications were so far completed as to furnish means for a strong defence. I give these rumours merely for what they are worth, and to show the temper of the populace.

As I write this telegram a report reaches me that French troops have crossed the frontier at Maubeuge and Valenciennes, and it is alleged that the small Belgian garrisons at Mons and Philippeville, after giving a wildly enthusiastic reception to their visitors, have valiantly offered their services to General Saussier.

THE MEETING OF THE FOUR FLEETS.

THE DUKE OF EDINBURGH IN COMMAND OF THE ENGLISH SQUADRON.

WE are favoured with another letter from Admiral Colomb, who has been fortunate enough—in one way—to observe the remarkable naval transactions in the North Sea :—

'Not knowing what would happen, or quite what to do, I lay at Colberg, as being a place less likely to be interfered with by the Russians by way of blockade than some of the other ports, and to get intelligence of what was going on. It was here I heard of the violation of the Belgian territories by France. I thought that the drawing of France into this step was equally an example of German shrewdness and of French rashness. I was not at all surprised that we should so suddenly have been brought into it, in the occupation of Antwerp, which is now being hastened on, and of course we were bound to mobilise everything we could put our hands on. I was sure we could never stop at the defence of Belgium. It seemed equally sure that we could not leave the Baltic, the Belts, and the Sound in the hands of the French and the Russians, for that would almost certainly sacrifice Germany. I had seen her hesitate to attack the Russian Fleet alone, and I was sure that against Russia and France together, she could only shut her main fleets up in her ports as she did in 1870, though she is so much more powerful now than she was then. There was a small German cruiser at Colberg; she trusted to get into shoal water if a superior Russian found her out—and her captain told me that he believed the German Government thought as I did in reference to the policy of attacking the Russian fleet; but that, beside this, they were alarmed at the crowds of small vessels with heavy guns, which, it was assumed, might be associated in any naval action in Russian waters. I only say this as I am told it,—I don't know anything of the real facts.

'I thought the appointment of the Duke of Edinburgh to the command in chief of the North Sea Fleet was a very natural one. His reputation as a tactician, I had always heard, was first-rate, and naval officers always seemed ready to depend on and follow him. I was told the command had been offered to Sir Geoffrey Hornby, but that his medical advisers absolutely forbid his accepting it; however, he seems to have had a good hand in the programme.

'The German officers entirely calculated on France making such an attack on their Baltic shores as she had proposed to make in 1870. The German papers rather made light of it, and hammered away on the two points that France would find it difficult to get transport and appliances, as Cherbourg and Brest were really her nearest ports; and that England would step in and prevent a descent if it got as far as that. But the Germans were everywhere full of preparation on land, and troops were concentrating at Colberg and elsewhere. I had read in one of our papers last year that for a long time the bulk of the French Fleet had been kept at Toulon, and so I was not surprised to see it stated in an English paper that only five battle-ships had left Brest for the North Sea, with, however, a good proportion of cruisers and small craft. If, then, this were really so, it would follow that, supposing the Germans had been able to bring forward any more ships in the time, and had repaired the *Oldenburg*, they must be either à cheval between the French and Russian Fleets—able to strike at each before the other could assist—or else between two fires; according to how they looked at it. I had seen them retire before the Russian Fleet on the apprehension of a French approach. Would they now, with more complete knowledge of the forces against them, reverse their policy and strike at either? Or would they remain quiescent; shut themselves up in Wilhelmshaven, and trust to their land defences to repel all attacks? There seemed almost an even chance, and I made up my mind to go on to Kiel, and to the Jahde, if I made out nothing at the first-named port.

'I had hoped to have made Kiel in daylight, but the wind failing me, it was dark when I got off the port. I could only guess where I was, for the Bülk Light did not show, and all I could make out in the way of lights seemed to be about the works of Friedrichsort, though the regular light there was also extinguished; thereupon I lay-to. I had the usual side-lights burning, and I suppose they were seen, for we had not been there ten minutes lying-to when a ship without lights of any sort came out of the gloom, and a voice hailed us in an unknown tongue first, and receiving no response, then in French, asking what we were. I answered, and presently a boat with a Russian officer boarded us. He was very polite; told us there were no German warships in Kiel except some small craft; that a squadron of Russian cruisers was blockading the place; and that I must get out of it. So there it was, and all I could do was to make sail for the Sound.

'Off the Jahde we found quite a strong combined French and Russian Fleet. We counted seven large French ships and six large Russians, so that it was clear that the Germans had made no attempt to interfere with the junction. There were many smaller vessels, chiefly French, and the whole fleet, except some small vessels, was at anchor.

'We made for the vicinity of a French flagship, and were soon boarded by a boat from another ship with some sort of flag up. The officer warned us that the Jahde was blockaded, and that though on our promise not to try to slip in, we might remain with the fleets, we should assuredly be captured or sunk if we tried to break blockade. As we only wanted to see what was going on, I readily gave a promise, and then we learnt that the Russian ships had only joined the French a few hours before we came in sight, and that no one knew what was going to be done, but it was ordered that the whole fleet must weigh before dark. The officer told us they expected transports and troops daily, but that he did not know what was intended.

'Immediately after dark; accordingly, the whole combined fleet got under weigh. Lights were shown during the process, but then all were extinguished and the ships disappeared without our having the least idea which direction they had taken.

'We were astonished soon after daylight next morning to see not only our friends the Russians and French steaming slowly in from the northward, but to see an apparently still greater fleet in the haze to the westward.

'There was an evident check and hesitation in the Franco-Russian Fleet, and presently we well understood why, when we distinctly made out the English white ensign flying in the Western Fleet. Our ships came on quite slowly. We could make out that they were grouped in three great masses. I counted fifteen in the most advanced portion, all very large ships, and I soon made out that they were in three lines, with a flagship at the head of each. Soon I made out the middle one to be certainly the *Alexandra* with an Admiral's flag at the main. On her right I supposed was the *Camperdown*, with Vice-Admiral Seymour's flag; and on the left the *Anson*, with that of Rear-Admiral Adeane. I had seen them both before I left England, and supposed they retained their commands. There were several small vessels near this great mass of ships, and then to the right of them was a group of seven large ships, three of them as if partly rigged, and four of them like turret-ships. Then, again, on the left of the main fleet I could make out what seemed to be a cluster of smaller vessels.

'We had barely made out all this, when out of the cloud of mist overhanging the mouth of the Jahde there came clearly the body of the German Fleet—ten of them I counted.

'Never was such an exciting time as this. It seemed to me that I was about to witness the greatest sea-battle that the world had ever seen, and when I noticed the Franco-Russian Fleet separating its bigger from its smaller ships, and drawing the latter into one long line, facing west, and stretching north and south, I made certain they were going to run right at the English Fleet pell-mell, in the way I had always read about.'

RETREAT OF FRENCH CRUISERS.

SINKING OF THE 'ELAINE.'

BUT yet I had not heard of any declaration of war by England, and it seemed a terribly reckless thing for the French and Russians—of whom I could only count fourteen in the line they had drawn out, to run down upon what seemed to be twenty-two English ironclads, when they could be joined, in a couple of hours perhaps, by the ten Germans. The three fleets were each about ten miles from my yacht, and I was in the middle part. There was not much wind, and what there was being from the southward, left smooth water, but brought down a good deal of mist from the flat land of which one could only get indications by buildings and trees sticking up above the horizon. I could not help thinking how wise the Germans were to have their fleet here rather than at Kiel. Nature sheltered them from attack at Wilhelmshavn in a way that no sort of art could do at Kiel, and here they were quite safe behind their shoals, and yet ready to fall upon their enemies at a moment's notice.

Nevertheless, they were hemmed in fast enough. That was made plain by the fact that at least five small French cruisers had turned up at daylight a long way inshore of where I was, and had evidently been there all night keeping watch on the port. While I was weighing, these cruisers, some of which seemed much nearer to our own fleet, appeared to be coming out—I supposed in obedience to signal—and then I saw that several German ships were evidently coming out after them, and steaming at speed. I had hardly realised the state of affairs when I saw I was in for a hot skirmish, and that we should be in the middle of it ourselves. However, we put on full speed, and steamed as hard as we could, straight for the *Alexandra*. Some of the French now passed us in retreat, firing their stern guns; and presently we were passing between an advancing and retiring line, and were between two fires. My wife gripped my arm tight and stood and

SINKING OF THE YACHT 'ELAINE.'

looked, but never a word she said. Nor I either, for I had a horror of what might happen, and was powerless.

'What's that?' cried my wife presently, pointing to the sky over the German ships. What, indeed? I was only conscious that some monstrous, roaring, and very relentless thing had passed me, and made a crash somewhere, and that my steward had torn up the hatchway, crying, 'Good God! the bottom's out of the ship!'

Then I knew that a German projectile had passed through our deck and planking below, and that we were sinking. I holloaed down to the engineer, 'Keep her going as long as you can!' dashed down for my wife's jewel-box, collared it, and was up again to find the men clearing away the boat. I knew the engine-room compartment was by way of being water-tight, and that we had a little time to spare in consequence; but I wanted to run out of the fire, which I could not do in the overcrowded boat. My engineer was as cool and white as marble. 'She'll go a bit yet, sir!' he called up through the skylight; 'the water's leakin' in through them sluices pretty, but there ain't more nor six inches yet.'

The boat was down, towing alongside, and I gave the word to quit the yacht as she was sinking markedly by the stern. The engineer came regretfully last into the boat before myself. 'Them blooming engines 'll go a bit yet,' he muttered as he passed me. 'I'm glad it worn't a Rooshian shot anyhow.' It was no use sticking to the yacht, but she had done us the good turn of carrying us out of the line of fire, which, indeed, was slackening by reason of the approach of the French to their own fleet.

The whole thing was such a scurry that one hardly knew what had, and what had not happened, but we understood it when my poor *Elaine*, with a great snort and splash, suddenly threw her nose into the air and went down stern first, leaving us in the overcrowded boat, clear now of the cross fire which had, indeed, nearly ceased. Then I became aware of two things; one, that a heavy English cruiser, with a flag of truce flying, was steaming towards the Franco-Russian Fleet; and next, that a smaller ship was steering direct for my boat. In a very few moments we found ourselves safe on board the *Blonde*, kindly welcomed and commiserated by Commander Pretyman, who told us he had been signalled to pick us up and take us to the flagship.

ON BOARD THE FLAGSHIP.

ACCEPTANCE OF THE ENGLISH TERMS BY THE RUSSIAN AND FRENCH ADMIRALS.

THE change was sudden and unexpected enough when we found ourselves greeted by the Duke the moment we put foot on board the *Alexandra*. My old friend Keppel had, we found, already turned out of his cabin to make room for my wife; and the Duke led us—still rather dazed—into his after-cabin, assuring us that we were his welcome guests till he could send us home. I could not help wondering at the moment at the quietness of his manner and his exceeding urbanity on the brink of such tremendous occurrences and with such awful responsibilities on his shoulders. I found I was by no means alone in my admiration of this amiable *aplomb*, but I soon learnt that not only the Duke, but most of the officers did not apprehend a collision.

For the situation was that war with France had not yet been formally decreed, and that the flag of truce had gone with the Duke's Flag Captain, Brooke, to 'invite' the French to withdraw their forces, in which case no attack would be made, and the Russians might retire unmolested to Cronstadt. If, however, in three hours the Russian Squadron had not separated from the French, and the French had not signified their acquiescence, the united English and German Fleets together would enforce compliance. The Duke's secretary, Mr. Rickard, showed me the copy of the message. It was exceedingly firm, but exceedingly conciliatory; praying the French Admiral Planché and the Russian Shestakov to reflect that, in presence of forces so enormously superior, their honour could in no way be touched, and that common dictates of humanity forbade the awful effusion of blood which would be so uselessly shed in the event of a refusal.

The ships were all prepared for action,—those with masts appearing to be nearly stripped,—and now I saw that the German Fleet was well out, and steaming directly for us. The officers all seemed a good deal more excited than the Admiral, but still I found that no one believed in the possibility of resistance. The latest news by a despatch vessel represented that the embarkation of troops at Cherbourg, which was closely watched by several of our cruisers, had apparently been stopped, and this, it was felt, gave additional cause to believe in a peaceable solution, as it was made clear that even if the English Fleet only stopped the transports, the whole Franco-Russian game was up. A last telegram from Paris, *viâ* Madrid, expressed belief that the French Admiral Prémesnil had sailed with orders to return to Brest if the English appeared in observation off the Jahde in greatly superior force.

Notwithstanding, there was not a glass in the ships that was not persistently directed upon the *Immortalité*—now about ten miles off, and stopped close to the French Flagship—and her great white flag, for it had been arranged that she should hoist the Dutch ensign under it as the signal that the terms were rejected.

The hours drew on, and for perhaps two there was no sign. The distance was too great to make out ordinary flag signals, but sometimes it could be seen that such were hoisted, and one of the signal midshipmen created a fresh stir by affirming that the ships in view were 'stoking up.'

My heart was in my mouth with the excitement of the moment, but if I was as cool and unconcerned in outward appearance as the officers and men surrounding me, I must have wonderfully belied my real feelings. Suddenly the head signal-man called out in a hurried voice, not taking his eye from his glass: 'The Russians are moving, sir!'

We could not in fact distinguish French from Russians at the distance, but I had told them that the Russians were on the right wing, and as they looked, they could see the right wing opening out from the left. A sort of disappointed sigh passed round the group, as by a single impulse they dropped their glasses and looked at one another. I am sure I saw an impatient gesture of the Duke's right arm, and a certain setting of his lips which confirmed it. There was no Dutch ensign. Common sense had overcome the sentiment of the allies; the terms were accepted, and the Russians were off to the Gulf of Finland.

All this surmise was confirmed when Captain Brooke returned on board; but I never saw complete disappointment so unmistakably betrayed as it was on his face, that of the Admiral and the other officers who received him at the gangway.

I have little more to say. The French Fleet presently passed us, steering to the westward. The Duke detached twelve of his battle-ships under Sir Michael Seymour with seven or eight cruisers—all newest types of ships—to follow up the Russians into their own waters, while he himself followed up the French with the remainder of his fleet. My wife and I were sent on board the *Thames* which came home full speed with the news.

I remain in a kind of mental paralysis. No one had ever suggested to me that in the presence of British power, naval war was to become but naval peace. All the naval people whom I had ever heard talk about it always seemed to have in their minds a certainty that in naval war, no two hostile fleets could ever see one another without rushing to a mutual destruction pell-mell. And yet I could get away from the fact that to every Frenchman and every Russian in the combined fleet I had seen, it must have been clear that no one but a madman could have pursued any other course than that which their Admirals followed. Of course it might have been different had war been actually declared.

PREPARATIONS FOR THE LANDING OF BRITISH TROOPS AT TREBIZONDE.

THE PROTECTION OF ERZEROUM—TURKS, LIKE THE ENGLISH, AS USUAL, TOO LATE.

(*From our Special Correspondent, Mr. Francis Scudamore.*)

KARAKURGHAN, *April* 29.

I OWE the opportunity afforded me for writing to you from this wretched place to an accident which has befallen my best horse, and will delay me possibly for another couple of days. The mischance is doubly unfortunate at this moment, inasmuch as reports from our front lead to the supposition that an important engagement is at hand. Any adequate analysis of the rumours that reach me constantly, contradictory as they are, continually varied, chequered with additions and omissions, and burdened with the extravagant local interest environing some wholly trivial circumstance, would be as entirely out of the question for me as for any of your readers at home. Indeed, your readers are certainly infinitely better informed than I am as to current events.

When I left Trebizonde, five days ago, the town was in a state of fevered anxiety, of enthusiastic anticipation, tempered in some sober quarters by a quiet but not ungenerous scepticism born of previous experience. The English were coming, cried the enthusiasts. Three English Army Corps (Heaven alone knows whence it was proposed to get them) were on their way to Trebizonde, to Samsoun, and to Shumla to aid their Turkish and Italian allies. The eastern division of the Mediterranean Fleet had already entered the Black Sea, as much to the surprise (and perhaps, somewhat to the chagrin) of the Turkish commanders at the Dardanelles and the Kavaks as of the generals of Russia and of France. In Trebizonde and the surrounding villages a certain basis of probability was built beneath these rumours by the fact that English agents had, for a week, been purchasing mules, sheep, and cattle, at, as is usual with British agents in times of stress, some five times their market value to any other purchaser. Nor have the native producers profited more than usual by this large-handed generosity, for some two or three Greek and Armenian traders, anticipating, as is their wont, honest English procrastination, have been beforehand with the army agents, with whom they are now dealing at altogether fancy prices. This, however, is after all but a small matter beside the great question of our intervention. That England's action should invariably be delayed

BRITISH TROOPS LANDING AT TREBIZONDE.

almost (but never quite) until too late—that her transports should reach their destination empty, her troops be either unprovided with cartridges, or supplied with those of some obsolete and useless pattern—that by every mistake ineptitude can secure or official ignorance produce, all arrangements connected with the disembarkation and provisioning, and general welfare of whatever forces have been tardily despatched, must inevitably break down but for the tireless energy, the unfailing resource, the unremitting good temper and never-flagging loyalty of all the officers and men thus maltreated, are matters which have long since come to be as well known abroad as they are beginning to be recognised at home. 'The English,' said the good people of Trebizonde, while awaiting the expected Army Corps, 'are good but careless. They are richer than the Russians, and they are less corrupt, but they are also more stupid.' This, as the independent criticism of allies, more than anxious to be generous, is worth at least a second thought.

I would gladly have witnessed the disembarkation of our troops (for aught I know it may have already taken place), but, after fruitlessly waiting many days in dreary Trebizonde, I no longer dared to delay. News had come that a large Russian force was advancing from Kars westward towards Erzeroum, and, although there are in and around that place some 50,000 Turkish troops, yet, save at Keupru Kui, a place about nine hours' ride from Erzeroum on the Kars road, little or no preparation appears to have been made to resist an enemy. Erzeroum, let it be remembered, is entered by three posterns, called respectively the Stamboul, the Ardahan, and the Kars gates. The roads from them lead to Ardahan, Kars, Van, Erzinghan, and Trebizonde. On the south of Erzeroum, at a very short distance from the walls, a mountain descends steeply towards the city, which it altogether commands, and a direct road runs from Van to Moush, and from that town to the mountain, from which two water channels lead into Erzeroum. If an enemy once had possession of the eminence —and, so far as I can learn, there is little or nothing to prevent him—he would be able to turn these water-courses off from the city. There are, it is true, a few wells within the walls, but the supply from them is already insufficient for the requirements of the population, without taking into account the troops quartered in and around the town. It seems typical of Turkish apathy that so little should have been done to secure this their last great stronghold in Asia Minor from attack. I am going, of course, merely by what I hear from Turkish officers, as I have as yet been unable to see for myself; but I have hitherto had no reason to discredit their information.

It appears that from time to time, since 1878, proposals have been made for fortifying various strong natural positions, but that, with a procrastinatory belief in the protection of Providence that is wholly Turkish and almost English, these plans have been continually set aside until it is now too late to execute them. Thus on the Van Road, about five miles from Erzeroum, there is an admirable position known as the Palandukain defile. This position was protected after a fashion in 1876, when a fort was constructed capable of offering sturdy resistance. Another fort had been built also at that time at Gereguzek, eighteen miles from Erzeroum, on the Ardahan road. Another position, that of the Devé Boinou Bogaz, five miles from Erzeroum, on the Kars road, was considered at that time to be a good place for a fort, and yet further defences were then constructed at the Loghana defile, which is some twenty-four hours from Erzeroum, on the Kars road. There are, no doubt, also important positions on the Bayazid road, as, for instance, at Deli Baba—a narrow gorge through high mountains, which the Turks declare to be impregnable—at Taher Gedi, five hours' march further on, and at Kara Kilissa, beyond which there is a level road to Bayazid. Since the war, however, it appears that little or nothing has been done to strengthen or even to maintain these positions in an adequate state of defence. There has been much talk of late in Constantinople of extensive armaments on this frontier. Krupp guns have, it has been said, been sent to supplement the bronze cannon manufactured at Tophané, with which the forts of Erzeroum were in the last war mainly armed. As to whether any such material has reached its destination I am as yet uninformed. People on this road, which it must surely have traversed, profess to know nothing of it. It is to be feared that we may expect a repetition of the famous story of the million liras expenditure said to have been incurred in the fortification of Erzeroum in the last war.

I did not journey from Trebizonde alone, but took advantage of the departure of a huge straggling convoy of mules and packhorses laden with ammunition for Erzeroum. There were also with us half a dozen English doctors who have taken service with the Porte, and have volunteered to attend the wounded under fire. Owing to the accident to my horse, who slipped, poor brute, through a ragged hole in the wide stone bridge across the Kara Su, close to this place (a terrible pitfall for artillery), and badly scraped both his own shin and his master's, these gentlemen have perforce abandoned me until such time as I can obtain another beast.

The traffic through this little place, which is the point of junction of the Trebizonde and Erzinghan roads to Erzeroum, and as a rule at this season is almost deserted, is in itself indicative of stirring events in our front. All through the day there has been a continuous passage of nondescript wayfarers in either direction. Turkish soldiers—stragglers or deserters may be—some sick, some slightly wounded; Koordish Bashi-bazouks, pure bandits for the most part, flashing great arsenals of gleaming weapons in their waist-belts, and armed, many of them, with Winchester rifles, remnants of the last war; slim, evil-visaged Circassians on lean, wiry horses, and gaunt Zaibeks, ferocious beneath their extravagant headgear, have tramped and clattered continuously past the miserable khan where I am established. Some of these gentry, I note, have Russian great-coats with regimental numbers on the shoulder strap, flung either across their cruppers, or around their shoulders. This is a sure indication that there has at least been some skirmish or reconnaissance in which Russian arms have suffered not a little.

REPULSE OF THE RUSSIANS.

THE TURKS PURSUE ESKI ZAGRA—THE GRIM REALITIES OF WAR.

NEAR KEUPRU KEUI, *May* 2.

I AM profiting by an opportunity to send you a hurried message by a Turkish officer on his way to Erzeroum with despatches.

Soon after writing last to you, I managed to pick up a horse—a poor beast enough truly, in place of my stalwart grey—and pushed on to Erzeroum. There I found all in confusion. Certain news had arrived of a Russian advance in force along the Kars road, and every available man had been thrown forward to meet it. It was but natural that the Russians should seize the earliest possible opportunity of hurling themselves against the Turkish stronghold, which they might very reasonably expect to find unprepared to receive them. More or less unprepared the Turks indeed were, but Ghazi Mouchtar Pasha—the hero of '77—who had himself reached Erzeroum but a few days since, was fully determined not to permit his traditional enemy to win an easy triumph. As I have said, every available regiment was ordered to meet the attack, and hurried forward to Keupru Keui, where the stand was to be made. I have as yet no details—indeed, as I stayed but an hour or so in Erzeroum to feed my horses, I have hitherto been able to see no one in authority; but so far as I can gather, the Turks, though outnumbered, were not greatly inferior to their adversaries, over whom they had the additional enormous advantage of being in a position which tradition has taught them to regard as well-nigh impregnable. In any case Turkish arms seem to have gained a signal victory.

Very soon after leaving Erzeroum, which I did shortly before mid-day this morning, I began to meet with unmistakable evidences that a big battle had either been fought or was in progress. First a knot of some twenty infantrymen, weary, haggard, and ragged, met me on the steep slope of the hill some five miles beyond the town. They were all jaded beyond expression—every one was wounded more or less grievously—several were using their rifles as crutches, and some who had lost or abandoned their rifles were helping themselves along either by the aid of their comrades' shoulders, or by stakes, or waggon-boards, or rammers, or indeed any of the miscellaneous articles of wood or metal that are to be found strewn along the line of a straggling fight. I gave them a water-skin, and offered a bottle of brandy (as *ilitch*—medicine for their wounds). The water they took, but none would touch the spirit save one gaunt, white-moustached veteran, who mumbled incoherencies about Algeria, by way seemingly of excuse. While they drank I asked them what was doing. 'A great battle was being fought,' they said, but their opinions were divided as to the course of the action; several men (weak from loss of blood) opined that the enemy was too strong for them. But one broad-shouldered, bright-eyed little fellow, who had had all the flesh of one cheek torn from him by a shell splinter, and had bound the wound with a strip from his rough serge jacket, was loud in his derision of this view. 'It was Eski Zagra again,' he said. The Moskoffs were driven back, beaten hopelessly, and pursued by agile Bashi-bazouks through the slippery passes, the precipitous fastnesses, the treacherous paths of the rugged route, a pursuit without cess or quarter—where every enemy, whether wounded or not, was exultingly slaughtered as soon as caught. The little veteran illustrated with horribly realistic gestures his own views as to the treatment of Russian wounded. With a foul gusto that raised wild enthusiasm in his weary comrades, he demonstrated how he would hew off the noses and lips of his enemy; how he would gouge out their eyes with his bayonet before he plunged it into their throats and twisted it till the victims died suffocated with their own blood. He outlined other horrors, but I had had enough, and left him posing in anticipation as a hero among his fellows, while I rode on towards this place.

That this fierce implacable Moslem had been right in his conjecture I soon had ample—ay, terrible—proof. In every mile, even on the rugged track itself, as I neared the spot from which I write, the horrible evidences of deadly carnage multiplied and repeated themselves. Disembowelled horses, broken limbers, little mounds of dead, fallen one on another, their still, calm, white faces in cruel contrast to the extravagant distortion of their scattered and twisted limbs; and everywhere traces of that ruthless hatred vowed by the Turk to his hereditary enemy. Hideous featureless corpses stared at me out of eyeless sockets from the roadside, their hands uplifted and bloody, showing that wounded, not dead Russians, had been thus maltreated; occasionally a movement, slight though perceptible, caused me to dismount, eager to aid some mutilated sufferer, but all to no purpose—the Turks had done their work too well. As I advanced, the spectacle of these recurrent horrors increased in its revelations of barbarism and malignant cruelty. The number of Turkish dead diminished step by step, as that of the Russians augmented, and by the time I reached this place I had had such a surfeit of ghoul-feasting (for the eye) as I envy no man.

While talking to Salem Bey Agris—the gentleman to whose good offices I am indebted for the conveyance of this hurried despatch, at least, as far as Erzeroum—a poor horse hobbled up, browsing its way along the thin coarse grass which covers the bank on which I was seated. Something in the animal's movements attracting my attention, I looked up and noticed to my infinite horror that the poor brute, which was still saddled and bridled, had but three legs—the off fore leg being from the shoulder downwards nothing but a sliver of white bone splintered to a pencil point. Horror-struck, I seized my revolver—my first thought being to put the poor creature out of its pain. But as it browsed on placidly, seemingly indifferent, I called Salem Bey's attention to its condition. 'Poor horse,' he said (and note that he had surveyed mutilated Russians with placid indifference), 'a suffering animal, indeed, tears the breast, but I have seen, only two hours since, a sight far more heartrending than this. I was charging with my squadron a troop of Cossacks. It chanced that a shell burst right over the first line, and, killing two troopers, tore away the whole muzzle of one of their horses. All was destroyed in the poor beast, right up to the eyes, and you might have supposed it would fall dead at once. Nothing of the kind. It held its place in the ranks, spouting torrents of blood and foam from its ghastly shattered head, until, fortunately, some stray Russian bullet laid it low. Until then, I will own,' he added, 'I was afraid for my men.'

The Bey, leaving me to digest this tale, strode away in the dusk to get his horse. 'Where is your army?' I have shouted to him, and his reply is: '*Bilémem* (I do not know). INSHALLAH, it has gone to KARS'

THE RUSSO-GERMAN CAMPAIGN—GREAT BATTLE AT SKIERNIWIÇE.

ROUT OF THE RUSSIANS AND THEIR RETREAT ON WARSAW—HEAVY FIGHTING ON THE GALICIAN FRONTIER.

(From our Special Correspondent, Mr. Charles Lowe.)

SKIERNIWIÇE, *May* 18.

STRANGE is the irony of events. In the month of September 1884, this was the friendly meeting-place of the Emperors of Russia, Germany, and Austria, who were accompanied by their respective Chancellors—Bismarck, Kalnoky, and Giers; and now the chateau where they so ostentatiously feasted, embraced, and exchanged their pledges of peace, is a heap of smoking ruins. After this, who shall say that there is any stability in human affairs, or any trustworthiness in human foresight?

The united Russian forces, consisting of the 5th and 6th Corps under General Gourko, and the 14th and 15th Corps under the Grand Duke Vladimir, have to-day suffered a crushing defeat at the hands of the combined German armies of the Vistula and Silesia, commanded by the King of Saxony, and are now in full retreat on Warsaw. As I predicted in my last despatch, this has been the Waterloo of the Russo-German portion of the campaign, and it has been brilliantly won by the Germans—thanks mainly to the disconcerting effects of smokeless powder on the tactics of an enemy who fights better in the mass than in detail, no less than to the fact of the Russians having committed the radical error of provoking a war before they were completely equipped with the new magazine rifle, which, even with the aid of the

French factories that received orders for half a million of the new weapon, will not be served out to the entire army of the Czar before the summer of 1894.

In my last despatch I recorded how the Grand Duke Vladimir, in spite of his victory over the German Army of Silesia at Czenstochau, had refrained from following up his success in consideration of Gourko's repulse at Alexandrovo, preferring—like Wellington, who had similarly beaten Ney at Quatre Bras, but was yet desirous of succouring the retreating Blücher, who had come to grief in front of Napoleon on the same day at Ligny—to retire towards Warsaw for the purpose of joining hands with his fellow-commander, on the latter being worsted by the King of Saxony. The distances, of course, were infinitely greater in the present case; but otherwise the principles of strategy were the same.

A glance at the map will show that the junction-point for Gourko and the Grand Duke Vladimir could only have been Skierniwiçe, where the railways from Alexandrovo and Czenstochau converge; and it appears that, though the Grand Duke's line of retreat to the common rendezvous was considerably the longer of the two, nevertheless the bulk of his forces had reached it first, by reason of the fact that he enjoyed a double line of rails, whereas Gourko had to move as best he could along a single track.

The German Army of the Vistula, with which I had thrown in my lot as a witness of the war, was not slow to gather itself together after the battle of Alexandrovo, and start in pursuit of Gourko's shattered forces, but much precious time was lost by us in repairing bridges which our retreating foes had blown up; and though at last, by dint of great exertions on our part, the railway proved not altogether unavailable to us for transport purposes, still the earlier stages of our advance on Warsaw simply assumed the form of an ordinary march along, and parallel with, the line, the engineers pontooning or planking any bridgeless stream or ravine which obstructed our progress.

At Vlokavek, which our advanced guard reached on the fifth day after the battle of Alexandrovo, though the distance is only about thirty miles, we were considerably hampered, and even hurt, by the flanking fire of a Russian battery, which had established itself in a safe position on the right bank of the Vistula—a battery, strange to say, which was unsupported by any body of infantry of which we could discover trace; and the King of Saxony, who, in spite of his sixty-four summers, is still almost as vigorous and alert as when he commanded on the Meuse, determined to imitate, though, of course, on a very much smaller scale, the celebrated passage of the Douro by Wellington (of which, by the way, this was, curiously enough, the anniversary, the 12th May). Accordingly, the 3d battalion of the 'Old Dessauers' Magdeburg regiment, under Major von Wusterhausen, was stealthily ferried over the Vistula, which is here both broad and deep, at the dead of night; and, performing a silent and circuitous march to the rear of the Russian battery, it opened a heavy fire on the bewildered Muscovites, just as the latter, profiting by the breaking dawn, were about to begin their usual day's work of pounding away at our advancing columns; and, charging with a cheer up to the emplacements, before the pieces could be reversed, the 'Old Dessauers' killed or captured every one of the gunners. For this smart and effective feat of arms Major von Wusterhausen will doubtless receive the Iron Cross of the first class and the rank of colonel.

This was the main incident which marked the course of our advance, though I might fill columns by recounting the minor vicissitudes of our march, especially the intolerable botheration which was occasioned us by the clouds of Cossacks and Dragoons —the latter little more than mere mounted infantry—who pertinaciously hovered on our flanks in search of fitting opportunities for harassing us, and had ever and anon to be brushed away like so many troublesome swarms of mosquitoes.

In the meantime the telegraph had kept us duly informed of the various stages in the forward movement of the army of Silesia along the other and longer side of the triangle, of which Skierniwice is the apex, and it was naturally enough our endeavour so to time our junction with it as to render it impossible for the Russians to attack our two armies severally and beat them in detail, even if they should have the stomach to assume the offensive, which we gravely doubted.

When our headquarters had reached Lowitz, which is only about fourteen miles from Skierniwiçe, and established itself in a pretty chateau, Arcadia by name, belonging to the Radziwill family, an officer of the Empress Frederick's Posen Hussars (Death's Heads), who had made a long and venturesome ride across country from Lipce, came spurring in with a despatch from Prince George of Saxony, announcing that the combined Russian forces under Gourko and the Grand Duke Vladimir had taken up a strong defensive position behind the Lupta brook (which runs into the Bzura, an affluent of the Vistula), with their left resting on a village, Stryzboga, and their right on another hamlet, Dromiloff, their centre being Skierniwiçe. The left half of their line, defended by the troops of the Czar's eldest brother, was formed by the Lupta itself, a brook about the size of the Bistritz at Sadowa; while the right half was thrown back from this streamlet at an angle of about twenty-five degrees, so as to profit by some ridgy ground in its rear. Prince George of Saxony, therefore, invited his royal brother to attack General Gourko with all energy on the morrow, while he himself would simultaneously assail the position of the Grand Duke Vladimir, a proposal which King Albert, after brief consultation with his Staff, declared his readiness to act upon.

Accordingly, two hours before dawn, all our troops were under arms, and in motion for the various positions which had been assigned them. On our half of the Russian front the 3d (Brandenburg) Corps, with the 7th Division, advanced to open the attack, while the 8th Division acted as reserve, and our two Cavalry Divisions were directed to keep a look-out on our left flank, adapting their action to the nature of the ground and the development of the infantry portion of the fight. Between us and the enemy the terrain was pretty wavy with occasional patches of crops and cover, while in front of Skierniwice it rose into a gentle slope, on the top of which spread the extensive wood forming the deer park and game preserves of the castle (famous for its Three Emperors' Meeting), of which the turrets were just visible above the tree-tops. This, as I said, formed the centre of the Russian position; and it was by opening our guns in this direction that we began the battle, with the view of making the enemy believe that our main objective was the middle of their line.

For a couple of hours or so the fight was nothing but an artillery duel at long range, and it was plain that although the Russian artillery was more advantageously posted, it had the utmost difficulty in finding the range, and even the exact position of our guns, owing to the comparative smokelessness of their discharges. On the other hand, after the Russian outposts had been driven in, the Jäger Battalion of the 3d Corps, which, courting every dip in the ground, had stealthily crept forward for some considerable distance in a hollow beyond our batteries, and lined the edge of a rye-field, within about 3000 metres of the Russian guns, opened fire at this very long range, and not without fatal effects; for with a good glass we could see the Russian artillerists dropping beside their pieces, a fact which made us realise the truth of the German Emperor's remark that, if field guns are to hold their ground as weapons of modern warfare, their range must still be further increased beyond that of the newest form of small bore rifle.

To emphasise the impression produced by this combined artillery and musketry fire—of such a galling and invisible kind—we made a show of manœuvring large bodies of infantry over against the Russian centre, as if in preparation for an attack in force; and presently we could discern that this feint movement on our part was responded to by the pushing up of more of the enemy's force from either flank into the woods of Skierniwice, for the purpose of giving us a reception lacking nothing in warmth should we have the temerity to essay an entrance there.

While this renewed concentration in the Russian centre was

going on, a curious incident happened, which puzzled us not a little at first. This was the sudden emerging from the wood of what appeared in the distance to be several squadrons of cavalry, which headed straight for our lines, and came careering down right on the rye-field where the Jäger Battalion before-mentioned, from its concealed position, was playing such sore havoc among the Russian gunners with their long range and invisible fire, and we doubted not that their whereabouts had at last been discovered. Accordingly, while our guns loaded with shrapnel, word was passed to the Stendal Hussars, who, acting as cavalry of the 7th Division, were standing ensconced in a hollow on the rear flank of our batteries, to prepare for hurling themselves upon these presumptuous horsemen. But this counter attack proved to be unnecessary; for presently we could discern that the Russian steeds were riderless, and, on coming nearer, they turned out to be only a huge herd of very fine deer, which had been scared out of their leafy haunts in the forest of Skierniwiçe by the infernal pother going on there. It may be remembered that, in his narrative of the battle of Königgrätz, the late Count Moltke referred to a similar incident.

Meanwhile, our real object, which was the delivery of our main attack on the right flank of the Russians, was being successfully attained. It can scarcely be expected that I, or any other single eye-witness, should be able to detail the incidents and development of a battle which extended along a line of more than six miles, as the reasons which preclude a General from exercising anything like unity of command over so vast an area form an equal restraint upon the War Correspondent's power of all-embracing observation. Even of conflicts like Königgrätz and Sedan, a pretty complete description of a general kind could always be given by one pen by reason of the smoke which betrayed the whereabouts of friend and foe and the fluctuations of the fight; but now that science has robbed war of one of its most picturesque appendages, a modern battle by day is a most bewildering spectacle. You hear the roar of cannon and the rattle of musketry, but this incessant thunder is accompanied by no lightning-flash. You see men flinging up their arms and falling around you, but know not whence they received their death-wounds any more than if they had been stricken down by the invisible arrows of the Sun-God Apollo.

Naturally enough this must have a most demoralising effect on all soldiers, and when Blücher at Lingy said: 'My men like to see the enemy,' he was only characterising the fighting men of most nations. Still, as far as I could discover, the German Infantry were less disconcerted by these unseen terrors of modern war than were their Russian foes, who are most dour and indomitable devils when they can fight shoulder to shoulder and in the mass, but lose much of their *morale* and their dogged powers of resistance when each man has mainly to rely upon his own intelligence (not a very marked feature of the Slavonic soldier), his own initiative, and his own isolated sources of courage. Indeed, we thought we could now and then detect traces of panic among the soldiers of the Czar; and in one case, at least, we distinctly saw an officer draw his revolver on some of his men who would rather have fled than fallen before a foe whom they could neither see nor feel.

In spite, however, of these demoralising influences which were at work among the scattered ranks of the Russians, they held their ground with singular tenacity; and the battle had thus raged for hours without our being able to carry out completely our main purpose, which was, under cover of the feint attack that we had directed against the enemy's centre, to turn his right and roll him up—a manœuvre, as we knew, which Prince George of Saxony was equally fain to accomplish with the Russian left.

About noon, however, the scales of victory were suddenly turned in our favour in the following manner. The day was bright, clear, and warm, and though the battlefield immediately in front of the knoll occupied by King Albert and his Staff (to which I had attached myself) was completely free from powder-smoke, the horizon behind the Russians all at once began to grow clouded with a long line of thick yellow dust, which floated ever nearer and nearer to us in dense billowy volumes like a huge, irregular wave of muddy sea foam. I saw the King exchange glances of intelligent meaning with the various members of his Staff, but did not myself comprehend the meaning of the phenomenon, until the rolling dust-cloud began to be relieved by sparks and glintings such as are emitted by mica from a grey hill-side, and then it flashed upon me all at once that these coruscations of light in a whirlwind of dust could only come from the flashing of the sun's rays on the sabres, helmets, and lances of our cavalry.

And so it was. For our Two Divisions of Horse, numbering in all thirty-two squadrons, starting betimes, had stolen away through Lowitz, up the right bank of the Bzura, and fording this stream above its confluence with the Ravka, had mounted this other brook and crossed it at Bolimoff, where they were fairly in the rear of the Russian right, on which they thus came thundering down. I had seen operations of this kind repeatedly carried out at the autumn manœuvres in Germany, but deemed them *Kriegspiel* in the literal sense of the word—and not to be thought of or hazarded in real warfare. Yet here was a vivid proof that the Germans are terribly earnest, even in their military pastimes, and that they only apply in war what they practise in peace. I daresay, however, King Albert would never have sanctioned so bold a venture had he not discovered early in the day that the Russians had shifted the bulk of their cavalry to their left flank as being the more exposed of the two, and only left a weak Brigade of Dragoons to strengthen the natural inaccessibility of their right. It had never occurred to them as a physical possibility that the Germans, unperceived by their Cossack scouts, could positively work two Cavalry Divisions round to their rear; but the Germans had done so, and, riding down the Dragoon Brigade in question, it rushed with a ringing cheer like a whirlwind upon the Russian battalions and smote them hip and thigh.

Becoming aware, though all too late, of this impending avalanche of squadrons in their rear, the Russians had faced about with wonderful alacrity and steadiness, and delivered a well-directed volley against their assailants, emptying a very considerable number of saddles; but though this staggered them a little, it did not in the least stop the long audacious wave of horsemen, who, couching their lances (for the German cavalry of all kinds are now armed with this weapon), rode full tilt at the lines of Russian marksmen, stabbing and spearing them as they so stubbornly stood their ground. The shock and *mêlée* were all over in less time than it takes to tell of it, and having thus performed their dare-devil and death-dealing ride through the shattered ranks of Gourko's infantry, the gallant squadrons put spurs to their jaded steeds, and with another rousing cheer came galloping across to our lines, through which they passed amid ringing salvoes of cheers, retiring into the hollow ground beyond to rally and reform—though very much thinned in numbers, it must be admitted. It was an heroic feat, executed at a great cost of life and limb; but it had completed the demoralisation among the ranks of the Russian infantry which our invisible musketry fire had begun, and paved the way for the crowning manœuvre of the day.

This was performed by our reserve Division of Infantry (the 8th), which, imitating the strategy of the Prussian Guards at Chlum, had edged its way round and taken the Russians full on their right flank, which it was now rapidly rolling up and forcing in upon the centre in huddled masses of demoralised and defeated troops of all arms. At the same time it was clear, from certain signs on the extreme right, that our army of the Vistula had succeeded in performing a similar turning movement in its particular part of the field (where the bulk of the Russian Cavalry had bravely, but vainly, attempted to stem the tide of our advance); and by two o'clock in the afternoon our line of battle had assumed something like semi-circular shape, which was ever narrowing down upon our out-manœuvred opponents.

By this time a general advance on our side had been ordered, and our Corps Artillery, after raining another most awful torrent of shells on the Russian position, now slackened and gradually stopped its fire, in order to let our infantry do the rest of the bloody work unhampered by the fire of their own guns. Our infantry, indeed, were only too eager to finish its terrible task; and although whole ranks were mown down before it could succeed in ousting the enemy from the field entrenchments, which ran bastion-like all round their position in Skierniwiçe, still Teutonic courage and discipline proved more than equal to Russian doggedness, and volley after volley of the Mauser repeater soon filled Gourko's trenches with heaps of dead and wounded.

THE STORMING OF SKIERNIWIÇE.

The townlet of Skierniwiçe was in flames, and no longer afforded shelter to its defenders; the chateau itself (with all its three-Emperor memories) had been converted into a heap of smoking ruins; the Russian batteries had been reduced to silence as much by our long-range rifle-fire as by our own field guns; the wood had also been rendered untenable by our encompassing it on three sides; and so nothing remained to be done but storm the position at the point of the bayonet. It is marvellous how troops can so dispose themselves as to escape observation in a terrain not over rich in natural and artificial cover; for the general advance had not been sounded long before reserve companies and battalions seemed to start from out the very earth and join in the universal rush forward upon the Russians, as they began to waver and finally give way all along the line. By one battalion a determined stand was made at the railway station, where there was some desperate hand-to-hand fighting that recalled the butchery of Bazeilles; but here, too, German obstinacy and valour carried the day; and as the 'Old Dessauers' had distinguished themselves by the capture of the Russian battery at Vlokavek, so now it was reserved to the 2d battalion of that same regiment to storm, with colours flying and kettle-drums beating, the final foothold of Gourko's gallant Muscovites on the field which had been selected by him and his fellow-commander as the Waterloo of this portion of the war.

By three o'clock the Russians were in full retreat on Warsaw and its ring of formidable forts, leaving us in undisputed possession of Skierniwiçe with all its stores and strategical advantages.

It will be impossible to estimate our own losses as well as those of our foes for some hours yet; but on both sides the carnage has been fearful, very much heavier, indeed, in view of the relative numbers of troops engaged, than were ever suffered by any combatants in the Franco-German or Russo-Turkish wars. But it is some little consolation, at least, to think that the ambulance arrangements of the Germans have kept pace with the improved methods of mass-murder called modern warfare, and the crowds of wounded, both Germans and Russians, are being well attended to.

The meeting between our victorious commanders, the King of Saxony and his brother, Prince George, after the battle, was of a most touching and affectionate kind, recalling the historic scene at Königgrätz, in which King William and his heroic son, 'Unser Fritz,' were the chief figures.

GREAT BATTLE ON THE GALICIAN FRONTIER.

LATER.

Just before sending off this despatch **news reaches me of a decisive battle** which has also been fought on the Galician frontier between the combined Russian forces thereabouts and an **Austrian army 250,000** strong, which **is said to have** resulted in the complete repulse of Dragomiroff, who is retreating towards Lublin, on the Warsaw line. Should this rumour prove true, it is probable that Dragomiroff will also **retire** on **Warsaw** to join hands with Gourko and the Grand Duke Vladimir, in which case it is not unlikely that the **present war will be** productive of another Gravelotte and another Metz.

ITALY MOBILISES HER ARMY, AND TAKES THE FIELD AGAINST FRANCE.

SCENE IN ROME ON THE DECLARATION OF WAR BY FRANCE— 'ITALY WILL FULFIL HER TREATY OBLIGATIONS.'

(By Post from an Occasional Correspondent.)

MONTE CARLO, *May* 30.

THE telegraph will have already kept you well informed of the various details in the development of the Franco-Italian portion of the present great European war; but having been enabled, by a series of lucky chances, to follow the main incidents of the Italian uprising until now, perhaps you might care to receive from me, by way of supplement to what you have already published, a brief general record of my observations.

I happened to be in Rome when the telegram was received there announcing that France had drawn her sword on Germany. I was first made aware of the fact by a large tumultuous crowd, which came surging and shouting past my window (a back one) of the Hôtel de Londres, on the Piazza di Spagna, shouting out '*evvivas*' for Germany and the Triple Alliance. This crowd had come rolling down from the Pincio, where the splendid band of the Carabinieri—second to none in Europe—had been discoursing delightful music, and where a special edition of the *Popolo Romano* had disseminated the news, which was not, indeed, wholly unexpected, that France, profiting by the embarrassments of Germany on her Eastern frontier, had risen with a cry of vengeance to spring upon the Rhine. One man had jumped up on the bandstand of the Carabinieri and read out this telegram to the listening throng, which then, as if by pre-concert, burst out into ringing cheers for King Humbert and the German Emperor; while the band swelled the chorus of these enthusiastic acclamations by playing the Italian Air and the '*Wacht am Rhein.*'

Then, starting off for the Quirinal, the crowd came rolling down by the Church of La Trinità dei Monti, and through the Via Sistina, where I hastened to join it, and where it stopped before the house in which Signor Crispi modestly occupies a third-floor flat. In compliance with the clamours of the mob, the ex-premier, the advocate and author of Italy's share in the Triple Alliance, presented himself on his balcony, and bowed his acknowledgments to the cheering mass below; but, declining in the circumstances to make a speech, he only waved his hand, and pointed in the direction of the Quirinal, to which, accordingly, the multitude now again headed with tumultuous haste.

After rushing up the flight of steps leading to the Quirinal, we found the spacious area in front of the Royal Palace already filled with similar contingents of the populace from other parts of the city; some of the demonstrationists having even clambered up and taken their stand on the pedestals of the equine masterpieces of Phidias, familiar to all visitors to Rome, while a very considerable element in the vast assemblage was formed by the black-robed and tonsured gentlemen from the other side of the river, who had come to witness the birth of events which might be pregnant with consequences for them and their aspirations. And from these priestly figures, with their pale and pensive faces, I could not help letting my eye wander across the intervening valley to the lofty windows of the Vatican, where perchance the self-imprisoned successor of St. Peter was trying, with the aid even of a telescope, to make out the meaning of all this popular commotion in front of the palace of the royal inheritor of all his worldly glory—to make out the meaning of it all, and wonder whether the stirring events now being fashioned in the crucible of war might possibly result in restoring to him some shreds and patches of his temporal power.

But these reveries of mine were speedily dispelled by another roar of acclamation from the multitude, which had parted and formed a lane, as did the waters of the Red Sea at the sight of Moses and his mantle, to let some one pass out from the Royal Palace. It was the Marquis di Rudini, accompanied by two of his secretaries, who had just left the Council presided over by the King, and was crossing over to the Ministry of Foreign Affairs. Cheer after cheer greeted this appearance of the man who, although he had stepped into the ministerial shoes of Signor Crispi, was known to have espoused his popular foreign policy; and the crowd could scarcely be prevented from shouldering him high and bearing him into his official residence. The crowd had barely closed round the portal of the Ministry when it had again to open up a lane to admit the passage of a carriage containing the German Ambassador, Count Solms, who had hastened hither from his palace on the Capitoline with a very grave face indeed. But when he re-emerged from the Ministry of Foreign Affairs in about twenty minutes' time, the clouds had lifted from his refined countenance, and he returned the salutations of the crowd with a grave smile of satisfaction. Quick to draw its own conclusions, the multitude set up another shout, and began to clamour for Rudini. Yielding at last to the loud and continuous solicitations of the Roman populace, the Marquis stepped out upon the balcony of the Ministry, and, after signifying his wish for silence, addressed his hearers to the following effect:—

'Gentlemen, this is at once a serious and a sublime moment, but as it is a time more for action than for words, my remarks must be brief. France, as you know, has drawn the sword on Germany, and Italy must be true to her loyal ally. (A burst of cheering.)

'Italy entered into certain treaty obligations, which she is now required to fulfil; and Italy will now fulfil them. (Frantic cheers.)

'The die is cast, and we must redeem our pledges at all risks; for our honour is at stake, and our national existence would be nothing without our national honour. (Loud "*evvivas.*")

'This is the first time that Italy, as a united nation, has been called upon to show the stuff whereof she is made; and with God's help she will justify the love that has been lavished, as well as the hopes that have been placed upon her.

'I need only add that orders have been issued for the immediate mobilising of all our brave army; and that the steps of this army will be accompanied by the fervent prayer of every true Italian—and we are all true Italians—from the sunny plains of Sicily to the snow-clad peaks of the Alps. (Great cheering.)

Italia farà da se. Evviva il Rè Humberto! Evviva l'imperatore di Germania! Evviva la tripla Allianza!'

Loud and long-continued cheering followed this speech of the Marquis Rudini (which was presently again to serve as the substance of a more elaborate oration in the Chamber); but with his exit from the balcony of the Foreign Office I may fitly drop my curtain on this opening scene of the Italian War-drama, which your space will only allow me to portray in one or two representative sketches, but not describe in detail.

. . . .

THE COUNCIL OF WAR.

THE scene of the next incident which I have to record was the Ministry of War, one of the hugest buildings in Rome (for in every country of the Continent is not the architecture of war rapidly dwarfing the structures of religion?), where King Humbert presided over a Council composed of his military and naval magnates, including the Generals commanding the twelve Army

Corps of the monarchy, and the Admirals of the Fleet, who had been summoned by telegraph to the capital to advise as to the course of action which should be adopted against France. The General Staff, it is true, had already worked out a plan of campaign for the contingency of such a war; but the situation, as it now stood, presented elements of doubt and difficulty which had not been wholly foreseen, and it was therefore necessary to deliberate as to how the Italian army should be divided and disposed of in existing circumstances.

The main question was: how many Army Corps could be hurled against France? and this question again was subordinate to the consideration of how many would be required to guard the coasts of Italy against a French descent. Moreover, the fact underlying both these questions, as pointed out by the King, was the absence of any hope that England would, for the present at least, see her way to give the aims of the Triple Alliance more than her mere moral support. Had England, for a due consideration, formally joined the Alliance, and placed her fleet at the disposal of Italy, thus securing her against all danger of French aggression, or counter-strokes, by sea, the whole Italian army would have been free to operate in the field against France; but, as it was, Italy had to face the possibility of a descent at various parts of her open and extensive sea-board by a French force of at least four Army Corps. France had already sent thirteen of her twenty Corps towards the Rhine; but the seven other garrisoning her Southern and South-western Departments had not yet received their marching orders; and at any moment some of them might be poured down to Marseilles and Toulon within a few hours' sailing of the Italian coast.

The opinion of the War Council was very much divided as to what should be done, Generals Pianell and Bariola acting as spokesmen of the two divergent parties; but at length, on the motion of General Cosenz, Chief of the Staff, whose view was supported by the King, it was resolved in the meantime to intrust the task of falling on the flank of France to the 1st, 2d, 3d and

4th Corps, while the 6th and 7th would act as a reserve, and the others remain behind to adapt themselves to the development of events, especially if the French were to suffer reverses on the Rhine and be thus compelled to denude the Southern Departments of their garrisons.

And then as to the line of attack, the line, that is to say, by which the Italians should seek to enter France, the Council—but here my informant, who was present, begged me to exercise the patience which I would now similarly seek to enjoin upon your readers. I may add that by the time the Council had finished its deliberations, the Marquis Rudini had sent to the evening papers the text of the German-Italian Treaty of Alliance, of which the terms are analogous to the Austro-German one published by Prince Bismarck a few years ago, stipulating for a mutual guarantee of territorial integrity, and providing that, in the event of either Germany or Italy being attacked by France, the other Power should at once take the field in its defence.

· · · · · · · ·

ITALIAN ROUTE—THROUGH THE RIVIERA.

FROM Rome I went to Spezzia, where a friend had promised to take me on board his yacht; and here I found a formidable ironclad squadron, consisting of the *Italia*, the *Andrea Doria*, the *Francisco Morosimi*, the *Re Umberto*, the *Rugiero di Lauria*, the *Affondatore* (turret-ram), and several other vessels of the second class, preparing to put to sea. What could be the objective of this fleet? On this point all the naval authorities were as silent as the grave; but a few more days were to solve the mystery.

Our own destination was Monte Carlo, where we anchored our yacht in the pretty little bay of Monaco, and, going ashore, found the army of the Prince—consisting of about sixty-five carabineers—in no small state of excitement, owing to the prospect of its being forced perhaps by circumstances to abandon its attitude of armed neutrality, and sucked into the whirlpool of hostilities, whereof the Riviera might so soon become the sanguinary scene.

But such a prospect had not the least apparent terror for the visitors to the beautiful Inferno at Monte Carlo—men and women of all nations—Jews and Gentiles, Elamites and Assyrians—who, in spite of the military bustle going on around them—French battalions of Chasseurs and Alpine troops arriving and departing by road and rail—continued to frequent the tables of the Casino with an all-engrossing passion for their occupation worthy of the abstruse philosopher of Syracuse. '*Noli turbare circulos meos,*' also exclaimed these lost-to-all-else worshippers of the roulette wheels.

It is not, perhaps, generally known in England, but the fact is that during the last few years the French have been busy constructing a formidable line of forts all along the Riviera from Marseilles to Mentone; and every commanding peak and mountain-top overlooking the sea and the seaside road is capped with one of these terrifically strong stone-works. Careless pleasure-seekers on the Riviera are not likely to take special notice of these mountain-crowns, with heavy long-range guns for their jewels; but there they are, all the same. They form, indeed, France's silent answer to the Triple Alliance, and were placed there since the conclusion of that pact to bar the advance of Italy, should that Power, in fulfilment of her treaty engagements with Germany, be called upon to assail the flank of France, and select as her line of attack the sea-board rather than the mountain route.

An important reason why the Italian army should prefer the Riviera road into France with all its perils was that, apart from the natural difficulties of the Alpine routes, which had rather increased than diminished since the time of Hannibal and Cæsar, they were unwilling—such was their loyalty to public law—to expose themselves to the charge of infringing the neutrality either of Switzerland or of Savoy. For it must be remembered that, even after it had changed hands with Nice in 1860, Savoy, this section, so to speak, of the Franco-Italian Alsace-Lorraine, continued subject to the Treaty of Vienna (1815) as neutral territory, part of which, Chablais and Faucigny, might even be occupied

with Federal troops 'in the event of Switzerland's neighbours being in a state of open or imminent warfare.' Indeed, a portion of the Federal Army had already made bold to brave the displeasure and even the reprisals of France by occupying as it was, theoretically speaking, entitled to do, the upper part of Savoy; and this had introduced into the military situation an element of complexity which the Italians would have been foolish to ignore. Consequently, they resolved to force the passage of the Riviera road—the more so as their fleet could cover their march to some extent, and even land troops at particular points, as long at least, at the other portions of the French navy, at present engaged in the Baltic and elsewhere, should not be free to make for the Mediterranean.

The Italians had also resolved to send another smaller army, consisting of their 1st and 3d Corps (whose places in the army of the Riviera were to be taken by the 6th and 8th), across the Alps by the Mont Cenis route, so as thus to attempt to turn the flank of the French Army, consisting mainly of the 7th, 14th, 15th, and 16th Corps, which were now pretty well all the French could spare from the further draft they had had to make on their military resources with a view to repair their reverses on the Rhine.

. . . .

BATTLE OF COSTEBELLE.

MOUNTAIN WARFARE.

I NEED not describe to you in detail, for that has doubtless already been done for you, the incidents of the preliminary fighting between the two armies—French and Italian—since the first outpost collision at Ventimiglia, and the first serious collision near Mentone. You are sure to have heard of all the thrilling incidents forming the prelude to the drama—the splendid but unavailing defence that was made by the 24th Battalion of French

I

Chasseurs from Ville-Franche against the irresistible onslaught of the Bersaglieri of the 4th Italian Corps; the brilliant cavalry encounter between the 5th Italian Lancers and the French Dragoons of Tarascon (Tartarin's native place on the Rhone); the exploits of the Italian Alpini, or Alpine Sharpshooters, in scouting and hill-climbing that would put to shame the records of the Alpine Club; the wonders of marching and 'milling' (if I may use a slang word) done by the mule-borne mountain-batteries of either belligerent: the obstinate artillery duels between the Italian iron-clads which steam along the coast and the bastioned stone-work batteries that crown the mountain-tops; with all the other novel features in this almost fascinating picture of bloody war set in such a beautiful framework of blue sky and purple hills, o'erlooking a paradise of flowers.

．　　．　　．　　．　　．　　．

The Battle of Hyères, or rather of Costebelle (where Queen Victoria lately passed a few quiet and peaceful weeks), though it resulted in the repulse of the French, and their retirement on Toulon, is not quite decisive of the campaign, as it will be next to impossible for the Italians to possess themselves of this formidable and important place, even with the aid of their fleet, before getting reinforcements from Italy, which cannot for the present be spared; and meanwhile the Brest Squadron of the French Fleet may be able to get rid of its embarrassments elsewhere and come round to the Mediterranean.

The situation, no doubt, will be simplified if General Ricotti, with his two Corps, manages to debouch from the Alps on the Mont Cenis side, and, disposing of all opposition in that quarter, come down the valley of the Rhone to co-operate with the army of the Riviera. But, in the meantime, the issue of the whole war may have been decided on the Vistula and the Rhine; and, if so, then the Italians will have accomplished their chief aim, which was to distract and hamper the forces of France, by creating a diversion on her flank and rear, and thus render her defeat by the Germans all the easier and all the more certain.

The Great War of 189—

In any case, the victories already achieved by the Italians show them to be possessed of splendid soldierly material, both in men and officers—material in no single respect inferior to that of France; and when, after the late battle of Costebelle, the German Emperor telegraphed to King Humbert that 'his troops had done things of which their Prussian comrades themselves might very well be proud, and which at least they had never surpassed even at Rossbach and Sedan,' it must have been felt by all the world that His German Majesty, in employing the phrases of compliment, was only using the language of truth.

To the Editor of 'Black and White.'

SIR,—I observe that some confusion has arisen as to the authorship of the letters from the Baltic and North Sea relating to the terrible war now raging. They are not mine. The author is my friend, Sir Rambleton Seaforth, who was on his wedding trip, and has certainly had a remarkable experience in that way. He is only a yachtsman, not a naval man, or he would have no doubt been able to give us fuller details, and a more correct view of the situation. The letters were written to me, and not intended for publication, and I much fear I shall be hauled over the coals when he comes home. But I shall answer him with the truth, which was that his sister stole them off my desk and sent them to you without asking my leave.

I am sorry to say that the pair did not come to the end of their adventures in the *Thames*. On her way into Sheerness she was ordered by signal to transfer her despatches into a picket-boat, which was sent out to her, and to proceed at once to Plymouth. As Sir Rambleton's place is in Devonshire, he and his wife decided to go on in her. Unfortunately, when she made her number off the Start, she was signalled to proceed at once off Cape Finisterre for the protection of commerce, and to coal at Ferrol, but not to call there till actually short of coal. She asked leave to land her passengers, and was refused, so Sir Rambleton and his wife are at sea off Finisterre now, if they have not been captured and carried into a French port, as it was stated that quite a cloud of French cruisers had been ordered to rendezvous at that point.—I am, Sir, your obedient servant, P. H. COLOMB.

May 10, 189—.

THE LANDING AT TREBIZONDE.

LORD SALISBURY ON **THE** SITUATION—DEBATE IN THE HOUSE OF LORDS.

LONDON, *Saturday, May* 14.

IT was not till May 7th that our Correspondent's letter (*see page* 102) announcing the reported arrival of English troops in Trebizonde was published in London. It had been delayed in transmission. Meantime, on May 3d, the day following the debate in the House of Commons, the proclamation calling out the Reserves was posted throughout the kingdom. It appears that warning notices, issued as secretly as possible, had been sent out four days earlier, following the precedent set in 1882. On May 6th Mr. Balfour gave notice that he should on May 10th ask for a credit vote in the House of Commons for ten millions, and for authority to call out the Militia. On the reception of the news received from our Correspondent, however, a hasty conference of the Liberal leaders, which met at Mr. Gladstone's house, decided that, as it would be inconvenient to have a debate in the House of Commons prior to that on the credit vote on May 10th, Lord Kimberley should on Monday night, May 9th, ask for explanations of Lord Salisbury, and notice was at once sent to Lord Salisbury to that effect. On the afternoon of **May 9th the House of** Lords was crowded from floor to ceiling. All the Princes were in their places. The House of Commons occupied the whole of **the space at** the bar in a dense mass. The galleries were filled with the Princesses and Peeresses.

Amid breathless silence, Lord Kimberley rose. In a few cautiously worded sentences he expressed a hope that Lord Salisbury would be able to give an unqualified contradiction to the ridiculous rumour which had reached England. He referred, of course, to the report of a correspondent that as long ago as April 29th, English troops, the forerunners of an English expedition, either had landed, or were immediately about to land, at Trebizonde. The House was ready to support the Ministry in every measure which they might take to safeguard the honour and interests of England. No part of the House was more zealous in that respect than those noble Lords with whom he had the honour to be associated. But a landing at Trebizonde implied something which in no way concerned the honour and interests of England It was impossible that their Lordships should not be led by it to suppose that the noble Marquis, the head of the Government, considered himself bound by that ridiculous compact, the Cyprus Convention, and that he now felt himself called upon to draw the sword of England in defence of Turkey, because Russia had crossed the Asiatic frontier of Turkey. However few the Liberal Peers in that House might be, they felt that they expressed the mind of England in declaring to the noble Marquis that, in behalf of the corrupt Government of Turkey, the sword of England ought never again to be drawn. As for the Cyprus Convention, it had been abrogated by Turkey herself. It was conditional, and the conditions had not been fulfilled. Speaking with the authority of many able military men, he could assure the noble Marquis that if he contemplated a campaign amid the mountains of Asia Minor, a campaign which, even if successful, could only lead up to a long and dreary siege of the Russian fortress of Kars, he was involving the country in military difficulties of untold magnitude and limitless duration. He was doing this at a time when, amid a universal conflagration, we required all our forces for the complications which were sure to arise both in Europe and in Asia.

There was rather a buzz of excitement than any definite ap-

as Lord Salisbury immediately rose to reply. He spoke as follows:—

'My Lords, I do not require the assurance of the noble Earl that your House is ready to support Her Majesty's Government in any steps which may be indispensable to safeguard the honour and interests of England. I cannot discuss with that freedom which the noble Earl, naturally as an independent Peer, allows himself, the character of the Government of our ally, the Sultan of Turkey, or the present position of the Cyprus Convention. Happily for the explanation which I am glad to have this opportunity of offering to your Lordships, it is wholly unnecessary for me to refer to either. We have never professed ourselves ready to support the Government of the Sultan against his Christian subjects, should that contingency arise. But there is one thing on which I think it is well that Europe should understand, that not only this House, but the whole of England, is agreed. We do not desire to see the independent Balkan States crushed beneath the heel of Russia. We do not desire to see the population of Asia Minor pass from the Government of the Turk to that of the Czar. I am unwilling to say all that I easily might say on that subject at the present moment. War between us and Russia has not been declared. Our relations are in so delicate a condition that I should have asked the noble Earl to postpone his question, but that I feared that might give rise to misunderstanding. We live in hope that such a dire calamity as a war between us and Russia may yet be averted by the wisdom and the notoriously peaceful disposition of the Czar. But the situation is this. Russia has commenced by sea an attack upon Bulgaria. In order to say nothing that may tend to aggravate the difficulties of the present moment, I refrain from referring to the circumstances which preceded that invasion. In any case, it has been impossible for us to allow Bulgaria to be crushed when the support of our fleet would be of the most material importance to her. We, on hearing of the Russian invasion, at once issued orders to Sir George Tryon to act under the instructions of our ambassador at Constantinople. With the consent of the Sultan, the fleet under Sir George Tryon entered the Black Sea five days after the Russians had effected their landing in Bulgaria. We then intimated to the Czar that we could not allow any further reinforcements to be carried to Varna, and we heard yesterday that the Russian fleet, yielding to the superior force of ours, had retreated to the harbour of Sebastopol. The roadstead of Varna is in occupation of our cruisers. The Russians have advanced inland, leaving a force to cover the siege of Varna, which is held by about 5000 Bulgarians. It was in consequence of the Turks having announced their intention of supporting their vassal State, Bulgaria, that the Russian troops, without any declaration of war, crossed the frontiers in Asia Minor. As it had been at our instance that Turkey had agreed to give support to the Bulgarians, it was impossible that we could leave her without a pledge of our support when this aggression took place. It is not a political question of the future destinies of Asia Minor as between Turkey and the Armenian population. It is simply a question of giving military support to a valuable ally during actual warfare. We cannot afford to throw away the assistance of thousands of most valiant soldiers, who are ready to support our just demand that the Balkan States shall be allowed to pursue in tranquillity that orderly development which has excited the astonishment and the admiration of Europe.

'As to the military dangers which the noble Earl apprehends, I think that it would be highly inconvenient, at a time when it is at least possible that actual war may follow, that we should discuss, for the information of those against whom we may have to fight, our military projects. It will, I think, be sufficient for me to say that we have intrusted the conduct of the whole of these operations to a member of your Lordships' House, in whom we have complete confidence, and whose name will be a guarantee to the country that nothing will be wanting in the command of the war, should it unfortunately be forced upon us, which will tend to the honour and success of the British arms. The gallant Viscount, the present Commander-in-Chief in Ireland, whom I am glad to see in his place to-night, will, I have no doubt, be quite prepared to accept responsibility for any dangers which trouble the imagination of the noble Earl. But I should suppose that he will prefer to discuss his plans with him after rather than before the war. It is not in presence of armies which, as we have recently seen, are conducted with absolute secrecy, and are able to deliver unexpected blows, because no one knows what is going to happen till the stroke falls, that we can afford to discuss our arrangements in the face of the world. The gallant Viscount has at least fully satisfied Her Majesty's Government that he has a complete grasp of the whole situation, that he knows his own mind, and we accept full responsibility for all that he proposes to do. If you do not trust us, replace us by those whom you do trust. But, in Heaven's name, let me implore you not to allow the strength of England at this moment to be weakened by divided counsels or by want of confidence in those to whom the conduct of military affairs is intrusted. At this moment it may make the whole difference between our obtaining by peaceful means the acceptance of our just demands and a war which must be terrible and may be long. In any case, should war break out, the firm attitude of the whole country, its patriotic resolve and a temporary abstinence from feeble criticism will have a most decisive effect upon the future.'

When Lord Salisbury sat down there was a momentary and most impressive hush, as of awed silence, in presence of the tremendous events which appeared to be imminent, and then there came from all parts of the House a burst of general and enthusiastic cheering, all the more striking because of the usually impassive attitude of that august assembly. The ladies in the gallery for a moment rose altogether as by a single impulse, and when they sat down not a few of them burst into tears from excitement, while a buzz of eager talk filled both House and galleries.

When the excitement had a little quieted down, Lord Rosebery, in a few short sentences, expressed his entire sympathy with the general policy enunciated by Lord Salisbury. He could not, however, refrain from hoping that we were not about to be committed to a dangerous and difficult campaign in Asia Minor, where the roads were bad, the country difficult, and the end uncertain. He had, however, complete confidence in the prudence and military genius of the gallant Viscount, and had no wish to hamper either him or the Government with untimely criticism.

The general effect throughout the country of the debate in the House of Lords decided the Liberal leaders to allow Mr. Balfour's application for the credit vote to pass unchallenged. Mr. Labouchere, however, moved the rejection of the vote, and was seconded by Sir Wilfrid Lawson. The credit was voted by a majority of 412 to 17. We do not propose to trouble our readers with the details of the debate. No one took Mr. Labouchere very seriously, and Sir Wilfrid Lawson's jokes, which by no means suited the temper of the House, may be found scattered through his previous speeches. With the exception of two or three peace-at-any-price members, nearly the whole of those who followed Mr. Labouchere consisted of Parnellite members, who avowedly voted only in order to show their independence of Mr. M'Carthy and of both political parties. The funniest incident occurred when Sir Wilfrid Lawson, whose own position was an absolutely isolated one, repeated his old proposals to boycott the army. The humour of the situation took the fancy of the House, and a general titter gradually broke into a roar of laughter as the honourable member, either not appreciating the point, or wilfully blind, exclaimed, 'Well, I shall!' It was the only opportunity which members had for relieving pent-up feeling, and they indulged it freely.

MOBILISATION OF THE FIRST ARMY CORPS.

CALLING OUT THE RESERVE.

MEANTIME the mobilisation of that portion of the 1st Army Corps, which was not moved with Sir Evelyn Wood to Antwerp, proceeded. It is necessary to explain what was and was not done in the case of the regiments that went to Antwerp. The troops at Aldershot were gradually increased, with a view nominally to the summer drills, till they numbered something under 12,000 men. To these, for the purposes of the expedition, were added three battalions of the Guards from London, two of the regiments of Household Cavalry, and two batteries of Field Artillery from Woolwich.

It must, however, be understood that in the proper sense of

THE MOBILISATION OF THE ENGLISH ARMY—TROOPS MARCHING THROUGH THE DOCK GATES, PORTSMOUTH.

the term these regiments could not be 'mobilised.' *There is at this moment no battalion in the whole kingdom, except those of the Guards, that is fit to go on active service as it stands on parade.* The battalions are filled with recruits who, when mobilisation is ordered, have, in the first instance, to be replaced with men from the Reserve. This cannot be done without a proclamation, and without the fact of the Reserves being called out being known to everybody. For such a sudden movement as Mr. Balfour announced in the House of Commons on May 2d, there are no troops but the Guards ordinarily available; but when application was made to the military authorities to know how soon it would be possible to carry out a move of this kind, it was pointed out, in the first instance, that the occupation of a fortress like Antwerp is a very different thing from a campaign in the field. It would do no harm to the young troops to be moved across sea to Belgium. There they would be comfortably housed, and when mobilisation was ordered it would be easy to send over to that quarter the Reserve men to take their place in the ranks. Indeed, it was pointed out that this course would be positively advantageous. For supposing that Sir Evelyn Wood's troops were required for a campaign elsewhere, it would be best to replace them in Antwerp by forming depôts there of recruits who with, perhaps, a few Militia regiments, who might be induced to volunteer for the purpose, would form a sufficient garrison; since it was in the last degree unlikely that, with all they had on their hands, any of the armies in the field would attempt a siege of such a fortress as Antwerp, occupied by English troops, even though young and raw. As soon as the probability of the Eastern expedition arose, we believe that Lord Wolseley pointed out that it was indispensable to carry out this plan. As the Reserves for the battalions now at Antwerp came in at the home stations they were shipped over to that town, and in fact all arrived there about the 9th of this month.

Sir Thomas Baker has, we understand, been sent over to Antwerp to take command of that garrison as soon as the depôts can be formed. Thus, about the time that we write, the whole of Sir Evelyn Wood's force ready to take the field will be available for service elsewhere. From the all-important point of view of facilities for embarkation and provision of shipping, this has been a decided gain. Enormous as are the mercantile resources of England, and patriotic as has been the readiness of all our great companies to place their vessels at the disposal of Government, it has always been assumed that we could not reasonably calculate on

The Great War of 189—

moving off from our ports at one moment more than about 35,000 troops, or the force of one *corps d'armée*. To move such a force, with all the carriages, horses, and stores necessary to make the army available for the field, will require 135 large steamers. Warning and provisional arrangements had, we understand, been made, for as many as this, by the transport department of the Admiralty, when the Government first began to apprehend the possibility of our having to employ them, nearly a month ago. But the facilities of the Port of Antwerp have enormously increased our means of transport. By far the larger portion of the shipping of that great port is in the hands of English firms, and the commercial relations between these firms and Germany have enabled the Government to charter, in addition to a large mass of Antwerp shipping, many German ships which have been laid up by the high war rates now ruling for insurance. Thus, virtually without touching our own shipping or the facilities for embarking at our ports, Sir Evelyn Wood's troops, forming about half of the 2d Corps which he is destined to command at the Seat of War, will be embarked probably before these words see the light.

Meantime the troops of the 1st Army Corps have already left our shores.

On May 8th the Duke of Connaught, who is to command the 1st Army Corps, sailed with the Headquarter Staff of that Corps and the 2d Battalion Scots Guards from the Royal Albert Docks, North Woolwich, in his old ship, the *Orient*, which had been recently docked. His Royal Highness had asked that, if it were equally convenient, he might travel with the captain and in the ship in which he had sailed for Egypt in 1882. It was a point of *punctilio* with the captain to clear out at exactly the same hour as in 1882; and accordingly, at twelve o'clock on May 8th, amid the cheers of a vast crowd, the *Orient* sailed from Woolwich as in 1882, just five days after the issue of the order calling in the Reserve men. The other portions of the Corps have sailed within the last week.

So far all speaks well for the efficient working of our system, but from our different correspondents at the points where mobilisation has been taking place, we hear of not a few blots which mar the harmony of the picture.

In the first place, an undoubted and severe strain has been put upon our resources. It is not usual for more than three battalions of the Guards to leave England at the same time for active service. The zeal and patriotism of the London Scottish, the Inns of Court Volunteers, the 20th Middlesex, the Artists' Corps, induced them to volunteer to take up several of the day guards in London; special arrangements having been worked out to make the duties as little irksome as possible, and to arrange for a free interchange of the men. With the exception of the Bank Guard, all-night duties have been handed over to the police, and it is hoped that this arrangement may become a permanent one. Thus relieved, the single battalion of the Grenadiers left in London will, it is believed, be sufficient for the indispensable remainder of the day duties, though we have seen solemn old heads gravely shaken from the windows of 'The Rag,' as they looked across the way at the policeman who, even for day duty, has assumed the protection of the War Office and Horse Guards.

Thus, in addition to the brigade of Guards which moved with Sir Evelyn Wood to Antwerp, a second Guard Brigade has been formed for the corps which His Royal Highness is to command.

According to the method intended to be the normal one for our mobilisation, as soon as the 1st Corps has moved off to the ports of embarkation, their places are to be taken at the stations they have vacated by the regiments of the 2d Army Corps, who will then be mobilised, and will subsequently be embarked from the same ports as the others. This arrangement has been disturbed by the fact that Sir Evelyn Wood's troops, forming about a division and a half of the 1st Army Corps, as originally intended, were prepared for movement in ample time, it having been known for nearly a year that such a movement might be required at any moment. When it was subsequently known that it would be necessary to send two Army Corps to the seat of war, as the troops from England would necessarily precede those from Antwerp, the places vacated at Aldershot were taken up by regiments of the proper 2d Army Corps, and their Reserve men sent to them there.

As regards the equipment of Sir Evelyn's force, there was nothing to find fault with,—the material for the necessary transport and stores was actually at Aldershot, and, for the Guards, in London.

RESERVE MEN SIRVED WITH THE NEW MAGAZINE-RIFLE, AND OFF TO THE FRONT TO-MORROW.

The troops embarked complete in every respect, except for the unavoidable absence of their Reserve men, which has now been supplied. On the whole, the Reserve men have come in very well, and the deficiency in the calculated numbers is very slight. The contrast in their age and physique to the boys of the battalions as we have known them, is very marked. On the other hand, it is reported that those who have left the colours for some years show sadly the defects of their not having been called out regularly for training. Many of them have certainly seen and handled the magazine-rifle. Others have not even done that. A certain falling off also in military habits and discipline is perhaps better indicated in a description which has been given by one of the correspondents of a trip he took in a railway carriage, with five men going to join their depôt from certain quarries in the north. We shall abridge his graphic sketch of the men in order to record the conversation he details.

One of them, a big man with sandy whiskers and indifferently shaved, but evidently a good-natured fellow, clapped him familiarly on the knee after certain gifts of baccy and a little nip from his flask, which latter was, however, refused by two out of the five, had made them all disposed to be communicative. 'Look ye here, sir, I doesn't mind a bit going back for a little soldiering, but it seems strange like. Why, a few months ago, one of the officers of my old regiment came down to see us at the quarries where we was. He was a very nice young officer, had been adjutant, and if I'd seen him by myself on the road, I'd have liked nothing better than to touch my hat to him, and get a bit of a chat about old times. But, lor' bless yer, if I'd saluted him down in the quarries I shouldn't have heard the last of it this side of Christmas. He seemed rather worried like at the way we treated him, though we was all glad to see him, and he asked me about it. "Well," says I, "the reason the chaps don't salute you, is just that they darn't for fear of the chaff." "What do yer salute him for? yer needn't, yer know," that's what all the other men in the quarries would want to know. Well, yer know, sir, 'tain't that. It's a kind of way of saying as you belong to the same body like as he does. He's got his dooty and you've got yours. But, lor' bless you, you never could make the quarry chaps see that. "See what John Morley says," they'd say, "he tells yer it's rank slavery, and that's just what it is. You make believe to like it, cos you've lost yer tail and 'ud like to see other chaps lose theirs." Well, yer know,

READING THE MOBILISATION ORDER.

sir, when you've been five or six years among that sort o' thing, and all the time you haven't had the chance of so much as seeing a regiment, and feel that you don't know nothing about this here blooming new drill, and about these yer magazine rifles and smokeless powder as they talks about, well, it seems strange like. You feel as if your blood had got changed since you was with the regiment. However, when we went off with a chance of going away to the war, and even when the Proclamation was fastened upon the village inn, and the women was howling fit to split, one old quarryman claps me on the back, and says he, "I'd like to be going with you, my lad; good luck for old England," for their blood got up pretty quick when they heard of the row, and they like fighting as well as any one.'

We must reserve for next week the reports we have heard from the Militia and the state of the proper 2d Army Corps, half of which will now become the 1st Army Corps under the Duke of Connaught, and the other half will, with Sir Evelyn's troops, form the 2d Army Corps under him.

At the last moment we hear that the titles of the Corps which Sir Evelyn and the Duke of Connaught are to command are changed. It has been naturally assumed that the Duke of Connaught would command the 1st Corps, and Sir Evelyn the 2d. All the correspondents during the week have so reported it, and we understand that, as a matter of courtesy, this would have been arranged if possible. But, as Sir Evelyn's troops all belong to the 1st Army Corps in the mobilisation scheme, and the waggons and stores were all marked for the '1st Army Corps,' it was found that to have changed this order would have introduced endless confusion. On the matter being explained to the Prince, he is reported to have said that 'he was a soldier, and could only wish that what was best for the Service should be considered. He was proud to serve as brother Corps-commander with so distinguished a soldier as Sir Evelyn Wood.'

RUSSIA DECLARES WAR AGAINST ENGLAND.

SIR GEORGE TRYON EVACUATES THE BLACK SEA.

LONDON, *May* 21.

EVENTS have ripened fast since last week. Russia, on May 16, on hearing of the dispatch of our troops to the East, declared war against us. The excitement against us in France has reached boiling point. There can be no doubt that our great fleet of convoys would not have been allowed to leave England had there, at the time of their departure, seemed to be any prospect of France declaring war against us, because from Algeria and her southern ports, she so threatens our movement through the Mediterranean that that opportunity is in itself an additional incentive to her to declare war. For a long time, however, it appeared as if the Ministry, prudently anxious not to add further to the enemies France already has on her hands, would temporise with us. Public feeling will, however, it is to be feared, prove too strong for the Ministry, and for some time the gravest anxiety was felt at home as to the fate of the expedition in the event of the fleet being attacked whilst escorting so great a convoy of ships, while Sir George Tryon was known to be fully occupied in the Black Sea. On the 18th, however, a telegraphic message arrived announcing that Sir George Tryon had withdrawn the entire fleet from the Black Sea immediately after the retreat of the Russian Fleet to Sebastopol; that his flag-ship had arrived at Malta, that the Duke of Connaught, in the *Orient*, had reached Cyprus after a very rapid and successful voyage; and that all the transports sailing direct from England had either arrived at or passed Malta. It is understood that the greater part of the troops of the 1st Army Corps will for the present rendezvous at Cyprus, where extensive preparations have for a long time past been made for their reception. Alarm was at first excited in some quarters lest the troops should suffer as they had done at the time of the first occupation of Cyprus. But according to the reports from the island it appears that a great improvement has taken place in its sanitary condition,—thanks to the British occupation; that the chief cause of the ill-health of the troops at the former time was the want of proper hutting arrangements, provided for them beforehand. Large quantities of roofing felt have been sent out, and labourers have constructed, under the direction of the engineers, large huts admirably roofed, and now practically ready for about 30,000 men. In case the necessary huts should not be ready for the whole of the troops, it is understood that the remainder of the force will land in Egypt. It is obvious that no expedition can be carried into the Black Sea until the great Naval action, which will almost certainly follow the French Declaration of War,—which is expected whilst we write,—has decided which flag is to be supreme in the Mediterranean.

Meantime, Sir Evelyn Wood's troops, which sailed from Antwerp on May 13th and 14th, have temporarily put into Gibraltar and Cadiz, where they have been received in the most friendly manner by our present allies the Spaniards.

The departure from England of the second half of the 2d Corps has been postponed. The ships are ready, but it is obviously inadvisable to accumulate more troops on the long line to the East till the question of the supremacy of the Alliance in the Mediterranean has been settled. The detachment of troops which was landed at Trebizonde has necessarily been withdrawn. They would have been exposed to attack by indefinitely superior force as soon as the command of the Black Sea passed into the hands of the Russians. It appears that the detachment never consisted of more than half a battalion, and a few sappers from the garrison of Cyprus, which had been reinforced with a view to such a movement.

DECLARATION OF WAR IN LONDON.

MOVEMENT BY THE CANADIAN PACIFIC RAILWAY.

London has had the excitement of a pageant unseen since 1854, and therefore unknown to most of our generation. On May 18th

The Great War of 189—

the Sergeant-at-Arms, attended by the whole of the city functionaries, declared war against Russia from the steps of the Royal Exchange.

It is obvious that we may have before long to expect some aggression of Russia upon Afghanistan. But Russia has already involved herself in such a number of campaigns, against Germany, against Austria, against Bulgaria and Turkey, and also against Turkey in Asia, that it seems in the last degree improbable that, with her resources impoverished and weakened by the effects of

DECLARATION OF WAR AGAINST RUSSIA FROM THE STEPS OF THE ROYAL EXCHANGE.

the great famine, she can employ great force in Afghanistan also. On our part, however, it is indispensable that we should in India not expect to carry on a great aggressive campaign against Russia. For, whereas for a forward campaign large reinforcements, both of men and officers, would be required, we cannot at present afford to send any large number of men from home, and even the possible supply of officers will be very limited.

We understand, however, that arrangements have been made

with the Canadian Pacific Railway for the immediate dispatch to India by that line of about 200 retired officers who have volunteered their services, and who having large Indian experience will be invaluable for many of the appointments that will become indispensable. One of our ablest and best known artists has made arrangements to accompany this party. We hope in a future issue to give a number of graphic illustrations of the new route, which, now that the Suez Canal is no longer available, from the risks attending it, fully shows its importance to the safety of the Empire. We understand that, also by the Canadian Pacific line, enormous stores of magazine rifles were, none too soon, dispatched to India about a month ago. Furthermore, about 500 million cartridges of smokeless powder for the rifles were dispatched about a fortnight ago by the same route. It was found impossible to obtain these from the Government factories, which up to the eve of the war were still experimenting on the form of powder. The 'Smokeless Powder Company,' however, undertook to provide 1000 million cartridges as a first instalment. Five hundred million of them have been assigned as the first provision for home and the Eastern expedition, and the second instalment was sent off in hot haste to the East, *viâ* the West, special arrangements for its security having been undertaken by the Canadian Pacific.

MOBILISATION OF THE SECOND CORPS.

Meantime it is certainly not to be regretted that we have been compelled to delay the dispatch from England of the second half of the 2d Corps. The trooping season to India being now over, nearly all the drafts had been sent out before the risk of war appeared imminent. A certain number were, however, kept back towards the end of the season. Nevertheless, the Reserve men have barely sufficed to make up the Corps and a half which have already sailed. It would have been impossible to make up the remaining half Corps at all, but for the fact that, specially for the

The Great War of 189—

war, a large number of Militiamen and of 'efficient volunteers' have offered their services. The 'efficient volunteers' have enlisted under a special clause which expressly limits their services to the period of the war, and, as a maximum, to a period of two years. Furthermore, the strength of the Artillery is deplorably deficient.

A short time ago there was fear lest the miscellaneous collection of weapons with which the Artillery was armed would produce confusion. This was remedied by activity in the Arsenal, and by giving out contracts to private firms. The result was the production of numbers of the so-called 12-pounder gun both for the Indian and home batteries. Unfortunately this gun has been condemned by the unanimous report of our ablest artillerymen. It is too heavy for the Horse Artillery, which loses mobility. On the other hand, the Field Artillery will have to meet the guns of Foreign Powers, no one of which throws a shell of less than 15 pounds. Most of the foreign field guns are even more powerful. The ammunition is most unsatisfactory. Everything has been sacrificed to securing an excessive muzzle velocity, which commends itself very much to mere experimentalists, but is regarded as useless by practical soldiers.

There has been a dangerous tendency to leave these questions altogether in the hands of an Ordnance Committee of men without experience of the requirements of an army. For a sporting rifle, the sportsman says what he wants, and the manufacturer applies his skill to furnishing what is asked for. For our Artillery the shopman decides. The men who have to handle the gun in war, or who have studied the experience of others who have handled it in war, are simply ignored.

EMBODIMENT OF THE MILITIA.

The general embodiment of the militia has shown serious defects in our system. These are glaring enough among the English and Scotch militia regiments, but among the Irish they are appalling. Many of the Irish militia battalions are now in the neighbourhood of Aldershot in a special camp. Some of them, like those of Antrim, Tipperary, Tyrone, are a splendid body of men. The great deficiency in some of the battalions is in the correspondence between their numbers and the muster rolls. One correspondent reports having ascertained that there are not a few Irish militiamen who have been in the habit of belonging to as many as five different corps at one time. 'The way the thing has been done is this: It has never been the practice to call out simultaneously the militia battalions for training; it would interfere inconveniently with the labour market. Certain men, taking advantage of this fact, have made a regular trade of getting the money allowed for one battalion after another as it has been called out. Indeed, so well has the fact been known that it is reported that not infrequently the Sergeant-Major has requested the adjutant of certain battalions to beg that the time of muster might be postponed till after the end of the training of another battalion, in order to ensure a full attendance. Now, however, that the battalions are gathered together the effects are visible enough. I am told that in some battalions nearly half the proper strength is wanting. Some steps are certainly required to cure this evil. The men, it must be observed, don't "desert" their proper battalion because they attend all their drills. Perhaps now that the militia is embodied it might be possible, legally, to try these men as deserters from the corps with which they do not appear. That, however, is a question for the military powers, not for your humble correspondent. What I am quite certain of is that they will not be tried. Our already slender numbers would be most formidably reduced if all these men were treated as criminals. Moreover, they are not at bottom bad fellows many of them. The idea that it is a crime to get a little more pay out of the public in return for doing a little more drill never entered their minds. The general effect of their action, of course, does not affect them at all. "Why, yer honour, didn't I put in me toime honest for me pay?" one of them with whom I was expostulating said to me the other day. They are, of course, the best drilled men we have. They have had so much of it. For this war, at all events, it is too late to devise a remedy for this sham.'

Just at present the headquarters of the militia are in the Staff College, that institution having been broken up for the war, and the sixty officers usually there have been sent to rejoin their regiments, or to fill up billets where they are badly wanted. The tents of the militia battalions cover the ground in the neighbourhood. Aldershot is occupied with the brigades that are being formed in hot haste to complete the force in the field. The stores for the 2d Army Corps were by no means in the same state of readiness as those for the 1st. But in Aldershot, at least, many of the waggons were actually ready, and, thanks to the delay which has taken place, and the costly and feverish purchases all over the country of stores, probably this portion of the two corps will be ready when it is required to move.

We hear from all parts of the world of enormous purchases of transport material of all kinds which will be hurried into the Levant as soon as it is safe to send them there. Mules especially are being everywhere purchased.

The horses that have been of late years registered with the Government for purchase for war have proved invaluable. Indeed, without them we could not possibly have equipped the troops. Many of them are splendid animals, and will greatly assist in making up our deficiencies in draught horses for the artillery and train.

CALLING OUT THE VOLUNTEERS.

As soon as the excitement in France began to be realised in this country two opinions strove for mastery. At first there was some little disposition to insist on the recall of the troops from all distant expeditions. But in a short time every one saw that for this it was practically now too late. A very large portion of our force was in the Levant already. That force had been dispatched with the full assent of the country, because in whatever way it was to be employed, as to which there were all kinds of conflicting rumours, it was felt that we were now bound in honour to assist in resisting the Russian attempt to crush Bulgaria. There was also a certain speculative interest of the ' What will he do with it ? ' kind, as to the nature of the campaign which Lord Wolseley has designed. On the whole, though croakers, some of whom were known not to be altogether exempt from personal and private pique, are to be heard here and there, a general confidence prevails. Men record how in '82, at a time when every-one thought that Arabi's power in Egypt was too great for the English force to overcome without a long campaign, he had announced and allowed it to be published, before he left England, that ' whatever resistance Arabi might offer, the campaign would be over in three months,' and how exactly that prediction had been fulfilled by the return of the English troops within that time. It is recalled again that, though, after all the delays that had taken place, it was impossible to say, before the Nile Campaign started, whether we should be in time to save Gordon, Lord Wolseley had announced before leaving England that we should reach hand to Gordon about Christmas time; and that this promise again, despite all the difficulties of the Nile, had been exactly fulfilled by the dispatch of Stewart and the steamer expedition, which, not by any fault of his, did not ' reach hand ' the few days earlier that were necessary to save Gordon. Others have recalled how this exactness of calculation and prediction had attended all his earlier campaigns. It is felt that now or never we must settle the pretensions of Russia on India and in the East; that if we did not take advantage of the rashness of Russia in attacking us whilst she was engaged with Germany and Austria, we could never again count upon the support of those allies. The alliance with Italy is immensely popular. A few manly sentences from Mr. Balfour in announcing his proposal to call out the volunteers, and one of the finest speeches which Mr. Chamberlain has ever made in reply to a rather snappish little speech of Lord Randolph, expressed the popular sentiment, and with general consent on May 17th, the day before the Declaration of War against Russia, the volunteers were called out.

The response to the call has been very remarkable. It has, of course, been necessary everywhere to make special arrangements

CALLING OUT THE VOLUNTEERS—PARADE OF THE SIGNALLERS OF THE
ST. MARTIN'S LE GRAND CORPS.

for the marshalling of the volunteers interfering as little as possible with business. But, whereas with the militia, unfortunately, the contrast between the peace effective and those who now show on parade is melancholy, with the volunteers it is almost startling. A few men have been with great reluctance, and probably only for a time, obliged by business necessities to withdraw from the ranks. Their places have been filled over and over again by passed 'efficients,' who have returned to the battalions. But that is not all. The change that has come over the spirit of the men is reported from all quarters. During quiet, peace times it was very difficult to get any response from the volunteers if appeal was made to them as representing the purpose of the British people to take the defence of the country on their own shoulders. Those did not understand the volunteers who so addressed them. They were volunteers because they liked it, because others joined, because they were good shots, and liked competing for the prizes, because they liked the fun of skirmishing and outdoor practice of all kinds, because it was a change from the sedentary habits of ordinary life. But now that the nation is roused, when all men feel that they would like, if they could, to play their part in the service *of England* here, when Scotland does not intend to lag behind, and when the blood of Irishmen is up, the talk is different. 'What other men want to do, *we* can' is rather the feeling.

At the same time the contrast between different corps is certainly a marked thing. The steady work of some, the indifference of others now tells. No past 'butter' compensates for present weakness. It is quite extraordinary what has been done by some corps to prepare for present events. The Lord Mayor's subscription has greatly assisted the Metropolitan Corps to be ready for the field. Generally, the town corps have had great facilities for turning out promptly. The Government grant, which has been defined already as payable on mobilisation, suffices to provide most that is required. In the big towns, where some steps have been taken beforehand to ascertain where waggons, carts, horses, stores, could best be obtained, and where some of the officers responsible knew just what was wanted and had it all tabulated beforehand, the battalions and brigades have formed up ready to move, so that they could live anywhere, with wonderful rapidity.

In the country districts, on the other hand, the differences between different brigades is most marked. Many of them have been telegraphing up to the Horse Guards to know where they are to obtain this, that, and the other. The Horse Guards is overwhelmed with work. Local knowledge is what is wanted. Here and there officers have been sent down from London to assist the more helpless corps; but few can be spared. The result in almost all these cases is slow and unsatisfactory. On the other hand, from some of the country brigades we hear the most encouraging reports. It appears that a system has been worked out in certain corps in accordance with suggestions thrown out in some articles in the *United Service Magazine*. It has even been practised during peace time. In accordance with this, first of all, long ago application was made to certain owners of carts and horses to know whether, in case of the volunteers being mobilised, they would be ready to dispose of their property at a certain fixed price, and whether they would undertake always to have a cart, for instance, of that description ready. There has been found to be no practical difficulty in making these arrangements beforehand.

Then a set of printed papers of different colours has been drawn out and kept in the Brigade office. These take a form of this kind :—

'Private ———. On receiving by telegraph the word, " Mobilise," you will . . . .'

On the lists of names kept in the office those men who are to fetch carts, horses, etc., are detailed. On the printed papers prepared for these it is recorded, 'You will at once go to No. X. Y. Street, where you will find a horse with such and such harness ready for you. You will take it to No. A. C. Street, where you will find a cart ready for you. You will harness in the horse and proceed to Mr. Jones's, No. F. E. Street. There you will find Privates Blank and Dash, who will have ready for you the stores to be loaded on the cart, and will load them. As soon as the cart is loaded you will drive to the rendezvous of the corps at Anywhere Park.'

This will give an indication of the method which has been pursued. The Government grant on mobilisation suffices to cover the necessary expenses. The contrast between the rapidity with which this system works and the confusion which exists where it has not been adopted; the ease with which the whole thing is done, is, from all the accounts we have received, most striking. Unfortunately, where no such preparation has been made the delay and confusion which result are not the only evil effect. The discouragement of the men from finding that they have not been as well looked after as others, the want of confidence in their officers, has a most demoralising effect. They hear that other brigades have already marched to the great camps which are being formed all over England, and they see that they have no prospect of being ready for a long time. The praises which are daily lavished on other corps for their extraordinary promptitude and smartness are gall and wormwood to them. The women chaff them mercilessly. It will not do to throw the blame on the 'system' or 'the authorities,' those convenient phrases which are commonly employed to disguise the absence of a man. Others have managed well enough under the present system and with the present authorities. British self-help, guided by forethought and knowledge, has been the secret.

THE POSITION OF AFFAIRS.

LONDON, *May* 28.

CERTAINLY we have been fortunate in the passages which our transports have made. It only shows what can be done under favourable conditions of weather, with selected coal and selected stokers. We understand that the Admiralty pressed on the Government the importance of attending to these points in a matter in which it might come to be a question of a run against time across a danger zone. As we anticipated in writing our last account of the events of the week, the Declaration of War by France was issued after we had gone to press on Thursday, May 19th. It was therefore only barely in time that our great mass of transports safely passed into the Levant. For, as will be seen from the telegraphic report of our correspondent—received last night, so that it has somewhat delayed our issue—the French Fleet has lost no time in following up the Declaration of War. The telegraphic dispatch, which was sent off on the very evening of the greatest naval engagement of modern times, explains clearly the sequence of events which has for some time to come made the Mediterranean once more a safe highway for us. We need not dilate on the vast importance of this event. In the present case it is not merely that our flag is once more supreme at sea; it means that the terrible anxieties, which had been awakened in the public mind as to the possible fate of our Eastern expedition, in case Sir George Tryon should not secure a complete triumph, are now at rest. With the Mediterranean secure it will be a very easy matter to regain possession of the Black Sea.

Whatever may be the ultimate purposes of the Italians in regard to an Algerian expedition, we think that there will now be no injury to the public service in letting it be known that the preparations which were recently made with that apparent object were only a *ruse de guerre*. Of course, in order that they might attain the object which they have so successfully achieved of drawing the French Fleet out into the open sea, it was necessary that these facts should be known only to Sir George Tryon. Our correspondent, therefore, telegraphs under the impression which prevailed in the fleet at the time. The rule is a sound one, even in regard to fleets where they have communication with the land, that what is believed among your own people will very soon be believed by the enemy. But the Italian Government, as much as our own, recognises the importance of the principle of concentrating its efforts at one point at one time as far as that may be at all possible. The Italians have quite enough on their hands in their war by land and sea with France. Our efforts are already directed to the East. All those most desirable objects, which the people 'who know,' or 'have been there,' or have been 'ten years resident' in various places, have been of late pressing upon the Government through the newspapers, really must wait till we have time, and armies, and fleets to attend to them. 'One thing at a time' is a simple principle of military and naval affairs, but it is one which the casual correspondents of newspapers never keep before their minds.

Meantime we have received news of the great battle between France and Germany, a report of which we have been expecting.

PREPARATIONS IN THE MEDITERRANEAN FLEET.

THE ALLIED FLEET AT PORT MAHON.

(From an Officer in Sir George Tryon's Fleet.)

I MAY begin the story of our great success by reminding your readers that when the French violated the Belgian Frontier, and we mobilised our fleet, Sir George Tryon had ten battleships with him, while the French were supposed to have about eighteen available for sea at Toulon, for they had withdrawn thither the Mediterranean and Levant Squadrons simultaneously with their demand upon Germany.

Sir George Tryon seems to have been very early informed that if war arose the Home Government must depend greatly on the alliance of Italy and Austria to maintain command of the Mediterranean Sea, for a great naval force would be necessary in the North to counteract the designs of Russia and France on the German sea-coast. Sir George Tryon, on his part, talked quite openly—which was said to be a wonder for him—of the fact that he was not desirous of large reinforcements. He did not believe, he said, that, if it came to the point, the French would bring out their older wooden ships, such as the *Colbert*, the *Suffren*, or even the *Richelieu*. The Italians, on the other hand, would most probably be able to complete eight of their very fine ships, while Austria might bring four or five vessels, which, though inferior, would not be ineffective. As it turned out, Tryon was only reinforced by two ships, the *Ajax* and the *Benbow*. Thus, supposing the eight Italians could be brought into line, and supposing the French produced eighteen ships, Tryon's fleet would be but two sail stronger than that of Admiral Ricunier. As events developed themselves, it was plain that Sir George grew anxious; but it was, both with himself and Admiral Markham, the anxiety of eagerness, and we were all very well assured that if it came to blows we should be daringly, as well as efficiently, led.

On the withdrawal of the fleet from the Black Sea, we were all assembled at Malta, where the garrison was labouring night and day in constructing out-works and exercising in the batteries. For us, on the other hand, there was absolutely nothing to do, except to keep our coals and stores complete day by day, which was not a very arduous undertaking. There were, however, constant and long conferences between the Admirals and the captains of the battle-ships, and it was no secret that every one of these took the form of discussions over possible or probable forms of attack or defence by the fleet at sea. It came to be accepted that if we met the French in open fight we should be numerically inferior, and the question was, how we should act from that point of view? The discussions amongst us, who were not directly responsible, took every variety of form. Sometimes a hot party would arise, claiming that it was perfectly useless to make plans until the enemy disclosed his. This was met by another party declaring that, if plans were not carefully made beforehand, there would be no plans at all. This, again, was taken up by a third party, which claimed that there was only one plan of any use, and that was, as soon as the hostile fleet was seen, to make a general signal, 'Ram the enemy,' and leave each ship to fight it out with its fellow. When it was pointed out that perhaps the enemy would not stay to be rammed, the general answer was, 'Well, it is all the same. There is nothing like the ram.'

Two things made themselves clear in these arguments; first, that hardly any one—even amongst the captains—had ever thought seriously on what now seemed to be drawing so very close to us; and, secondly, that the Admirals were beginning to lay down certain definite principles, which the captains were inclined to accept as being very likely to turn out sound. Before very long the whole result came out in a general order which was confidential to the captains, the commanders, and the first-lieutenants of the battle-ships.

Without professing to give the exact wording, I am able to say that the first principle laid down was the necessity of avoiding giving a friend the ram, or firing into him either by gun or torpedo. The second principle was the desirability of so arranging that, if possible, an enemy's ship should sustain the fire of more than one of our own ships; or at least so guarding things that no one of our ships should find herself opposed by two of the enemy's.

The memorandum went on to say that, as a consequence of these principles, ships attached to one another were on no account to separate unless forced to do so; but that if confusion arose, ships were to keep their speed and pass out of the enemy's fleet in the direction opposite to that from which they passed into it, with the view of re-forming out of the smoke, in order to renew the attack.

In any case, said the order, the enemy will be approached by the fleet in two or three columns in line ahead, at a speed of about ten knots. The flag or senior officers will lead their columns, and in whatever form the enemy may approach—if he does approach—they will endeavour to cut through at different points, using their guns, torpedoes, and rams indiscriminately as circumstances offer. In order to avoid all chance of injuring friends, the columns will be arranged in echelon. The Commander-in-Chief will lead the first column, and the leaders of succeeding columns will not be expected to enter the enemy's fleet until the rear ships of the preceding column may be supposed to have passed through. After passing through, the ships not disabled will re-form and renew the attack in the same way.

If the enemy retires, making use of his stern guns, the fleet will be formed in line abreast or quarter-line, and every endeavour must be made to close with him, to ram his ships upon their sterns or quarters, or, in the event of failure, to carry them by boarding from that position.

The general opinion on this memorandum was that it said quite enough, and yet not too much. It was quite clear and plain, and nothing seemed wanting but the declaration of war and the attack of a superior French Fleet.

We were very much surprised to hear from England that troops were on their way out, with the idea of operations in the Black Sea. It seemed very risky, when France might declare war at any moment. But the general belief is that the Ministry must have had some assurances from the French Government which we know nothing about. Anyhow the transports began to arrive at Malta in a continual stream, and there received orders to proceed to Cyprus, where we hear preparations are being made for the reception of the troops. The *Orient*, with the Duke of Connaught on board, did not come in; she only closed sufficiently to receive a signal changing her destination to Cyprus, and went on. Several cruisers from the Channel appeared at intervals, watching over the safety of the troopers; they were not interfered with, and went on to Cyprus.

News of the Spanish alliance and orders to proceed to Spezzia to form a junction with the Italian Fleet came simultaneously, and as the ships steamed out of the harbour the whole population swarmed over the forts and walls and cheered in the wildest way, which, on a signal from the Admiral, the ships returned heartily. At Spezzia we found six ships ready, with orders from home to watch Toulon, but not to make any attacks upon the French unless they should attempt to attack Italy by sea. Simultaneously with these orders we heard of the Duke of Edinburgh's wonderful and bloodless success in the North Sea. But there was a general sound of congratulation that our force in the Mediterranean was not powerful enough to compel such obedience as we had enforced in the North. The Italians, ashore and afloat, were in a wonderful state of enthusiasm. They crowded our ships during the few days we lay at Spezzia, and the women were so demonstrative of affection that some of the older officers did not half like it.

It soon became known that Sir George Tryon had decided to make Port Mahon the headquarters of the fleet, and to send cruisers only before Toulon. I should have said that we were now very fairly supplied in this way. They had been arriving from England almost daily while we were at Malta, and we had now fourteen, large and small, with the fleet.

For a reason which I did not at first understand, we only took four out of the six Italian ships that were ready with us to Port Mahon, namely, the *Andrea Doria*, the *Francisco Morosini*, the *Re Umberto*, and the *Rugiero di Lauria*. Moreover, we left at Spezzia the *Thunderer*, *Ajax*, and *Agamemnon*. We noted that the Italian ships we took with us were the newest, and that those of our own we left were, in a sense, 'lame ducks.' But still there was a good deal of wonder that we should deliberately reduce our force to fourteen sail when we were almost closing with the enemy. It was whispered about later that orders from home had dictated the detachment, that war would be immediately declared by England against France, and that an attack would be made by Italian troops carried chiefly in the *Italia* and *Lepanto*, and supported by a combined Anglo-Italian squadron against Algiers.

However, we steamed away to Port Mahon, and in this magnificent harbour found a fresh relay of colliers and two more cruisers, the *Apollo* and *Sappho*, which showed us that there was a good deal of foresight at headquarters. We had the declaration of war immediately, and then we began to see where we were. We were, in fact, at bay. In no case was the French Fleet strong enough to hope to prevent our putting to sea, and there was practically nothing that France could do with her fleet, as long as ours was intact. And now, too, I began to see that we were, at Minorca, in a position to cover the proposed attack on Algiers. Any attempt of the Toulon Fleet to drive off our attacking forces would be liable to be met by a counter attack from ourselves. Yet if France could really produce eighteen battleships out of Toulon, while we could only furnish thirteen, we were running very great risks.

However, we went to work in a very business-like way. Tryon placed five of his largest cruisers, including the *Amphion*, *Australia*, and *Undaunted*, on the line to Toulon, giving orders that Lord Charles Beresford in the *Undaunted*, with Dunlop in the *Australia* to back him up, were to undertake the watch on the Toulon Fleet, closing with the harbour after dark, and drawing off before daylight each morning, but not so far as to lose touch with the port. Then the other three were to spread themselves towards Minorca, and to work backwards and forwards, so as to signal to each other and to Minorca at least once in every twenty-four hours.

For us at Port Mahon it again became a time of inaction; nothing to do but exercise and keep our coal supply up. But we now lay with fires banked and steam at half an hour's notice.

We soon learnt that the seven ships had left Spezzia with several transports and cruisers; and we began to think that if France had any chance at all, she might have it by falling suddenly and swiftly on this weak detachment. The Admirals seemed sure that she would, and the utmost anxiety attended the reports from the signal station.

THE BATTLE OF SARDINIA.

THE RAMMING OF THE 'AMIRAL BAUDIN.'

IT was just after daylight on the morning of the fourth day that a sort of cheering cry of 'The enemy are at sea!' ran all through the ships. Up went the simple signal, 'Weigh,' and there was really a horrible contrast between our anxiety and eagerness and the unmoved grind and crunch as link by link the cables came slowly in. But this was soon over, and we were at sea, forming at once in two lines ahead, as before arranged. The report was that the French had left Toulon twelve hours before, steering about S.E., but it had not been possible to count their numbers owing to the darkness. We steamed due east at half-speed; but it was plain to us all that if the French passed through the Straits of Bonifacio we might easily miss them, even though our cruisers were well spread out both ahead and astern. While we were in the middle of debate, down there rolled upon us as dense a fog as ever I saw in the Mediterranean. The Admiral had provided for this as for everything else, and we knew that we must preserve order with the steam syrens only, without the aid of guns; but as it was no use keeping speed, we slowed down. We were like this all day and all night, and at daylight it seemed as thick as ever. The ships had of course been all cleared for action, and we were ready to open fire in a minute, though one naturally prayed that the fog would lift before the enemy appeared. At 8 A.M. it began to clear, and at 9 we distinctly counted twenty-one steam-ships to the south of us. The flag-ship immediately made the signal for eight knots, and gradually altered course towards the strange fleet. We were soon able to make them out as sixteen French battle-ships, in the indented line abreast, steering south, with five cruisers in front of them. They were smoking up a good deal, but at ten or twelve miles distance we could not tell whether they were going at speed.

We soon found they were not, for we began to gain on them, and the signal was made for ten knots. We could tell by the position of the steam cones, that every ship had steam to spare, and I suppose it was the desire of making sure of a compact fleet which kept us at comparatively low speed. Even at ten knots we continued to gain considerably. We were quite two miles off when the French began to open fire from their stern guns, and I am bound to say we were all very much surprised at the bad shots. They fell short and over, right and left, but after quite an hour few ships apparently had been badly hit.

We were still in two lines ahead and were making no reply at all to the French fire. We could not understand, when we had got within 3000 yards, why the Admiral did not put us in line abreast and open fire. But in the middle of our wonder we suddenly saw the French ships open out to right and left, and before we knew where we were the whole mass of the battle-ships were coming right down upon us. We saw at once that it was in anticipation of some such manœuvre that we had not quitted our first formation.

But the wisdom of our Admirals was at once shown. Orders were given to train the guns abeam and to let the enemy have it at the closest range, abstaining from fire till then. The French, on the other hand, never ceased to fire; but the smoke they made so surrounded them that it was plain they were wasting their ammunition, and did not see so well where they were going. But their rapidity of approach was tremendous, and I could note it as I had no guns to look after and could see nearly all round from the sheltered spot I had chosen.

My ship was near the middle of the port line, and I soon saw the great jet of smoke from the *Trafalgar*, followed by the roar which denoted the simultaneous discharge of a whole broadside. In less than half a minute there was the puff and the roar of the second ship, the *Collingwood*, and almost immediately I saw that the *Nile*, at the head of the other line, had fired. But then I directly saw what I had not been prepared for. I saw the *Nile* turning round sharp to port, and, looking to the head of my own line, I saw the *Trafalgar* steaming along our line on the opposite course to ours. It flashed through my mind like a shot, that every ship was turning round after she had fired her broadside, and that consequently the heads of the French lines or groups, after running the gauntlet of our lines, would be met by the ships that had first fired on them, and that as the battle had begun by the ships passing in opposite directions, it would be continued by all the ships with their heads in the same direction.

I do not pretend to say that I knew what all this meant at the moment; indeed, I did not know anything in another minute, for the roar and shake of the whole of our guns, trained on the port beam, knocked the power of thinking out of me. Recovering myself in a cloud of choking smoke, I was first aware that there must have been very little reply to our fire, but two signalmen were stretched on the deck beside me, both quite still; one with his shoulder torn entirely away, and the other bleeding profusely from a wound in his head. There were also, as if through the ship, new sorts of voices which, in hurried and confused utterance, warned me that there were death and wounds elsewhere.

But there was no time to think of it. We were wheeling round after our next ahead; and out of the dense smoke which we were leaving, issued stray missiles tearing past, and sometimes striking davits or stanchions, or shattering the planking of a boat. There was nothing, in fact, now but a roar of guns all round us, and we were covered with a canopy of smoke. The sole design perceptible was that we were only firing into the smoke to starboard, and no missiles were coming from the port side, while every now and then we got a glimpse of our next ahead and next astern.

As we steamed on, messages went from the captain to the lieutenants not to fire any more till they could see the enemy; and it was becoming clear that the French fire was ceasing, though whereabouts they were could hardly be ascertained. Presently, however, we found ourselves quite clear of smoke and could see then that the French ships must, most of them, have stopped, for our vessels—as well as could be seen—were nearly in their old formations, while the French were well astern, still somewhat entangled by the smoke, and evidently in some confusion.

Out of this smoke there quickly emerged a ship, which we made out to be the flag-ship *Formidable* with a considerable heel to port and steering to the N.W.

With the general signal flying that the Division was to continue its course, the *Trafalgar* suddenly put on steam and went after the *Formidable* full speed. The two ships were now in close action and enveloped in smoke, so that we could only make out their positions occasionally, the *Trafalgar* apparently hanging on the starboard quarter of the *Formidable*. The firing did not last more than ten minutes or a quarter of an hour, when, the smoke clearing away, it was seen that the *Formidable's* colours were down.

What had happened we only knew afterwards. The *Formidable* had been badly torpedoed in passing, and was steaming as she hoped out of action when we saw her. As the *Trafalgar* approached, she made a short gallant defence with her guns, and fired two torpedoes at her; but the water was rising in the stokeholds, and it was impossible to keep steam. Admiral Markham, seeing plainly what the case was, passed close under the *Formidable's* stern, and hailed to claim surrender in the interests of humanity, or he would ram and sink her. It was the chance of war, and there was nothing but surrender before our gallant opponent.

Meantime it was plain to be seen how well Sir George Tryon's orders had worked. Some of our ships were frightfully knocked about, and the *Benbow* was almost in a sinking state from a number of shot-holes between wind and water; while the *Edinburgh* was all down by the head, having caught a torpedo near the stem, but the whole of the ships were in two lines as they entered into action, and they now re-formed and headed towards the French, leaving the *Benbow, Edinburgh*, and the prize French flag-ship together, attended by two or three of the cruisers.

But the most frightful incident of the battle took place in the other line, and I was not an eye-witness of it. I have not mentioned the *Polyphemus* before, but she was with us and sailed with us. It seems Sir George Tryon's orders to her were simply to keep out of the way in the first instance, and to strike home should any opportunity offer. Captain Brooke, it appears, running out to starboard of the Admiral's column, saw his chance in the smoke, and ran straight at the nearest French ship, whose attention was taken up by the fire of our ships on her other side. The shock was horrible, and she scarce had time to extricate herself, when the *Amiral Baudin* reeled and sank.

FLIGHT OF THE FRENCH SQUADRON.

It did not appear that the rest of the French ships were as much knocked about as we were, but we afterwards learnt the cause of this. It was simply that the heavy shell of the French had made a greater show on us during our first approach than we had been aware of; but, in passing, our light guns had made terrible havoc amongst the unprotected guns' crews in the French batteries, while, as they had not reserved their fire, it was not so destructive to us. Then, too, it seems that our manœuvre was entirely unexpected, and paralysed the action of the leading ships after they had, as they supposed, passed through our fleet. It was, again, our light guns which produced effect, but without making it so visible to outside observers.

The loss of the flag-ship, of the *Amiral Baudin*, and the great loss in killed and wounded did, however, act in demoralising the ships' companies, so that three or four of the ships had already drawn off to the north-eastward, and there was for the time a good deal of confusion; but they turned their heads from us and gradually drew out into a line abreast, nearly as we met them at first.

No doubt fearing a repetition of their former manœuvre, Sir George Tryon kept his fleet still in two lines; but as the French swept round, steering first N.E. and then nearly due north for Toulon, we were broken up into four short columns, and these were presently put into quarter line.

And now we had a game of long bowls for some time, without apparently much damage to either side. We were always being checked in our pursuit by the failure first of one ship, and then of another, to keep steam; and it seemed to be precisely the same with the French, so that darkness closed upon us without either the French being able to draw out of action, or our being able to make it a close one.

Before daylight, our reckoning brought us so close up to Toulon, that, as we had lost sight of the enemy three hours before, signal was made to slow down, and at daylight we could just make out the French closing into the land and disappearing.

Such was the Battle of Sardinia, as I made it out. The French risked it in the hope of falling on the weak Anglo-Italian squadron, and so saving Algeria. It was almost as great a risk for us, being so numerically inferior; but, accepting the position all along, our Admirals so managed that we suffered much less loss in the end. But the feature which struck us all as most remarkable was the fact that while we had two ships practically disabled, and the French had suffered but the same loss, yet we were victorious by reason of the terrible carnage which our lighter guns had caused in the enemy's ships.

P.S.—I have just learnt that the real cause of the French retreat was news that reached them by a cruiser of the approach of the squadron from Algiers. This Sir George Tryon expected all along, but we knew nothing of it. We met the ships next day. News from England has just come by the *Blonde*. The German Fleet has joined that of Sir Michael Seymour in the Gulf of Finnland, and he has sent home five of his ships. The Duke of Edinburgh has detached two of his, and the whole seven are making the best of their way, with several cruisers, to reinforce us. All idea of further attack on Algiers is given up, and Admiral Markham will sail with ten battle-ships and six cruisers to the Levant, to convoy the troops into the Black Sea, and then to mask the Russian Fleet in Sebastopol. So the Black Sea expedition is to go on. Yet the general opinion amongst us is that our Government are running considerable risks, and that we are relying on the principle of 'Nothing venture, nothing have.'

THE FRANCO-GERMAN CAMPAIGN—CAVALRY ENGAGEMENT NEAR LIGNY.

DEFEAT OF THE FRENCH.

(*From our Special Correspondent with the Germans.*)

NAMUR, *May* 5.

A REPORT reaches me to-night that the Germans from Metz

light siege train since early on the morning of the 3d. The guns in the annex batteries of the French defences not being mounted yet, each fort was surrounded by a circle of fire, to which it could only return a divergent reply. The forts are now shapeless heaps of ruin, the cavaliers cut down, and the guns either dismounted or buried under the earth thrown out by the bursting shells. No attempt at assault has yet been made.

An attempt at a raid by the German cavalry from the direction of Luxembourg—Dun is also reported, without great results. Two squadrons have managed to slip round the Verdun defences, and re-entered German territory near Mars-la-Tour, last night, destroying railways and wires as they went.

NAMUR, *May* 9.

There has been a smart cavalry action to-day in the vicinity of Ligny and St. Amand, names so well known in the Waterloo campaign, in which the French have very decidedly had the worst of it.

Before commencing my account, I will add that the censorship here is very strict indeed, and that no mention whatever is permitted of numbers of corps or regiments, or of the names of their commanders; as these data are invaluable to an enemy in enabling him to check the truth of information received, and it is always possible that the wires between here and Brussels may be tapped.

Yesterday afternoon I found a place in a train going to Gembloux, where our Cavalry Division had arrived during the morning. Arrived there, I met an old friend in the Hussars, who told me that he and three other officers had been selected for a reconnaissance ride next morning, and that a place in their carriage was at my service. The idea of driving out to a real cavalry action struck me as singular, so I asked for information, and was told by my friend that he and his comrades, who were all noted steeplechase riders, had had several horses in training for a meeting, to which the war had put a stop, and had been told by their colonel to train the horses a little 'fat' and bring them along to the front—he would be glad of their services, and find them an opportunity for distinction greater than any to be won between the flags. They were to have their horses led out for them, and, as soon as the expected collision occurred, to mount, slip through the enemy's scouts in the confusion of the scrimmage, and ride as far as possible to the south and westward to see what was going on behind the cavalry screen.

Needless to say, I accepted the offer, and 2 A.M. found me with my friends driving out along the road to Ligny, where lay the outposts.

Latest reports indicated the enemy's cavalry, at least a division strong, between Fleurus and Charleroi. The advance-guard of our Division, the Hussar brigade, moved off about an hour before sunrise, following the line of the great road. We stayed behind to await the arrival of the main body, and presently moved over in the direction of St. Amand. Soon the main body was seen approaching, and about the same time we could see the Hussars falling back across the railway, and a report arrived that the French were coming on in force.

The Divisional Commander rode forward to reconnoitre the ground in front, and left orders to the main body to form for attack under cover in a hollow in rear; the same, by chance, in which Blücher had stationed the reserves of his right before the battle of Ligny in 1815.

It was a perfectly faultless morning, and the sun was just beginning to rise when we saw three batteries of French Horse Artillery cross the railway and come out into the plain. Our own batteries were in the act of unlimbering, at double intervals, to allow for the melinite shells; and as they crossed the sky-line the French, too, saw them, and came into 'action front.' The two first shots on each side fell almost simultaneously, and the duel began. The hollow in our front and the blinding rays of the sun full in the eyes of the enemy gave us an immense advantage, and in five minutes our side had 'ranged,' and one French gun was sent flying. Meanwhile our Hussars had been falling back, and were wheeling up into position as second and third lines to the two heavy brigades.

The French Cavalry were now crossing the railway in line of squadron columns and immediately afterwards formed 'line,' and the signal to advance was given by our Commander. As our horse crossed the plateau on which the guns were in action, 'Troops half left' was sounded, and the French hearing the signal, no doubt, and seeing also that we were not quite in line, must have guessed our intention to attack their left, and endeavoured to meet it by 'Shouldering.'

Reaching the hollow our cavalry again wheeled into line, crossed the little brooklet without disorder, and then, by silent signal, broke into column of troops to the right, and galloped up the hollow in a long sweeping stride—their distances perfectly preserved. This movement promised to bring them out right on the flank and rear of the French left, but the next moment we saw the French Reserve, which had hitherto been hidden by trees along the lane from Perwin to Bry—moving in a direction that would bring them right on the flank of our first line. The situation was most critical—we all held our breath—but the next moment we heard the regimental call of the leading regiment, followed by the long 'G's' of 'line to the front,' and we knew that the danger was seen and met.

Simultaneously also the tail of the column still in sight wheeled into line, and came dashing forward to the attack.

The French were already in a poor condition to meet it. The attempt to 'shoulder' the long line had loosened their order, and from the moment they came in sight our gunners had turned their full power upon them with results almost indescribable. Out of the dust and smoke of the bursting shells we saw limbs and bodies thrown high in the air, and the right and second line of the enemy was already in hopeless confusion before the blow fell on their left. This wing had escaped our shells, for to fire on it would have imperilled our own men. They saw the danger coming, and two squadrons endeavoured to wheel up to meet it, but they were too late, the next moment our trumpets rang out the 'charge,' and with a roar of cheering our men dashed forward; we heard the crash of the collision, for a moment saw horses rear up and fall backward, and then the dust rose and shut out all further vision. But the French did not bolt, the wreck of their right and second line wheeled up, rallied on their officers as best they could, and dashed into the *mêlée*, where they too were lost to sight. From time to time we saw groups of our white-coated Cuirassiers and the dark blue Uhlans emerge from the dust-cloud, then wheel and go back again, and for some moments the fight here became stationary, for the French on this point outnumbered us two to one. Then suddenly from out of the hollow we again heard the charge sounding, and for a second or two caught sight of the left of our third line, as with perfectly closed ranks they dashed into the *mêlée*. This blow settled the matter. The mass again came into motion; first a few files, followed by more, began to drop off to the rear, and presently the whole cloud, gathering pace as it went, swept down right on to the flank of their horse batteries, who, seeing the danger coming, had endeavoured to limber up in the full fire of our artillery. But they were too late, the crowd swept over them, and when it had passed we saw eight guns still on the ground, with some Hussars and Uhlans busy around them.

What happened on our right I could only partially see, the trees interfering with my line of vision. I am therefore dependent on the testimony of others.

The regiment that had 'front formed' was one of the heaviest in the army, and prided itself on riding even closer knee to knee in the charge than the regulation sanctions; and well was it for them that they did so, for the odds against them were very heavy. The shock was perfectly direct; the French wavered a little at the last moment, and the Cuirassiers burst through them, maintaining their formation almost intact; then, wheeling round, attacked the overlapping French squadrons, and drove them back towards the hollow, where the second line of Hussars, warned of what was happening in front, had taken ground outwards, and then charged the *mêlée* from the northwards, setting it in motion again towards the south.

By degrees the forces began to disentangle themselves, and the Germans rallied again in closed squadrons, while the French got away as best they could towards the woods of Lambusart.

The losses due to the lance appear to have been trifling, for at the moment of actual contact the men could not reach each other; the horses fairly breasted one another, and the lighter ones went over backwards, many being found with fractured spines. In the *mêlée*, too, the lance proved useless,—the crowd was too dense. Men wrestled and fought with their fists. The French loss caused by our artillery was perfectly appalling; but, thanks to the dexterity of our leader, who managed always to keep the enemy between him and the guns—thus effectually masking their fire—we have escaped their shells almost entirely. I may also call attention to the advantages we secured by having the sun at our backs, which gave the French gunners—excellently trained as they are, and gallant beyond a doubt—hardly the chance of inflicting injury on us.

No one can accuse the French this morning of showing anything but perfect gallantry, but we have again an instance that more than gallantry is required for cavalry efficiency. The reason why the Germans won is because they manœuvred with perfect precision, and were so thoroughly in hand that even the most unexpected occurrences could be met and dealt with. Here the French were outmatched, and their leader, too, seemed hardly equal to his task. He formed line too soon; had he stayed in squadron columns a little longer he could have changed front without the unsteadiness entailed by the endeavour to do so after the line had been formed.

Whilst writing this one of the General Staff has kindly come round to tell me that there is room in a special train starting to-night in two hours—destination not to be breathed—and I fancy within a very short time you will hear of something startling; more I dare not say at present.

My friends of this morning are back again safe and sound, having ridden some sixty miles. They tell me the French had thirty-six squadrons against our twenty-four this morning. But about the rest of their information I must be silent.

VOUZIERS, MIDNIGHT, *May* 12.

THE curtain has at last fallen on the first act of this great national tragedy—the first strategical problem has been solved, and I am again free to write.

Briefly what has happened is this:

All the available troops of the Metz (or 3d Army) have been drawn off under cover of the operations described in my telegram of the 5th inst., to the neighbourhood of Luxembourg—Thionville.

The five Corps of the 1st Army have been concentrated from Namur, and districts northward, behind the frontier north of Mezieres, Sedan, and the 2d Army (four Corps) has formed between them. Three other Corps are following in rear.

These movements were completed on the 9th inst., and at daybreak on the 10th the frontier was crossed by the leading troops of all three armies.

Two French corps, distributed for the defence of the Meuse, were caught by the 3d Army whilst endeavouring to concentrate, and compelled to fall back in considerable confusion.

The Second Army met with no opposition, and their cavalry reached Buzancy.

The cavalry divisions in advance of the First Army had a sharp and victorious encounter with French horse on the plateau between the Meuse and Aisne, who retreated afterwards towards Laon, and our leading corps made good the passage of the Meuse, between Mezieres and Sedan, and upstream towards Mouzon, their advance guards bivouacking on the line, Rancourt—Omont—Poix. It was a day of hard marching, but the weather was cool, and the men in good training seemed to make light of their twenty to twenty-five miles.

I was not present at any of the collisions this day, being unable to overtake the cavalry screen; from what I can learn, however, the success of the latter was due to much the same reasons as in the fight at St. Amand—Bry, viz., mobility in the troops, *coup d'œil* in the leaders, and closed files in the charge.

The fight of the next day I saw capitally, and send it herewith as I wrote it the same evening.

ENGAGEMENT AT VAUX CHAMPAGNE.

DRICOURT, *May* 11.

I OVERTOOK the main body of our Cavalry Division (*i.e.* the one attached to the immediately following Corps, with which I have for the present joined fortunes) near Tourteron—a village lying some seven miles north of the Aisne—late last night, and learnt that there was certain to be a sharp tussle next morning; for patrols reported large masses of French troops in the valley of the Aisne about Vouziers, and from a neighbouring hill we could see the reflection of their bivouac fires, while southward we heard the noise of trains passing constantly and at short intervals on the line from Rheims to Monthois.

At 3 A.M. the headquarter orders reached us, and at 4.30 we were on the move—pretty smart work, considering the number of hands through which orders had to pass. I followed the General's staff, who had kindly given me permission to do so.

Our mission was evident, viz., to seize the high land beyond the Aisne, to cover the passage of the stream by our infantry.

On the way reports came in that a large body of French troops, at least a Corps, was moving to meet us by the same road, and it became evident that it was a race between us who could reach the long stretching downs of Vaux Champagne in our front first, and in sufficient strength to hold them. That our cavalry could be there in time was clear; indeed, our scouts were already far beyond it, but how to hold it was another matter, about which I should have liked information, but did not dare to ask for it.

We cantered forward, and drew up on the downs about 7.15. I found the situation very much like one I saw at the French manœuvres last year near Lesmont, when infantry and artillery, both without scouts in advance, raced for a similar hill, and met at the top with results disastrous for the artillery.

The ground was exactly similar, and deserves a word or two of explanation. The downs of Vaux form, as it were, a T piece to a long central ridge. We were standing on the cross-head, and looking southward a corresponding transverse ridge limited our vision at 2500 to 3000 yards, and between the two lay two valleys trending east and west from the central neck, the slopes gentle and unbroken, with a slight convexity in cross section. If we were ten minutes too late the infantry would be in the hollows out of the line of sight of our batteries, and our fate would be a matter of minutes.

We had only three batteries on the spot, and where were the others? I did not know, and dared not ask, and as etiquette prevented my going in front of the General, I had not the consolation of studying his face; all I noticed was that he was smoking very quietly and reflectively. Northward, a mist lay over the river, and all the valley was still; the minutes seemed like hours. At length my ear caught the sound, so well known to me, of the roll of gun-carriages and clatter of harness, and out of the sea of mist below I suddenly saw the helmets and heads of the gunners arise, and then I knew that, confident in the reports of the cavalry, our General was going to try, and to succeed, in the same manœuvre in which the French last year, without cavalry, had so conspicuously failed; for these new comers could only be the Corps Artillery, and with eighteen to twenty batteries in line on this height in time, I felt certain no infantry could hope to capture it. The enemy, however, was not far off, for isolated shots were now heard from the southward, and our cavalry videttes came in view, falling back before his advance.

Our guns were brought up behind the brow and unlimbered, but kept back below the sky-line, and every one was ordered under cover, where we waited for some ten minutes. Then suddenly the order was given to load and run forward by hand. I crept to the front and there saw extending half-way down the opposite slope the leading lines of a whole French Division deployed for action. A more perfect target it would have been impossible to devise. Next moment eighteen batteries at least were pouring their fire into this defenceless mass, and the further hillside became a scene of

OUR CORRESPONDENT AT THE BATTLE OF VAUX CHAMPAGNE.

slaughter unequalled in the annals of warfare except, possibly, at Eylau.

The guns were all laid for the leading line, there was no question of ranging at all—for the distance was not more than 1200 yards—some of the French threw themselves down and attempted to reply, but in a few moments the smoke and dust from our bursting shells enveloped them, and their bullets began to fly higher. The following lines pressed on to the leading ones, thus making the target denser, and now the gunners changed from shrapnel to common shell, with high explosive bursters, and we saw limbs and trunks of men thrown high in the air above the dust-clouds, whilst even the screams of the wounded reached us above the din. It was ghastly beyond the power of description, and I dropped back to look the other way, and there saw the whole of our Cavalry Division trotting forward to reap the harvest the guns had sown.

They were at this moment in column of regiments, each regiment wheeled up by troops, and moving perpendicularly to the prolongation of the enemy's line. I lost sight of them for a moment as I cut across the hill, and when I next saw them they had wheeled into line and were bearing down on the enemy obliquely across his front, so that six successive lines were available to ride down all resistance. The first two lines increased their squadron intervals, and opened their files to about half a horse's length, and then, at about 500 yards from the enemy, the gallop was sounded. The outer sections of the French endeavoured to wheel up to meet them, but a last salvo from the two flank batteries with shrapnel seemed to tear them away, and the next instant the cavalry were on them. For a moment the line was a bit unsteadied, but its pace did not check. The French rose and fired after them, and many fell, but the second line, 300 yards in rear of the first, was on them, and then the third and fourth, and now I understood why the German cavalry carry lances. The first line kept up its pace to the end, and then rallied beyond it and came back through them again; the fifth, not yet engaged, trotted round and charged in from the front, and the sixth moved off up the hill to watch the flanks. The confusion now defied description, the French firing-like lunatics in every direction, and the whole mass taking an uphill direction, thus masking the fire of the French guns, which had been in action within a few minutes of the commencement of our fire, and had replied pluckily to the guns on our side specially reserved to deal with them; but now, in the confusion, our lancers got amongst them and succeeded in destroying most of the teams. It was 8 A.M. when the first gun fired, it was 8.20 when the cavalry charged, and since then, perhaps, twenty minutes more had elapsed—a whole Infantry Division had been destroyed. But our position was by no means without cause for anxiety, nor could we hold the ground we had won; we knew French reinforcements were at hand, for we heard guns open on our cavalry beyond the hill, and these soon began falling back in disorder.

What would we not have given for a brigade of Bersaglieri or of French Chasseurs—I thought of one I had seen last autumn that marched nine kilometres in forty-five minutes, and wished we had it with us now.

Our leading companies were still a couple of miles away; heading more to the left, I moved along the ridge till I reached a point whence I could overlook what was going to happen.

About two miles to the south-east I saw a French brigade with six batteries of artillery, moving forward, formed for attack in their conventional manner. The guns came into action to the eastward, and almost at the same moment the Prussian divisional batteries also unlimbered, but the French found their range first, and so occupied the attention of the Germans that the infantry this time passed unscathed down the same slope which, on the other flank, had proved so disastrous to them. It was now evident, from the form of the ground, that the two infantries would butt up against each other at about two hundred yards, and victory would probably fall to the side which was quickest 'on the drop,' as the Americans say. Both sides were rapidly approaching one another, the Prussians still in line of company columns, the French in a dense line of skirmishers. Presently the former 'front formed line,' their drums began to beat, and the whole advanced in 'parade march,' dressed as on the passing line. Suddenly, and simultaneously, the French line dropped to the ground, the Prussians halted and came to the ready; for a moment they stood motionless. Then the French, finding, I suppose, that on the ground, they could not see, sprang to their feet, and that instant there was a glint of light along the line as the rifles came to the present, and the next second the scythe of death swept over the French, and they fell in swathes. But the Prussians began to fall too, and the French supports were closer at hand, and fed the fighting line more rapidly, but their fire was not equally in hand. I could hear the Prussian volleys and mark the course of each distinctly. For five minutes the struggle raged—the roar of musketry was deafening—but above it I again caught the beat of the drum, and saw the second Prussian line advancing. When it was almost close on the first, the shrill whistles sounded, the fire partially ceased, and, headed by their officers, the whole sprang forward with a rush. But the French did not give; their reserves, too, were close at hand in company columns; the fighting line rallied on these, and all dashed forward together. But no bayonet encounter followed. Both sides halted at about thirty paces, and again the magazine fire blazed out, telling on the French clumps much more rapidly than it did on the Prussian line—for a single bullet pierced ten or a dozen bodies. Then presently the French masses became ragged towards the rear—they bagged outwards like sacks, and began to move with increasing speed down the hill, and at this moment two squadrons of divisional cavalry, who had slipped out between the guns and the infantry, swept down on them from flank to flank.

They probably did not do much damage, but they separated the infantries—and a number of French batteries now appeared on the further hill, and compelled the Prussians to fall back also.

The artillery duel now began again—but lasted only a short time, for the French evidently only meant to break off the fight, and as soon as the wreck of the infantry were in safety, the firing ceased, and the guns withdrew.

The Germans were in no condition for immediate pursuit. They had to wait for the remainder of the corps to close up, and to rally the cavalry.

It was now about 11.30—and to the eastward on the high ground overlooking the Aisne about Vouziers we could see the flashes of a long line of guns, and in the plain below dark masses of troops.

About four we moved forward, and about six bivouacked near a place called Dricourt, whence I write this. I learn that our scouts discovered a whole Corps moving down on our flank this morning from St. Remy, but about 10 A.M., hearing presumably of the result of the action at Vaux, they bent off southward, and are evidently now on our front. It appears the French Corps we fought to-day came on with one division deployed for action on its left, a brigade in echelon on the right. The corps artillery between the two and the remaining brigade in reserve. Where the cavalry was we do not know.

Another French corps was defeated about Vouziers. So we have the wreck of two Corps, and the whole of one for certain, in our front for to-morrow, for our outposts are in contact along the whole line. How many more we may find I cannot tell, but we are two days clear ahead of their calculated mobilisation, and these two days' fighting must have seriously deranged their plans.

The men are rather sober; they have seen death for the first time, and the slaughter caused by our new shells is most horrible to look at. Besides, only few of them were engaged in the actual fighting line, and the remainder do not yet know from experience the intensity of the passion for blood which seizes them when once they have taken active part in the slaying.

It has been a wise measure to let the massed bands play to-night, and I have never experienced anything more moving than the sound of the last great hymn, sung by all the men, with which the 'Zapfenstreich' winds up.

THE BATTLE OF MACHAULT.

GREAT GERMAN VICTORY.

(From our Special Correspondent with the Germans.)

DRICOURT, *May* 11.

THE gunners were moving long before daylight, and I went with them. Dawn was just breaking when we reached the summit of the rolling ridge which marks our front, and we could still see signs of bivouac fires burnt low on another and almost parallel wave some 2000 to 3000 yards to our front. The bottom of the hollow is steeper and we cannot see into it, but they tell me our Infantry are down there.

Our position faces N.N.W. by S.S.E., so again we shall have the sun at our backs. Some of our guns are entrenched, and I notice the intervals between them are wider than usual, probably, as before, to ward against the melinite shells.

Of our strategic position all I know is that we have a Corps on either flank, and two within supporting distance—what the 2d Army is doing I don't know.

. . . . . .

VOUZIERS, *May* 12.

I was obliged to break off my dispatch abruptly, owing to the sudden development of events. I had just written the last line when the first gun went off about ten minutes before sunrise, and for an hour an incessant roar of artillery raged. The French shot well, but the sun in their eyes gave them never a chance.

I had now time and daylight enough to look round. Our troops were all carefully under cover at least 2000 yards to the rear, mostly in rendezvous formations, waiting. Of the enemy I could only see his guns, and when the sun rose high enough, one could distinctly make out the line of an entrenchment just at the break of the long slope into the hollow. Even then I might not have noticed it but for the indiscretion of its occupants, who would keep moving about. It may have been about six o'clock when I saw, out of the hollows away to the rear, three great columns rise up, which proved to be six batteries of Artillery each. They trotted forward, forming line to the front, and then I realised that I was at length about to see a real Napoleonic battle, the blow to pierce the centre or fail.

Nearing the outer edge of the zone, where the splinters of bursting shells meant for us began to be dangerous, the gallop was sounded, and the whole eighteen batteries dashed forward in superb form. Our guns increased their fire to the utmost ex-

tremity, shrouding the enemy's front in the smoke of their shells, and then ceased for a few moments as the new arrivals passed

The Great War of 189—

through the intervals, resuming it again as soon as they were clear, and maintaining it at this extreme rate till it was seen that the others had unlimbered and were ready to take their part in the action at a range of about 1500 yards. This move brought them, however, to within 1000 yards of the enemy's advanced Infantry, and we saw many drop; but our own advanced posts had been reinforced by small driblets, too insignificant to attract the enemy's artillery fire, and these with the aid of a few guns that could now be spared soon took the edge off the French Infantry fire.

In fifteen minutes or less, the effect of these eighteen fresh batteries was plainly apparent; to stay where they were meant for the French gunners annihilation, and that was not their business, and presently we saw their teams come up by alternate batteries. In the crowd of men and horses thus assembled our shells made terrible havoc, and probably not one-third of the guns were successfully withdrawn. Then the whole power of our sixty batteries was turned on the Infantry, and we had the 'defender's dilemma' before us. He could not retire his Infantry up the slope, for that meant beginning the action with a retreat; and he could not leave them there unsupported, for that would mean annihilation; his only chance was to move troops down the slope to reinforce them—and presently we saw them coming. Then a repetition of yesterday's slaughter began.

Had we known for certain what was going on out of our sight, we might have been content to let the foe bleed himself to death in these fruitless efforts; but we did not, we could only guess that he would be moving forward his reinforcements of all arms with all haste, and our game was to crush what was before us as quickly as might be.

Our Infantry were now rapidly coming up, the two divisions side by side, the brigades of each in the same order, with their regiments each one behind the other. The leading regiment had two battalions in first line and one in support, and the foremost battalions, each two companies in front and two behind, in company column. As the troops approached our guns they formed line and came forward, their drums beating, with the strictest possible discipline, for the bullets were flying in showers overhead, and men were constantly dropping.

The lines went down the slope with about 500 paces between them, and as the leading one reached the advanced posts, the latter rose, and, with a cheer, dashed down into the hollow, where they found shelter for a moment in the dead angle at the foot of the slope. Our gunners now turned their fire on the Infantry trench for a few moments with high explosive shells, and then the whole crowd of men in the hollow rose and rushed it at the point of the bayonet, clearing it in a moment and pursuing beyond. Then came the turn of the French, and gallantly they availed themselves of it. Our rapid advance had masked our guns, the French falling back before it had been taken up by their supports, and now having only Infantry to deal with, the whole of them turned and came on again.

It did not come to cold steel, however, for again both sides stopped and blazed into each other with magazine fire and astounding inaccuracy. The air above our heads seemed alive with bullets—but our reserves were coming up under cover, and those of the French moving down hill caught many of the missiles that flew too high. Soon, perhaps in five minutes, the whole body, both assailants and defenders, began to move slowly up the hill, the movement never ceasing till our Infantry reached the top. Our Horse Artillery, followed by our Divisional Cavalry, galloped forward in support. What happened for the next few minutes I am unable to state from observation, for I, too, was moving across the valley, and looking for a reasonably secure spot from which to see further. I found one at the junction between two French Corps, where a copse came right up to the edge of their line—both Corps being hotly engaged in front had wheeled inwards a little towards the centre, and there was a gap of some 500 yards, and not a soul on the look-out. From here I could take in the whole situation. To the south-eastward guns flashing and heavy masses of troops showed the battle extended for miles beyond the left of our corps, and south-west of us I saw at least thirty French batteries in line along a low crest that ran about parallel to the ridge we had now reached, whilst up the slope towards us, but from our left front, a whole French Division of Infantry was moving towards their comrades on the hill already hardly pressed, from whom they were yet about one thousand yards distant.

Their guns were still silent, for their Infantry masked their view, and it was fortunate for our battalions that they were so, for the fight for the moment was stationary, and we were only just holding our own.

For some moments it continued so, and the effect to the spectator was very curious. The air was so filled with the roar of musketry that it seemed to come from nowhere in particular. There was nothing, in the absence of all smoke, to connect it with these two long lines of men, whose rifles spasmodically rose and fell. Along the front of the French, owing, I suppose, to the angle at which I saw them, a row of little blue sparks scintillated like the spark discharge from an electric brush, and over both there lay a blue, grey mist which gave a curious mirage effect to the whole. The shooting must have been vile on both sides, for according to practice-ground results, thirty seconds should have sufficed for mutual extermination; but, though men fell fast, the net result appeared wonderfully small.

This may have lasted some three minutes, but it was impossible to keep the run of the time, and then above the roll of the musketry I caught the beat of the drums, and a reinforcing line, closed and in perfect order, came over the brow to our assistance. The sight of these closed lines was enough for both sides; the French gave way, and our fighting line dashed forward. But only for some 300 yards or so, for again French reinforcements brought the movement to a check. And now the French Artillery opened fire on our following lines, and we had a taste of what it means to come down hill in the sweep of shrapnel.

Our gunners were, however, quickly on the spot. They had

been waiting behind till room was made for them, but till they picked up the range our losses were terrible, and I think that that following line must have lost a larger percentage than any other troops this day.

The French fighting line was now sagging to the rear, and their last reinforcement—a still intact division—was yet some 500 yards away from them, when I noticed a couple of cavalry officers pass close to where I stood in the copse, take in the whole scene at a glance, and gallop away.

I knew then what was coming; it would be the death stroke if given in time, before the fresh French Infantry had actually joined the fighting line. These were now not 300 yards away from their comrades when the first squadron passed me galloping straight down the hill in column of troops. The first squadron no sooner had its last troop clear of our Infantry front, than it wheeled into line, and went right at the flank of the French, who attempted to fall back to meet it, but gave way at the last moment and ran right back on the reinforcements, and pell-mell fugitives and pursuers crashed right into the angle of these fresh troops. The second squadron followed, then a third and fourth. The confusion became indescribable, and now by the same track an endless succession of squadrons began to emerge, for the first arrivals had been only the Divisional regiment, and two whole fresh Cavalry Divisions were now to follow. On the French side, too, a Cavalry Division appeared coming out through the line of guns in line of squadron columns, and a cavalry duel was now imminent.

There was not much time on our side to prepare for it. The first regiment of the leading Division joined in the charge on the Infantry, but that blow sufficed, and the whole mass began to break up and fall to the rear with increasing velocity. The remaining squadrons, as they arrived, formed line to the front, and awaited the arrival of their fellows.

As soon as the 1st Division had completed its formation, it trotted forward to meet the enemy, who were now only some 800 yards distant. Both sides were suffering from Artillery fire, and there was no room for manœuvre. The gallop and charge were sounded simultaneously, and the shock took place all along the front; but the German files were not closed as well as on former occasions, and the two lines fairly threaded each other, then wheeled about by troops, and went for one another again. Then a closed, locked, *mêlée* arose, and the fight became stationary. But our 2d Division was now rapidly arriving, and its leading brigade delivered a shock which set the mass in motion towards the French guns. Then another brigade was sent in, and this fairly started it on the run, and in a few seconds the whole confused mob of over 6000 horsemen was flying in wild confusion right down on and over the gunners, who again tried to limber up, but were again too late.

The battle was over, the French line pierced, their last closed reserves broken, and we had a brigade of Cavalry and masses of Infantry, who had not yet pulled a trigger, in hand.

I looked at my watch, it was just 8 A.M., and I turned and rode for the nearest wire. Crossing the ground over which we had come, I was able to notice that our two divisions had both still a regiment in hand, and of the following Corps only the Corps Artillery had been engaged, so we were in ample strength for the pursuit.

THE LESSON OF THE FIGHT.

What the effect of this victory will be on the course of the war it is too soon to prophesy. It may very well prove decisive, for we have now driven a wedge right in between the French Armies, behind their eastern and northern defences, and stand with five Corps on either face of the wedge, with three more in between ready to move to the support of either. The French must either move against us by lateral roads and railways, in which case we can always meet them on a broader front, or attempt to concentrate far away to the southward, and in any case our strength is morally more than doubled by our successes. The Germans took the field with no overweening opinion of themselves. They are a modest people, as a whole, given to pessimism about themselves, and ready to believe the overdone reports as to the regeneration of their hereditary enemy that reached them through the public Press. The French, on the other hand, had again learnt to believe in themselves; their journalists, who were not going to do the fighting, had lauded them to the skies, while the nation and rank and file had believed all they were told, even if the experienced soldiers had not. They have fought with the greatest gallantry, but for the second time it has been their want of thoroughness that has ruined them. In each arm and every branch they were just a little behind their adversaries. They lost two clear days in mobilisation, and hence were strategically unready when the blow fell. Their Cavalry was brave, but not a match for the Germans in mobility, and consequently was beaten. The defeat of the Cavalry led the Infantry to blunder into a trap where no human courage could avail them, and this again entailed a concentration backward, with the obligation of standing on the defensive to await the arrival of a reinforcing Corps which came just too late; and the consequences we have seen in to-day's fight. I do not believe the Germans have lost very heavily, though isolated bodies may certainly have done so. But the three arms played into each other's hands so perfectly, and the arrival of the supports was so well timed, that none were ever called on for exertions beyond their strength. Such tactical handling has never been seen since Napoleon's days. But there is this difference to note, that this time the troops have handled themselves instead of being handled by the General.

It is too early yet for a list of casualties to have been made out, but at the last moment I learn that our Cavalry yesterday lost 20 per cent. of their strength.

THE WAR IN THE FAR EAST—THE CAPTURE OF VLADIVOSTOCK.

DETAILS OF THE ENGAGEMENT.

A CORRESPONDENT at Hong-Kong telegraphs under date July 18th as follows:—

Every one is engaged in discussing what we shall do with Eastern Siberia, now that we have got it. The fall of Vladivostock was so sudden, and so apparently easy of accomplishment, that it almost seems as if the Admiral, Sir Frederick Richards, and General Barker are likely to lose the credit of the success which they themselves achieved.

It is known that the 1st Battalion Leinster Regiment, together with the 1st Battalion of the 4th Goorkhas, the 21st Bombay Rifles, another Bombay regiment, and two batteries of Artillery, were dispatched to Hong-Kong from India at the very beginning of the troubles, and that they were joined there by 1000 of the finest men ever seen from Australia, with distinct orders to the Admiral and the General at Hong-Kong (who was given the military command) to operate against Vladivostock.

The *Leander* and *Mercury* were instantly sent to the north to reconnoitre, while the remainder of the squadron was brought to Hong-Kong, it being understood that cruisers would be detached from the East Indian and Australian stations to guard Singapore and the Straits.

Except two ships which claimed protection in the neutral waters of Japan, it was known that all the Russian squadron had retired to Vladivostock. Telegrams had further informed the Admiral that four ships from the Pacific station had been ordered to Yokohama to wait his orders.

It was frightful work getting the necessary armaments and stores on board the transports, from the intense heat prevailing; but there was much less sickness than might have been supposed the new troops being roomily housed on board the steamers which were to take them north, and kept employed, except during the greatest heat, in assisting in all the work of preparing and loading the transports. In rather over five weeks everything was finished, and the *Archer* and *Swift* being left to guard Hong-Kong in the event of any stray Russian cruiser appearing, the remaining thirteen ships of the squadron, headed by the Admiral in the *Imperieuse*, who had the General with him, and convoying fifteen or sixteen transport, store, and collier steamers, sailed for Vladivostock.

The harbour of Vladivostock is one of the finest in the world. It lies east and west, and is about two miles long in those directions, while it is about half a mile wide from north to south. All over this fine space there is a clear depth of from five to nine fathoms —precisely that of greatest convenience for an anchorage. The town is situated at the north-west angle of the harbour, and the latter is everywhere overlooked by high ground, but especially from the south. The immediate entrance to the harbour is by a passage a mile and a half long and three-quarters of a mile wide, lying about N.N.E. and S.S.W., and opening into the west part of the inner harbour. This passage is formed by a peninsula not more than half a mile wide at any part, and more than three miles long. It is generally high ground, rising in parts to 300 feet. The entrance to **Vladivostock** is wholly covered by the large island of Kazakavitch, which measures five or six miles either way, and contains in itself the very fine and extended harbour of Novik Bay. The strait between this island and the mainland, which must be entered to pass into Vladivostock Harbour, narrows gradually, but with much indentation and many anchorages, to the west entrance, formed between the Shkota Peninsula before described, and the island. At this point it is only about one-third of a mile wide, and the north shore is the end of a very narrow, sandy spit, about a third of a mile long

It was known that for years past the Russians had been erecting batteries and placing mines to guard the approaches to their harbour, and were there no other way of advancing to attack but by sea, up the channel and into the harbour, no place is so easily defended. But as it turned out, and is now recognised, no place is more difficult to defend when attacked in the proper way. It is near the end of a peninsula itself, and troops landed from anchorages at the heads of the two bays which form the peninsula, can easily isolate and cut the town off from the mainland, and so take it in the rear.

It was at first thought that our expedition would follow this plan of attack, but the rendezvous made by signal immediately on leaving Hong-Kong, namely, Novik Bay, set that question at rest.

It took the fleet ten days to reach Novik Bay, but, off Korsakov Island, it was joined by the *Melpomene*, *Daphne*, *Champion* and *Garnet*, from the Pacific, and so made up to seventeen sail in all. A few hours after, the *Leander* and *Mercury* rejoined, reporting that there was a small garrison—perhaps 150 men—occupying the two batteries covering the entrance to Novik Bay, and probably protecting a mine field, but no other batteries or garrisons were known to be on the island. The ships had been twice chased by four ships coming out of Vladivostock, but in obedience to orders had not attempted to bring them to action, and had easily out-steamed them each time.

The whole squadron now lay-to off the entrance to the bay, while 500 men of the Sutherland Highlanders were landed south of the entrance with directions to capture the southern battery, assisted by the fire of the *Leander* and *Mercury*, and to turn the guns on the northern battery, also assisted by the ships.

This turned out to be a very small affair. The Russians taken in rear and engaged in front, fled into the forest long before our troops closed; and the northern battery, seeing what had happened, fired one or two shots from the very light guns which the battery contained, spiked them, and retired. The cables to the mines were discovered and cut, and within four hours afterwards the whole armament was safely anchored in Novik Bay.

The next two days were entirely occupied in filling up with coal from two colliers, and settling the final arrangements for attack. The Admiral himself, taking the General with him, hoisted his flag in the *Alacrity*, and ran up the west shore of the Shkota Peninsula, drawing the fire of a small battery at its south end, and of one or two heavier ones at the back of the town.

On the third day, all was astir at daylight. Most of the boats of the squadron were alongside the transports, and troops to the number of nearly 3000 were crowded into them, besides the field-pieces of the ships, and their crews. The steam launches and pinnaces soon took lines of these loaded boats in tow, and steamed out of the bay, whence five or six of the war ships had preceded them. In a very few minutes these latter were engaging the little battery on the end of Cape Tokarofski, as the low sandy spit is called, which made but a very feeble reply, and soon hoisted a white flag. There were only twenty men in it, and three small guns, so that resistance would have been hopeless. It was ascertained to be the mine station for a line of mines across the Strait.

The plan of attack was now cleverly developed. The landing was effected all along the west shore of the Shkota Peninsula, and in spite of the rough scrub with which it is covered, the seamen dragged the field-pieces along the shore to the north. No resistance was offered; it was impossible to offer any under the guns of the ships, and by noon the whole body were halted for dinner.

There is a valley about half-way along the peninsula lying about N.E. and S.W., opening on to the harbour at the northern end, and on to the sea at the southern end. It was supposed that resistance would be encountered here, though it was not intended to march through it, but to adhere to the shore and the cover of the ships until the town could be turned.

Accordingly, after dinner the advanced guard had no sooner opened this valley than it was met by a heavy rifle and gun fire from a strong detachment posted and entrenched across the head of it. But the General was not to be caught napping. He had sent four field-pieces up the hill on his right, which from its brow poured a wholly unexpected and murderous fire down upon the Russians. This they did not stand for ten minutes, and our march went on. Then the field-pieces on this height found themselves overlooking the harbour, and at once turned their attention

THE TAKING OF VLADIVOSTOCK: GOORKAS PROTECTING THE GUNS.

to shelling the ships in it, though the distance was too great to admit of effective fire.

At this time the ships, ten or twelve of them, spread themselves in a long line ahead of the advancing column, and searched every foot of ground, which could be easily done as it was generally low.

There were several batteries discovered facing seaward, which the ships engaged. The Russians stuck to their guns most manfully, and some of our ships suffered very heavily, but none of the batteries had any efficient rear defences, and as the gunners caught sight of the head of our column advancing by the shore, they invariably abandoned their works and retired to the northward, along the road that leads round that part of the harbour.

Fearing an attempt might be made to dislodge the field-pieces on the height, a wing of the Goorkhas was sent up to reinforce them, and it was quite a sight to see these little fellows swarming up like so many ants.

And now the signallers with the field-pieces got to the highest point of ground, and very soon telegraphed to the Admiral that the ships might shell the Russian troops by firing on the signal station, which the troops surrounded. Some of the ships could see the station, and in obedience to signal from the Admiral began to shell it. The signallers directed the fire from the ships, so that, without seeing the object, it was immensely destructive, and ultimately forced the Russians to retreat.

This being again communicated to the ships and to the landing party now mustering in strength at the back of the town, a general advance was made, before which the Russians fell back, and ultimately sent in a flag of truce with terms of surrender.

Our loss was very small; only one officer of the Bombay Regiment, and 42 men killed; 5 officers and 134 men wounded. Nor was the Russian loss much greater, being estimated at 67 killed and 203 wounded. It was the skill of the attack in turning the Russian defences, and the immense use that was made of the fire from the ships, which produced a result astonishing to those who had not inquired into its causes.

EVENTS IN THE EAST OF EUROPE.

THE BELEAGUERED GARRISON IN VARNA.

LONDON, *June* 11.

THE course of events in the Black Sea, since our fleet for the time evacuated it, has been as follows:—It appears that as soon as the Russian Fleet was driven off the sea into harbour, immediate steps were taken by the Russian authorities to withdraw the troops which had been gathered for the purpose of reinforcing the troops already landed in Bulgaria. Unable to pass by sea they were useless for that purpose; and it was hoped, if they were sent off at once to reinforce the armies opposing Austria, that a successful action against that Power might enable the victorious army, co-operating with the army already in Bulgaria, to make the passage through Roumania by land and, at least, ensure the safety of the expeditionary force in Bulgaria. Perhaps it might be possible in that case to secure the object, dear to the heart of the Czar, of so strengthening that expeditionary force as to enable it to crush the Bulgarian Army. The deepest anxiety prevailed in Russia as to the fate of those troops, somewhat rashly committed to the sea expedition, no sufficient allowance having been made for the prompt action of the English Fleet.

It was some time before the Russian Fleet, which had retired to Sebastopol, discovered that the English Fleet had actually evacuated the Black Sea. Sir George Tryon had left some cruisers as long as possible to disguise the movement. When these also disappeared, a fear was entertained that this was a mere ruse to draw the Russian Fleet away from Sebastopol in order to crush it in the open sea. We regret to say that it was through the telegraphic dispatches to the English newspapers that, by various indirect channels, the news first reached the Russian Government that Trebizonde had been evacuated and, subsequently, that the English Fleet had passed into the Mediterranean. It was, however, not till Sir George Tryon had actually reached Malta that they were fully aware that the Black Sea had been evacuated. Then it was, after a day of hesitation as to the best course to be pursued, decided to establish touch with the Russian Army in Bulgaria, all communication with which had been cut for some time. As, however, that army—not without difficulty—had maintained its telegraphic communication with the sea, this was effected soon after the cruisers had reached the coast, in the neighbourhood of Varna.

It was then ascertained that the Bulgarian force in Varna itself was still holding out; and that the Russian Army, reduced to about 35,000 men by the force left to guard the lines to the sea, by the covering force at Varna and Shumla, and by sickness, had been able to effect very little. It had at first advanced inland as far as Tirnovo, where it remained in an entrenched camp, waiting for information. It was believed that the Austrian force in Servia had been too much reduced to be able to advance, and that the Bulgarian troops were fully occupied in Macedonia. Had the force landed been carried up to the figure that was intended, an immediate advance on Sofia would have been attempted. As the case stood, however, General Karanoff did not feel himself strong enough for this, and as now his only hope was to have the way through Roumania opened, he had turned northwards, having sent messengers through to communicate by land with Russia. He had, however, found it impossible to effect the passage of the Danube up to the moment when he received the joyful telegram announcing that, in consequence of the departure of the English Fleet, it was possible either to withdraw him by sea in safety, or to reinforce him. As there seemed every prospect that a great success might yet be achieved, if the force originally intended could now be landed in Bulgaria, the cruiser carried back proposals to that effect. Meanwhile, however, much time had been lost. The greater part of the Russian troops had been sent inland by train from the sea-board. Though they were at once re-embarked on all available lines, very little had been done more than preparing for embarkation at Odessa, Sebastopol, and other ports, when the news of the Battle of Sardinia created a sudden alarm that the Black Sea would not long be a safe place for Russian ships. For the next ten days tremendous efforts were made to hurry the embarkation of the troops, but by the end of that time news reached the Russians that large numbers of English cruisers had already appeared in the Black Sea.

ARRIVAL OF BRITISH TROOPS IN THE SEA OF MARMORA.

LORD **WOLSELEY IN** CONSTANTINOPLE.

NEWS of the dispatch of the reinforcements to the Mediterranean Fleet, announced by our naval correspondent a fortnight ago, had reached the Russian Government, unfortunately again through the enterprise of some English correspondents, whose information was telegraphed *viâ* New York, and thence by a route not as yet clearly traced to some Russian agents, who managed to get it to their Government very rapidly. It was therefore taken for granted that the cruisers would be promptly followed by such ships as Admiral Tryon could spare. When then the first of Admiral Markham's line-of-battle ships appeared, the Russian Fleet, afraid of being caught whilst involved in assisting in the transport of the troops and stores to Varna, once more retired, part to Odessa, and part to Sebastopol. Our own cruisers immediately re-occupied the littoral of Bulgaria near Varna. They were successful in capturing one of the transports that was attempting to escape. We have been favoured with these particulars, which have been gathered from the prisoners captured on this transport. As far as can be ascertained the reinforcements landed on this occasion have, in consequence of the delays recorded, not exceeded **15,000** or 20,000 men. Nearly all of them are reported to have marched to join General Karanoff who is

supposed to be between the Danube and Tirnova, at which point he is expected to effect his junction with the reinforcements.

The greatest alarm exists at Sofia. The Bulgarian troops are still much involved in the Macedonian campaign, and, though as many as possible have been recalled for the defence of the capital, it was feared that, with the sea open, the Russians would be able to pour in irresistible numbers. And, though that danger is now over, if General Karanoff has once more under his hands an effective force of 60,000 men, or nearly so, it is believed that he may yet make a bold dash for the capital. The moment the news of the Battle of Sardinia reached Spain, Sir Evelyn Wood's troops,—which had been held in readiness to sail at two hours' notice from Cadiz and Gibraltar,—passed eastwards. The news reached Alexandria and Cyprus on the same day. Embarkation was very rapid at Alexandria. The garrison there had been largely reinforced in order to facilitate embarkation, in consequence of the difficulties of keeping a large fleet of transports for a long time in the open roadstead at Famagousta. The whole of the Army of Occupation will be temporarily employed on the Eastern expedition. Sir Francis Grenfell has announced his confidence that he will be able, for the time the war lasts, to ensure the safety of Egypt, provided that, should any serious movement be threatened by the Mahdi, he is supported by a certain number of native troops from India. This has been provided for. Within twenty-four hours ten thousand troops in all were ready to sail from Alexandria. On the other hand, progress at Cyprus has been much slower. The wind not having been favourable for some days, a large part of the transports were obliged to put to sea; and when the embarkation began, the difficulties of embarking were very serious.

Every one in the island is groaning over the fact that nothing has been done to develop the splendid old harbour of Famagousta during our occupation. However, the first of the transports were ready to sail in a day or two. As it was necessary to await the arrival of Admiral Markham's Fleet, or, at least, of the cruisers, before passing out of the Sea of Marmora, the ships sailed as they were ready, and the rendezvous was formed after passing the Dardanelles. The first troopers to arrive in the Sea of Marmora were those from Alexandria. These were followed immediately by about 5000 men from Malta, who had been detained there when the alarm due to the French Declaration of War caused the check to the expedition. The garrison has, like that of Gibraltar, been reduced to a very low ebb, and will be made up by the Militia regiments, who have most patriotically volunteered for service in the Mediterranean garrisons. A portion of the troopers from Cyprus followed; but as soon as they had entered the Sea of Marmora, Admiral Markham's battle-ships passed through. The cruisers sent on to protect the movement had already entered the Black Sea, and been followed by those from Admiral Markham's Fleet.

Sir Evelyn Wood's force from Gibraltar and Cadiz, rather less than eight days from thence, arrived before nearly the whole of the force from Cyprus had come in. On the tenth day after the battle of Sardinia—that is, on June 4, the fleet of transports, headed by Sir Evelyn Wood's troopers, began the entry into the Black Sea. At the moment we write, we hear that the whole of the transports carrying all the troops, except the half Corps originally detained in England, have been lost to sight from land, sailing east. As soon (as was recorded in our issue of May 28th) as the seven battle-ships and cruisers from the Baltic were known to be on their way to England, the remaining half Corps was embarked from the home ports, and the entire fleet, with the troopers, reached Gibraltar about forty-eight hours after Sir Evelyn Wood had sailed. The troopers have accordingly now entered the Sea of Marmora, and will, no doubt, follow the rest of the fleet.

Lord Wolseley has been in Constantinople for some time. He was there in telegraphic communication with all the different bodies of troops and with England. He was more conveniently able to obtain fresh information from all quarters, and to be in communication with our Ambassador and the Porte. He watched

THE SULTAN, LORD WOLSELEY, AND SIR CLARE FORD WATCHING THE PASSAGE OF THE BRITISH FLEET THROUGH THE BOSPHORUS FROM THE STEPS OF THE DOLMA BAGHTCHE PALACE.

from Dolma Baghtché the magnificent sight of the passage of our
fleet and troopers towards the Black Sea. Admiral Markham
embarked in the Ambassador's yacht, after a long conference with
Lord Wolseley, and followed up his own fleet; but we learn that
just before the first troopers of the detachment from England
began to pass the Dardanelles, the yacht returned, and Lord
Wolseley embarked in it, leaving sealed orders for the detachment from England. We hear that Lord Wolseley talks much
of the advantages of a campaign in Asia Minor, and that actually
Trebizonde has again been occupied by an advanced detachment.
Moukhtar Pacha, having been largely reinforced, is still holding
his own very well on that side. Further than that we know as
yet nothing of the nature of the future campaign. Another week
will, however, no doubt throw much light on the subject.

FEELING IN AUSTRALIA.

PROPOSAL TO SEIZE NEW CALEDONIA.

(From our Special Correspondent, Mr. David Christie Murray.)

MELBOURNE, *June* 2.

THE *Age* and the *Argus* of this day's date publish the results
of several interviews. I wire you a synopsis of the ten newspaper
columns which feed the curiosity of Australian readers. Lord
Hopetoun and Lord Jersey are essentially and quite naturally
non-committal. They unite in declaring that, so far, the Colonial
attitude and action have the full approval of the Home Government, but they both decline to lend countenance to the combined
action of the Governments of Victoria and New South Wales.
Mr. Justice Windeyer, of Sydney, and Mr. Justice Way, of
Adelaide, are at one in the opinion that, France and England
being at open warfare, the Australian Fleet may at once be
legitimately employed in operations against the enemy without leave obtained from the Home Government.

Sir Thomas M'Ilwraith exults in the prospect of the fulfilment of his life-long dream. He, more than any other Colonial statesman, has been interested in the preservation of purely British influence in the Southern Hemisphere, and he sees in the present European conflict a certain promise that the blundering ineptitude of Lord Derby and his successors will be finally rendered harmless. The fact that England is fighting shoulder to shoulder with Germany will, Sir Thomas thinks, facilitate a friendly exchange by means of which the north-eastern portion of New Guinea may be brought under the dominion of the British Crown. He insists, with some vehemence, on the undoubted fact, that if his own policy had not been obstructed by the Home authorities, the northern waters of these seas would have been given over to the undivided empire of Great Britain, and he urges strongly the advisability of seizing the present moment to undo the blunders of the past. He approves warmly of the combined action of New South Wales and Victoria, and declares that their proposal to seize New Caledonia is not merely statesmanlike and patriotic, but could hardly have been avoided in the circumstances.

In New South Wales Sir Henry Parkes and the Hon. Mr. Dibbs sink, for once, all party differences, and the venerable Leader of the Opposition supports the action of the Government as warmly as if it had been taken at his own initiative. Here, in Melbourne, the Government and Opposition are, in quite as pronounced a fashion, at one with each other. In short, outside the Governors, whose official position condemns them to neutrality, there is not a dissentient voice to be heard. New Caledonia has long been a thorn in the Australian side. It is only 700 miles from the coast of Queensland, and the northern colony and its parent neighbour have long since tired of being overrun by escaped French convicts of the vilest type. You, in England, have little conception of the resentment which is inspired in the breasts of the most loyal Australians by the supineness and folly which allowed the Home Government to sit idly by whilst a French penal settlement was established so near our shores. Australia complains, and complains with justice, that she has been treated from the first as a reservoir into which might be poured the most abominable draff of English society. It was bad enough, and more than bad enough, to be compelled to receive the refuse of the Home Country. But when the escapes from New Caledonia began to be so numerous as to prove a decided nuisance, the indignation of the public was naturally aroused. Whatever you may think of us in England, we Australians are, at least, a patient and enduring people. We have made mild demonstrations in the way of departmental remonstrance, and have done nothing more. Had we been stronger than we are we should long since have made the presence of the French Government in New Caledonia a *casus belli*.

The Mother Country is so indifferent to our aspirations and our needs, that she has never given herself the trouble to recognise the gravity of this special cause of complaint. At least 300 cases of escape from New Caledonia to Australian shores are known and recorded. In the case of the 'exiles' we naturally rejoice. We have given home and a glad welcome to that distinguished artist, M. Henri, who was banished from his native France for his political opinions, and who has now achieved for himself a perfectly unique position in Australian art. There is, assuredly, not one man in the Australian Continent who would willingly have put an obstacle in the way of escape of M. Henri Rochefort. It is not men of this type to whose presence in our neighbourhood we object. But it is undeniable that the French criminals who now people New Caledonia, are men of the most abominable of all conceivable types. The grievance—the true grievance—is not merely that the French Government should have been allowed to defile our neighbourhood by the deportation of these people, but that they should positively have determined to perpetuate the race. How many people in England are aware of the shameful and stupid fact that the French Government, having massed its most awful male outcasts in New Caledonia, deliberately sent out to them female convicts of the most abandoned type in order that the men might marry and reproduce their own likeness? The mere incidental question of bigamy by government authority need scarcely be considered. Amongst the women sent out were parricides, simple murdresses, and creatures soiled by all the crimes of which nature is capable. One of the brides had murdered both her father and her mother, and another, on the outward voyage, threw her own baby out of a port-hole. The sires of the future French settlement were, of course, worthy of their partners, and one may fairly ask what could possibly be expected of a race so founded. I have myself spoken with Englishmen upon this question, and have been met with a laugh, a shrug of the shoulders, and an allusion to an ancient proverb about a pot and kettle. It is undeniable that Hobart Town and Botany Bay welcomed in their time a great deal of human evil, but it never came unalloyed, and an examination of facts will teach any inquirer that a good fifty per cent. of the so-called crimes for which men and women were expatriated, were no more than the ebullitions of an impatient patriotism, or the escapades of unguided youth. Leaving that aside, nobody pretends that the Australian population of three and a half millions is seriously tainted. We are troubled by certain forms of rowdyism and brutality, and we have a dangerous class rooted amongst us. That a great law-abiding population should be handicapped in that way by the past action of the Mother Country was hard enough to bear in all conscience, but that England should have sat supine whilst a foreign power doubled, trebled, and quadrupled, the curse upon our borders is intolerable.

We Anglo-Saxons are everywhere a long-suffering and rather stupid people. Australia herself has been somewhat to blame for her own partial acquiescence in this injustice, and there are vast numbers of her inhabitants who know little and care less about the question. The Australian citizen who had suffered from the inroads of a gang of foreign desperadoes has a sympathetic interest in the matter, but he is only one in ten thousand, and the fact is that we have been far too tame.

o

The distance between New Caledonia and Australia is, as I have said already, about 700 miles. That between the Sandwich Islands and the United States is about 2000 miles. But those islands are directly under American control, and the United States have always held that the presence of a foreign power there would have to be regarded as a menace. Just as she warned away France from Mexico, she would now warn away any foreign intruder in the South Seas. It is easy to conceive that England herself might have been equally wise. The French treatment of the Canaques, whom they dispossessed when they took forcible possession of the island, has been wrong-headed in the extreme. They have had the absurdest panics about impossible native risings, and have sent out numberless expeditions to destroy the food supplies of the wretched natives. Things are quieter now, and the Canaques are effectively cowed.

It was decided last night by telegraphic communication between the Premiers of Victoria and New South Wales, that the two leading Colonies should jointly invite Queensland, Western Australia, South Australia, and Tasmania to lend their authority for the immediate dispatch of the Australian squadron to Noumea. An intimation of the fact has been sent to the Home Government, but no permission has been asked. It is not in the least likely that England will interfere with us at such a moment, and on such a question, but even if she did, the question is one so vitally affecting the destinies of Australia that we should be compelled to take the matter into our own hands.

LORD CHARLES SCOTT OBJECTS.

June 6.

There is a rumour abroad to the effect that Admiral Lord Charles Scott has put his veto on the dispatch of the fleet until such time as instructions can be received from England, but though this report has been angrily seized upon by the populace, no credence whatever appears to be attached to it in quarters where the most trustworthy information might naturally be looked for. It has served, however, to enliven the city to a very remarkable extent, and the mere hint of opposition to the popular will has created a widespread excitement, and has made it evident that the men of the colonies are bent on having their own way. Collins Street and Bourke Street are patrolled by vast bands, who groan loudly at the name of the Admiral and cheer the local leaders of public opinion. It is quite a fortuitous occurrence that the various bodies of Melbourne cadets had arranged to march with their bands through the principal streets this evening, but the event has given colour and stir to the *al fresco* entertainment provided by the populace for their own delectation. Special editions of the evening papers confirm the rumoured action of the Admiral, and the excitement is growing to fever heat. Lord Charles Scott's position is that the squadron of which he holds command is intended for defensive purposes only, and cannot be legitimately employed in offensive operations without the direct sanction of the war authorities at home. He is likely to be technically in the right, but the fact that England and France are already actively engaged is generally held here, amongst the most moderate men, to abrogate this rule, and to make it the immediate and obvious duty of Australia to take her place in action. In the meantime, so the Sydney telegrams inform us, the squadron now lying in the harbour there is making every preparation for active service, and it is entirely probable that, after all, no real delay may ensue.

INSTRUCTIONS FROM THE ADMIRALTY.

DEPARTURE OF THE EXPEDITION.

MIDNIGHT.

AFTER all, there will be no waiting. A telegraphic dispatch has been received from the Admiralty, and the instructions are that the squadron shall take instant action. A special train to

Sydney has been chartered by the Premier. He will be accompanied by three or four members of the Ministry, and I have succeeded in attaching myself to the party. The train starts in an hour.

June 7.

The Ministerial train has broken the record, and at four o'clock the Ministerial party is steaming across the beautiful harbour towards the flagship. Driving hurriedly through the streets of the city, we have had time to see no more than that the main thoroughfares are gay with bunting, though the streets themselves are empty. The whole population has turned out to witness the departure of the squadron, and from the deck of the launch a crowd of many scores of thousands is visible about Lady Macquarrie's Chair. The great harbour is thronged with every kind of craft. All the merchant ships are gaily decorated everywhere. The weather is heavenly, and the harbour, with its sparkling waters and majestic lines of headland, can rarely have been seen to more advantage. The spirit of the people is evidently and entirely in the enterprise on which they have embarked. The four ships of the Australian squadron lie in sight of the vast crowd, and are already volleying clouds of smoke. As I lift my eyes from the note-book in which I am rapidly scrawling these lines, I can see that the great hulk of the flagship has begun to move. Flash goes a gun from her black side, and a hundred rolling echoes bellow from the surrounding heights. The crowd sends back a heart-stirring cheer, and a gun from the fort responds to the Admiral's salute. Vessel after vessel salutes, and the fort answers each in turn. Like leviathans afloat move our bulwarks on the brine, a score of times huger than when Campbell sung the prowess of the British arms at sea. Before we can reach the flagship they are all well under weigh, and forging grandly towards the open waters. Aboard some of the yachts and launches are brass bands, not all of the finest quality. They play 'God save the Queen' in all manner of keys and in different times. The result is not what one might fancy, for everybody seems to find it wildly exhilarating. The cheers from the immense concourse near Government House grow fainter and fainter as we recede, and at last die away altogether. There is a fresh breeze in the open, and a roughish sea, and so in a while even the most enthusiastic of the pursuers are willing to turn back again. The spectacle is over. The squadron has steamed away, and Australia stands ready to strike her first blow in the cause of the British race in the seas of the Southern Hemisphere.

THE FRANCO-GERMAN CAMPAIGN—THE GERMAN ADVANCE.

RENEWED FIGHTING—ROUT OF THE FRENCH ARMY.

(From our Special Correspondent with the Germans.)

SUIPPES, *May* 19.

A WHOLE week has passed and we have not moved. Our cavalry and most of my Corps are enjoying the hospitality of the French barracks at the camp of Chalons, horribly dirty, still, better than a bivouac in the pouring rain we have been enduring. Our officers' patrols go daily south of Chalons-sur-Marne and eastward to Bar-le-Duc.

Rheims is observed—practically invested—for our scouts tear up the railways leading to it from Paris as fast as the enemy can lay them down again, and further to the westward patrols are in touch with the French Army of the North, and we learn that troops are daily being moved by rail to the southward, which corroborates other information that they are again going to try on us Bourbaki's stroke of 1870, and, under the circumstances, it is about the best thing they can do.

In our rear the Reserve Divisions are working day and night to complete our road and railway communications with the

Namur-Luxembourg Railway, and as everything has been foreseen to the smallest detail years in advance—even the girders for bridges made and kept in stock—and the country, moreover, presents no serious difficulties (certainly none to frighten our engineers of Afghanistan experience, and the Germans are but little behind us), I have no doubt that our halt here will be but of short duration; indeed, some of the roads are evidently through already, for our Reserve ammunition waggons came up yesterday. The line through Mezières-Givet is also expected to be open in a day or two, and then our siege train will be able to take the works of Rheims under fire in earnest. This delay, I need hardly say, is very much against the feelings of our Hotspurs, and I have listened to many an oration from young subalterns to prove how differently old Moltke would have led them. With due deference, I think it can be shown from his own works that he would have done nothing of the kind. His own saying was that the art of war was only the practical application of principles to the attainment of the end in view—viz., the subjugation of the enemy to your will—at what knowledge of the circumstances shows you to be at the moment the cheapest possible cost to the country.

In 1870, with a vast numerical superiority, no fortifications to speak of on the enemy's side, and no allies on his own, the principle of extermination by a series of battles was the best policy to adopt. Now, against almost equal numbers, backed by fortresses not to be despised—the first victory having been won and the fighting value of our troops thereby doubled—our best game is not to break our heads against the enemy's strong places, but in a central position to await his offensive returns and move out to meet him—not stand to be attacked—as soon as his plans are sufficiently indicated by our cavalry outposts.

It was a wise stroke on the part of the enemy to lead off with a first blow from Russia; but we countered it by the immediate assumption of the offensive, which enabled us to score first blood against France. For the present we can await the decision in Russia in comparative security.

The troops are not idle meanwhile. After a day's rest and the reorganisation of the regiments in consequence of losses—which, by the way, amount to only 10 per cent. in the Corps engaged—they were at work again drilling with the same intensity of purpose as if the spring inspections and not a battle lay before them. That was a lesson they learnt from the last war—viz., that the command of men in the squadron or company is personal property, and cannot be handed over like charge of the quartermaster's store. A leader must know his men, and they must know him by actual contact on the parade ground if the full fighting worth is to be got out of the men.

11 P.M.

News of our victory at Alexandrovo has just come in. That will set free a couple of Corps at least for this, the *decisive* theatre. If only they had our Midland and North-Western traffic managers!

SUIPPES, *May* 25, 10 P.M.

We move at 5 A.M. to-morrow, direction Bar-le-Duc—*i.e.* S.E.

HEITH LE MAURUPT, *May* 27, 10 P.M.

Another most decisive victory for the Germans. Censor will not allow any more.

CAMP OF CHALONS, *May* 31, 10 A.M.

Another victory; now I may tell you all that has happened in the order in which it occurred. As I had anticipated, the French have again tried Bourbaki's move, with much the same results. As far as we can learn, three Corps were transferred from the line of the northern fortresses, by Paris—Lyons, and the whole of their Army of the East moved northward to meet us, their right on the line of their eastern defences.

Our 2d Army moved up both banks of the Aisne to meet them, it was theoretically wrong, no doubt, but we could not help it. The 3d passed troops over the Meuse, to form on their left, and we—*i.e.* the 1st—detached three Corps to reinforce the right.

leaving two 'field' Corps and a number of Reserve Divisions (I understand six) to hold the Army of the North in check, and retire slowly before it if seriously attacked.

My Corps rendezvoused on the 26th at 4 A.M. around Suippes. The country had been thoroughly reconnoitred, and, guided by officers of the Topographical Staff, all combatant branches moved straight across country, in the good old Napoleonic method, trains and Corps Artillery only by the roads. The rain had ceased, and the going was fairly good; anyway, we all agreed that it was infinitely preferable work to stewing in dusty lanes in closed columns, with never a breath of fresh air, even though in the bottoms the soil was somewhat heavy. The men were in the best of spirits at the start—reviving the good old march to Sedan joke, 'Mit Armen links schwenkt! Gerade aus'—but the sun came out, and by 5 P.M., when we had covered nearly twenty miles as the crow flies, faces began to look drawn and weary. Then we caught the sound of the guns in front, and the men stepped out again briskly.

About 6.30 we got the order to halt and bivouac; fortunately we were close to some ponds and a stream. Our cavalry had this time come little into conflict with the enemy, but after driving in a few patrols had come on the French infantry, practically deployed for action, heading a little west of north, and had not attempted to make any impression. Indeed, there was no reason why they should, for they could see everything perfectly from some neighbouring ridges, and so had fulfilled their duties. We, at least, knew where the enemy was, and he did not know where we were. So far we had the advantage.

The fight began with a race for the ridges. We had no particular advantage, and a scrimmaging fight began at once all along the line. Our artillery was in great part neutralised; so was that of the other side. It simply became a struggle of endurance—the Germans, relying on the superior discipline of their men, could afford to feed the fighting line more slowly (*i.e.* with greater distance between the following lines), and thanks to the perfection of their Staff, trained to work as nearly as possible under war-

The Great War of 189—

time conditions, the mechanism of the feed worked with less friction and more certainty; fresh troops were always forthcoming when they were required. On the other side the machinery wanted lubricating, owing to their radically defective conception of the nature of the infantry fight, which induced them to move to the attack in a succession of extended lines following one another too quickly; their strength melted away almost before they reached the actual fighting line, and then the Staff failed to send support quickly enough. It was soon evident that they were bleeding to exhaustion more rapidly than we were.

Thus hour by hour our attack pressed home like waves of an incoming tide, and from a distance the effect was most curious to watch. Two long undulating lines—a light blue haze hanging over them—each seemed to be backed by some elastic force; as the equilibrium at one point was disturbed, one line recoiled and the other pressed forward till flanking fire brought it again to a top for the moment.

By noon the edge of the high ground overlooking the valley, through which runs the Rhine-Marne Canal, was reached, and now the flood was running strong in our favour. Then we could see, too, how these disturbances in the equilibrium of the two lines were occasioned. The smaller units of the French thought too much of their flanks, too little of their centre. Thus, where two battalions or companies touched, the men balled up and crowded together, offering a better target; then the fire from the centre relaxed, and the moment the pressure of the enemy's fire gave way, the Germans dashed forward to fill up the vacuum. Soon, too, the French endeavoured to bring up their reserves in column, for their men would no longer advance in extended order; and now the small calibre rifle and its great penetration justified its existence; I had not thought much of it before. But the employment of columns induced a new feature—viz., a tendency in the larger units (*e.g.* divisions) to close on their centre—and presently before our eyes we saw a great gap opening out behind the enemy's fighting line. The time for the final blow was close at hand. Our gunners, coming up under cover of the hills, were crushing the artillery of the enemy out in the plain, and had some attention to spare for his reserves. I saw a cavalry aide-de-camp leave the Staff of the Army Commander, who was close at hand, and I made tracks as fast as I could for some broken ground, where I hoped to be safe from the coming storm.

Twenty minutes afterwards, heading straight for the gap I described above, came at least eight squadrons in line at a gallop. Their ground scouts yelled at their own infantry in front to lie down, and they mostly did so. The cavalry checked for a moment at them, as if at a fence, and then swept down on the infantry in front, not two hundred yards distant, rode over and beyond them, wheeled outwards, and bore down on the reserves. As they passed our infantry, the latter threw themselves into groups to let the second line of cavalry—which still remained in squadron columns —through, and then four more lines of cavalry followed, and the whole plain became a sea of dust and confusion. Our infantry rallied into company columns, and dashed forward with the bayonet in pursuit, and we had the last tableau of Waterloo over again. The canal and the stream in the hollow put a stop to our advance, and fresh infantry with the pioneer companies moved forward to make good the crossing, which might have been a troublesome business enough, had not the troops to our left—*i.e.* west—already carried the passages at Revigny.

Darkness was now rapidly coming on, and the fight here died away. I rode back to the rear, and found food and a welcome with the Headquarters of our third Corps, which had only just reached the ground and had not been engaged.

About five next morning the troops again stood to their arms, but in the night news of an advance of the French Army of the north had come in, and we began to retrace our steps over the same ground already traversed. As we were starting, intelligence of the British victory in the Mediterranean arrived, and with it rumours of Communistic disturbances in Paris. I was also told that two Corps had been detached from the 2d Army from near

St. Menehould, and two more from the Russian frontier had arrived about Pont-a-Mousson, and with the four Bavarian reserve divisions were preparing to strike the French Army of the west in their right flank. At night we reached the line of the great road Chalons-sur-Marne—St. Menehould, and about 4 P.M. fell right on the flank of a French corps moving from Epernay on the Camp of Chalons. Part of the Corps from St. Menehould marching by Suippes was on our right, and together we drove the French back in some disorder into the complex of hilly ground about Moronvilliers, cutting them off from Rheims.

The Corps left to watch this latter place had fallen back fighting the previous day, and lay along the road from Suippes by Somme-puis-Attigny—i.e. about north and south.

At daybreak we advanced again, and soon a struggle began which, in the hilly, wooded ground we now were in, utterly defies description. As before, it was mainly decided by superior endurance of loss and a better-trained Staff. Of tactical combination there was none on a large scale, but divisional artillery and cavalry suffered heavily in endeavouring to support their comrades of the infantry.

We reached the culminating point of the plateau after five hours' successive fighting, but the exhaustion of our men was extreme; hundreds dropped unable to go a step further, and we afterwards picked up at least an equal number of French in the same condition. Indeed, during the last hours of the afternoon, it had become a struggle of the survival of the fittest. The French fought with a determination they never before displayed—probably because the ground, by giving scope to our cavalry on previous occasions, never gave them the opportunity.

But this time every copse and bush gave them the chance to rally, and many are the instances recounted of how superior officers on the French side emulated the example of Ney in the retreat from Russia, and rifle in hand stood to the last.

The battle was actually decided by a blow delivered some six miles to the north, where the ground did give our three arms a chance of co-operation, and about 6 P.M. the resistance in front of us gave way altogether. The fighting broke off, and the men lay on their arms where they stood, too weary to move another step.

During the night, however, a cavalry division belonging to the 2d Army—which had moved round our rear while the action was going on—beat up the bivouacs of the French, falling first on the artillery and some cavalry and stampeding their horses, who took

GERMAN CAVALRY ATTACK BY NIGHT ON THE FRENCH BIVOUACS.

flight right down the extent of the line. And this last blow turned the French retreat into rout. It was York's manœuvre at Laon, in 1814, over again, only more thoroughly carried out.

Our Corps were too weary to follow, but the one next on our right, which had been squeezed out of line by our converging movement the day before, took up the pursuit before daybreak in the direction of Rethel.

ADVANCE OF THE SECOND AND THIRD ARMIES ON PARIS.

THE BOMBARDMENT OF RHEIMS.

WARMERIVILLE, *June* 6.

THE general situation is as follows:—On the eastern wing the Germans eventually made some 30,000 prisoners, and drove the wreck of the Army of the East into Epinal and Belfort.

Leaving three Corps and the Bavarian reserve divisions to watch them—the remainder of the second and third Armies are moving by the valley of the Marne on Paris, their advance guards to-day reaching Epernay. The available troops of the western wing drove the enemy before them northwards into Laon and against the Belgian frontier, making 40,000 prisoners; but at least 60,000 are known to have escaped by rail into Paris.

Rheims has been closely invested—my Corps, which lost 25 per cent. in the last action, is in reserve round and about the village from which I write. The light siege-train arrived here to-day, and the remainder is expected shortly.

RIOTING IN RHEIMS.

RHEIMS, *June* 14.

The siege-train arrived here complete on the night of the 10th, on the 11th it was put in battery; and at daybreak next morning opened fire against the three forts, Brimont, Fresnes, and Berru. It was just the same here as before Verdun; within a few hours our converging fire from covered positions knocked the forts to pieces, and the French guns were buried in the *débris* of their own parapets. Some of their guns, firing by indirect laying, remained unsilenced; on the other hand, their fire hit nothing to speak of. The advantage of smokeless powder, combined with indirect laying, turned entirely in favour of the attack.

At daybreak on the 12th we moved forward to the attack of the intermediate positions—not against the forts themselves, for these were mere mudheaps, so saturated with the carbonic oxide due to the explosion of our gun-cotton shells that they were equally untenable by friend or foe.

The fight presented no special features of interest. It was noticeable, however, how much the *morale* of the other side had been shaken, and how devastating is the power of 40 and 60 lb. shrapnel fire. The hills on which Berru and Brimont stand were

SCENE IN THE STREETS OF RHEIMS : GERMAN TROOPS CLEARING THE STREETS OF FRENCH RIOTERS.

both in our hands by about noon. Fresnes was surrounded, and surrendered shortly after. We could pursue down the slopes with fire only, for Rheims itself was still protected by hasty entrenchments which, as the sun was beginning to decline, it was hardly possible to see.

During the night the light siege-train was put in battery on the captured heights, and our outposts reported sounds of firing and tumult in the town, and, indeed, scarcely had our guns opened fire next morning when the white flag flew out from the Cathedral tower; and about 10 A.M. we marched in as peacemakers, for a number of territorialists and armed workmen had broken out in the night, shot the Commandant, and began to plunder the inhabitants, and as all discipline was at an end the second in command yielded to the pressure of the inhabitants and consented to surrender. We cleared the streets without much difficulty, the rioters bolting like hares as we entered them; and the good people of Rheims, remembering the good behaviour of the troops in '70, welcomed us as friends rather than enemies.

THE MARCH UPON THE FRENCH CAPITAL.

THE REVOLUTION IN PARIS—ARMISTICE DECLARED.

MEAUX, *June* 21.

AFTER a day's rest we marched to Dormans, and thence down the valley of the Marne, through the most lovely scenery. At every halting place, fresh news of Anarchistic trouble in Paris reaches us, and I fancy the end cannot now be far off, everything depends on the time our engineers and railway troops take to restore the communications, and I have seen no single case of injury which will require more than three days at the outside to make practicable.

CLAYE, *June* 27.

At daybreak this morning, after a preliminary bombardment of twenty-four hours, the position between the forts of Vaujours and Chelles was stormed. The effect of the bombardment was just what it had been before Rheims, and we left the forts untouched. The garrisons had taken shelter in the bomb-proofs, and at first refused to come out; but seeing themselves completely surrounded, and as the deadly fumes of our bursting shells began to penetrate into their retreat, they at last came out and laid down their arms, seeing the impossibility of further resistance.

The line between the two forts was closed with every resource of field fortification; but they proved of no avail, and only gave a fresh illustration of the old saying, related of a British soldier in the Crimean days, who, when taunted by a superior officer with being afraid of the Russian trenches, replied, 'It ain't the —— mud heaps, its the —— that stands behind!'

The line depended on the forts for flank defence, and when these were silenced, the struggle degenerated into a purely frontal one, in which the immense superiority of our fire in accuracy told. It was, perhaps, in its commencement, the nearest approach to an ideal skirmishing fight we have yet had. Covered by the fire of every available heavy gun—maintained to the last moment possible—our skirmishers crept in to within the edge of the obstacles and entanglements, potting every Frenchman as he showed his head, so that the working parties who followed immediately behind could cut the wires, etc., at their leisure. In places dense lines of abattis could not be thus easily dealt with, but the value of these fell when once the flanks were turned; and when the troops told off for the actual storm broke cover there was practically nothing in front to stop them. We carried the place almost at the first rush; then ensued many long hours of wood fighting, and at the fall of night our outposts finally held the line, Dugny, Le Bourget, Raincy, Neuilly. Many of the officers had been there before. We are now within easy bombarding range of the city.

As I write a report comes in that great fires are raging in Paris. This cannot be caused by our shells.

CLAYE, *June* 28, 9 P.M.

All firing has ceased at the outposts. A report is current that a *parlementaire* with a white flag has come in, and an armistice is looked on as certain.

LATER.

The report **is confirmed.** An insurrection has broken out in the city; the Government is deposed, and some members of it massacred. We are moving forward to the line of the old forts which will be given up to set free the garrisons to act against the Commune, and from them we hold the whole city at our mercy.

BRITISH CAMPAIGN IN BULGARIA.

DECISIVE DEFEAT OF THE RUSSIANS.

LONDON.

AT length we have great news to report from the British Army. A great battle has been fought and won. Nay, more—the whole Russian Army in Bulgaria, caught like rats in a trap, has, after two days of fierce fighting, laid down its arms. It will be seen, therefore, that the British Army has, after all, not turned up in Asia Minor, but in Bulgaria. All the rumours and apparent demonstrations which led to the belief that a great campaign in Asia Minor was intended, were merely designed to distract attention from the real objects of the expedition. Those who are familiar with Lord Wolseley's methods now profess to have been always made suspicious by the fact that, as we reported in our issue of June 4th, he had been talking a great deal of the advantages of a campaign in Asia Minor. They say that it is notorious that he holds strongly to the belief that what is supposed in your own army to be about to happen will soon be believed by the enemy. He succeeded in this way in imposing on Arabi so completely during the '82 campaign, that (extraordinary as it may appear) the Egyptian leader was a prisoner in Ceylon, when he was for the first time made acquainted with the great movement of the English expedition from Alexandria to Ismalia. Lord Wolseley then succeeded in deceiving Arabi because he had imposed upon the world at large, although precisely in a similar manner he had, by spreading reports of a call from Captain Glover during the Ashantee campaign, managed to embark his troops for the surprise of the coast towns from which the Ashantees were drawing their supplies, without any one suspecting the direction in which he was going to strike. The former ruse had been forgotten, and caused no suspicion as to the second. If we may judge by the comments of our contemporaries on the reports which have been hitherto furnished of the war, they have been either very discreet and loyal, or have been completely bamboozled. And yet it was tolerably plain that the direction in which an English Army could at the moment be most effectively employed was in clearing Bulgaria of the aggressive force of Russians, which, from the peculiar circumstances of the case, she had not force to dispose of alone.

Seeing that it is immediately in behalf of Bulgaria, and only secondarily in behalf of Turkey, because of the support she had offered to Bulgaria, that we were engaged in the struggle, there was, independently of the military advantages of the movement, an important political object to be gained by exercising our strength at once in support of the gallant Bulgarian forces. Even if it had been altogether politically convenient to allow the Turkish Army to enter Bulgaria and move upon Tirnova and Shumla, the material obstacles in the way were very serious. On the other hand, twenty-four hours' easy steaming would bring our troops to the place at which the Russians had originally landed. It was almost certain that as soon as the Russian General found that our ships had again cut his communications by sea, he would abandon his attempt to move upon Sofia and endeavour to make good his retreat by the Dobrudja. From Kavarna we could easily cut across such a movement, which it was to be hoped that the Roumanians would endeavour to delay by every means in their power. It appears that Lord Wolseley, all the time that he was at Constantinople, was in full and direct communication with the Bulgarian Generals, and that all movements were concerted in connection with them; while the Roumanians, assured of English support both by sea and land, were ready to do their utmost to hamper the Russian movements should any attempt be made, either from north or south, to force the passage of the Dobrudja.

The Great War of 189—

Without entering into further details, it will be sufficient to say that Lord Wolseley's delay at Constantinople was mainly in order to receive the very latest reports from Bulgaria as to the exact position and movements of the Russian Army. From the nearest point on the coast to which telegraphic communication has been carried from Constantinople swift dispatch boats were to bring off the cypher messages, either to the fleet or to Kavarna, whence, as the army advanced inland, the news would be carried. A second line of communication was also established by way of Kustenjeh and Bucharest. Thus the General had the great advantage of knowing more precisely than would usually be the case what the exact movements of his enemy were. To a certain extent those movements were tied. Detachments of too large force to be left to take their fate had been placed to watch Shumla and Varna. From the reports which reached Lord Wolseley, it was clear that the Russians having broken up their camp at Tirnova were marching by way of Shumla—either intending to call in their detachment from Varna and move from Shumla direct upon the Dobrudja, or to advance upon Varna.

In either case, an immediate landing at Kavarna would apparently be out of reach of any serious disturbance from the Russian forces until the landing was effected, and was extremely likely to tempt the Russians to move to attack us in that position. In that case, if we were only able to hold our own in a position already examined and surveyed, it was probable that our force would be amply sufficient to deal with the Russians, even alone, and that within forty-eight hours the Bulgarians who had undertaken to hang closely upon the Russian rear, might be expected to arrive and make the position of the Russians impossible.

Immediately after the ships had passed out of sight of land, the whole fleet changed its course to the N.-N.-West—and by mid-day following that on which the fleet had left the Bosphorus the greater portion of it was in the bay which extends from Caliakra Cape towards Varna.

The landing had already been begun before our Correspondent

arrived—but he was fortunate enough to be allowed to join Colonel French's Hussars, who were landed soon after it was ascertained that the debarkation of the troops would meet with no immediate resistance. This regiment was pushed southwards supported by a body of mounted infantry under Colonel Hutton the second day after the arrival of the troops, and as soon as possible a couple of Horse Artillery guns, which were accompanied by Colonel Marshall, with a small cavalry escort were sent after them in support. The orders for the cavalry were to ascertain the condition of affairs at Varna; if possible to capture a few prisoners, and, taking advantage of the friendliness of the inhabitants, to endeavour to obtain reports of the movements of the enemy.

THE BOMBARDMENT OF VARNA.

AERIAL WARFARE.

OUR Correspondent's description of this march is most interesting and graphic, but we must abridge it in order to come to greater events. It will be sufficient to say that they ascertained that the Russian headquarters had arrived near Shumla without having had any news of the landing of the English Army. The Russian Army was moving on Varna. The Varna force had, however, evidently received orders to make an attempt, if possible, to induce the town to surrender. Just as the cavalry arrived on distant hills within sight of the town, they saw a balloon hanging over it. This at first gave them some anxiety lest their movements might be watched, and their position discovered. In a short time, however, they had reason to perceive that the balloon was there for a very different purpose. A sight, as our Correspondent describes it, at once appalling and magnificent met their view. A black mass of some kind was seen to drop from the balloon; as it about reached the level of the tallest building in the place it suddenly burst into a lurid glare which lighted up the minarets and pinnacles of the old Turkish town. Its course was marked by crashing buildings and falling ruins. It was evidently a dynamite shell of vast proportions, which had been deliberately dropped from the balloon.

The object could only have been to terrorise the inhabitants by a cruel and wanton destruction of property. If it had chanced on a magazine it might have produced some effect upon the defence. As it was, it could and did produce none. It indicated to the Englishmen who watched it, rather the parting attempt of Russian hopelessness than a serious effort of war. Nevertheless, a tremendous cannonade was simultaneously opened from all the works near the town, and was not put an end to until some of our ships, which had maintained communication with the garrison, closed in, to within range of the works, and though at a considerable distance threw such a mass of shells against the Russian field-guns that they were glad to cease their fire and withdraw.

We give in our Correspondent's words the next scene. 'Not so, however, the balloon. To our amazement we saw it deliberately change its course over the town and steer in teeth of the wind, which was at the time a comparatively light breeze setting seawards. As it reached the position which it was evidently seeking—nearly over the magazines of Varna—we again saw another shell drop out of the balloon, and as it burst on reaching the buildings, what seemed like a universal conflagration of all that part of the town, accompanied by frightful detonations and explosions, showed the effect it had produced.

'Colonel Marshall was standing next me at the moment, and exclaimed, "Good God! I will tell you what it is; I remember hearing, just before I left England, from an engineer named Delmard, that the French were in possession of a war balloon capable of being steered backwards and forwards even against a light wind, and that they had an arrangement by which a particular form of shell, with a steel casing and some arrangement of liquid oxygen and blasting gelatine, could be dropped from the balloon. They expected great results from it, and must evidently, as a special favour to the Russians, have sent this specimen of the thing over to them."

'The evening sun had long set in the direction of Shumla. A crescent moon had risen, and some brilliant stars shone in the sky. As we looked over the undulating ground which separated us from the burning town, the flames lighted up the ships in the offing to the east, making a picture difficult indeed adequately to represent.

'One thing, however, was clear to us, that the attention of the force round Varna would be entirely occupied by the attempt to take advantage of the destruction they had produced, which, disastrous as it was for the inhabitants, did not seem likely, as far as we could judge, to enforce any surrender.

'The cavalry, finding themselves not observed, maintained their position for the following day, sending scouting parties in all directions, and reporting to headquarters.

'This was the evening of the third day since the debarkation had begun. Another cavalry regiment, with the remainder of the Horse Artillery battery, had been sent up to support us; and early the following morning Lord Wolseley, with several of his Staff, including Sir Baker Russell, who is in command of the Cavalry Division, joined us. About 6 A.M. I was looking down over the plain, when I saw two Bulgarian peasants apparently in fierce altercation, coming up towards the position where we were, escorted by one of the Hussars, who was vainly endeavouring to make himself intelligible to them. Presently they came in, one of them holding up a letter in his hand. One of the interpreters with Lord Wolseley in a short time made out their story. It appeared that a Russian officer, who had missed his way, had been seized and murdered by the villagers in the place to which these two men belonged. One of the Hussars had found them in possession of certain property of this officer, and had noticed that a bag of letters was part of it. Being an intelligent fellow, he had managed to make them understand that they should accompany him to Colonel French. The letter the man was holding up proved to be one of no importance, but it was only intended as an indication of the purpose for which he had come. His companion had what was evidently an officer's sabretash, and on this being opened, several letters were found in it, evidently dispatched from the Russian headquarters to the commandant of the force before Varna. It informed him of the fact that the English troops, which were reported to have entered the Black Sea, were believed in Russia at the latest news to have all gone on towards Trebizonde. It informed him further that the Russian General proposed to make a direct march to the Dobrudja, and gave him the different halting points on the march. It informed him of the point at which he was to join the march, and told him that the greater part of the Cossacks and the remainder of the Russian cavalry would be required to watch the Bulgarian force, which, though inferior to the Russians, and at some marches distant, might be expected to follow up their retreat. It would therefore be necessary for the rather considerable cavalry force which was attached to the troops at Varna to protect the right flank, and to watch the advance of the main army when it arrived. Without troubling your readers with the very ample information which this dispatch conveyed, I may say generally that the period at which the Russian Army, marching in two columns along two roads at some distance from one another, would arrive at about the level of Kosluji with its left column, was still about four days off. All this information we received later. At the moment I saw Lord Wolseley carefully reading through the translation of the dispatches as it was put into his hands.

'Admiral Markham had ridden out with the party, and the first person to whom Lord Wolseley turned, after he finished, was the Admiral. A short discussion took place between them, the nature of which I did not at the moment hear, but which I have reason to believe related to the question of the amount of transport and supplies that could be landed in the next day or two. At all events, it was evident to all of us in a very short time that the plans had been changed. Orders were immediately issued for the march that afternoon of the three brigades which had first landed; fortunately they were in the neighbourhood of Baltjik, so that they were the nearest to Varna. The Cavalry, with the mounted Infantry, were at once brought up, and extended so as to cut off all communication between the main Russian Army and Varna.

'Fortunately the country in this neighbourhood consists of a series of undulating uplands, with numbers of features permitting the concealment of large bodies of men.'

To tell the story as we now know it from various sources, the opportunity which presented itself to Lord Wolseley's mind as he read the intercepted dispatch was just this. It was evident from the information brought in by the Bulgarians, and from other sources, that the Russians were still ignorant that an English force had landed in the country. If he could immediately surprise the camp at Varna, he would have at least a highly probable opportunity of breaking in upon the Russian columns on their march, and annihilating one before the other could come to its support; especially seeing that they were relying upon the Cavalry of the Varna force to cover their movements. This was a far more brilliant opportunity than that which had been at first hoped for when the taking up a position, which would oblige the Russians to attack, had been designed. The intention was for the three Infantry brigades to move up that night in two marches into a position within reach of attack of the Russian camp at Varna, and actually to make the attack at grey dawn on the following morning.

Lord Charles Beresford was, according to arrangement, to land in the evening with no particular attempt at concealment with a party of Blue Jackets and Marines, and to arrange with the Bulgarian Officer in command at Varna, for a sally of the whole Bulgarian garrison so as to attract the attention of the Russians towards the Varna side at the moment when our attack was made. Watches having been carefully compared, three o'clock in the morning was fixed upon as the hour for the simultaneous attack. The three brigades were to attack respectively the right, left, and centre of the Russian position.

A powerful force of Artillery was kept back about two miles from Varna in a favourable position in order to give support to our troops in the event of any disaster. But it was to be a pure Infantry attack, not a gun was to be fired, unless any of our troops were forced to retreat. The sole duty of the Cavalry was to cut off fugitives and prevent any knowledge of what had happened from reaching the Russian General.

We have reason to believe that some of the inhabitants brought off by the fleet had supplied Lord Wolseley with most accurate information as to the nature of the ground in the neighbourhood of the Russian camp, and that this had given him considerable confidence in arranging the details of the attack. Sir Evelyn Wood had charge of the whole of the actual attack, and very great advantage was found to arise from the practice in night marching which had been carried out under his orders at Aldershot.

It cannot, however, be said that the fighting on this occasion was a very severe trial for our troops. The British Army had to all intents and purposes dropped from the clouds upon the Russians before they were aware of its arrival. No very serious preparations had been made to resist attack from the north since there was no reason to anticipate troops coming from that side. The surprise the following morning was complete. That is to say, not that the Russians were caught in their beds, but that the English troops fully organised and ready for the attack were upon them, and into their lines, before the Russians had been able to prepare any organised resistance.

Only on one side, where an active Russian General had cautiously entangled the front of his position with obstacles, was the right brigade checked for a time, and, though some losses were occasioned here, the general effect of the attack on all sides of the Russian position, and the numerous places in which the works had been entered made it impossible for the troops who had resisted the attack of the right Brigade to hold out for any length of time.

The Russians fought most gallantly, yet showed very little power of acting for themselves in a case where superior orders could not reach them.

ROUT OF THE RUSSIAN ARMY.

THE RELIEF OF VARNA.

By noon the whole of the works were in our hands, and as the Cavalry intercepted all who attempted to make their escape, the Mounted Infantry holding all such places as were inconvenient for the Cavalry, we had every reason to believe that no one had escaped to tell the tale. The slaughter on neither side was very great, the Russian position being, from the beginning, so obviously hopeless, greatly outnumbered and surprised as they were, that nearly 10,000 men laid down their arms. The prisoners were the following day embarked for Constantinople, considerable supplies and very valuable transport waggons, horses, and mules fell into our hands. To make assurance doubly sure, Lord Wolseley had brought up a fourth of Sir Evelyn Wood's brigades nearly to the position occupied by the batteries. Meantime, on the same morning that the fight was going on, nearly the whole of the remainder of the force had marched to occupy the high lands which overlook the two roads leading up from Kosluji and Varna upon Bazardjik.

It was evident that, assuming the march of the Russians to be carried out in accordance with the captured dispatch, the two Russian columns would, during a certain period of their march, be not only some ten miles apart, but be separated by some very difficult country. And, moreover, that as the roads converged towards Bazardjik, an English force occupying the uplands would have its two portions much closer together than the advancing Russians. A valuable capture of the papers of the Russian General in command at Varna showed that a duplicate of the intercepted dispatch had reached him the previous day. Apparently a reply had been prepared, but none as yet sent off. This indicated the movements he was intending to adopt in order to join the main force. As it had been ascertained that Kosluji, though not as yet in the possession of the Russians, was in telegraphic communication with the Russian headquarters, it was resolved to repair the telegraph, which had only been cut by the peasants between Kosluji and Varna. As soon as this was done a telegraphic dispatch was sent through in the Russian cypher to the General commanding, 'Yours of the 10th, Cavalry will be pushed on to cover right flank, and advance of army on Bazardjik. The Infantry and Artillery will join rear of column after the right column has passed the junction.' The British forces were now distributed as follows: Of the Duke of Connaught's Corps, the right division occupied the high ground which the road from Kosluji towards Bazardjik crosses shortly after passing Kosluji. The second division similarly occupied the high ground above the Varna-Bazardjik road. The Artillery of the entire army was concentrated on the high ground in such a way as to be able to bring its fire upon the columns debouching from the roads. The whole of Sir Evelyn Wood's Corps lay in a position between Varna and the high ground, ready to attack the right column as soon as its march should be sufficiently developed to give an opportunity. Advantage had been taken of the number of captured Russian uniforms in the camp at Varna to put up dummy sentries, so as to leave the impression from a distance that Varna encampment and neighbourhood was still held by the Russians. The whole of the ground over which the fight was likely to take place was carefully reconnoitred beforehand. On the morning of June 14th the Russian right column, which, having a considerably longer march to perform, moved off first, had arrived at the point where the road turns sharply to the north leading towards Bazardjik, when a party of Cossacks, who had been sent on to communicate with the cavalry from Varna, which was supposed to be before them on the road, galloped in and reported that they had been stopped on the road in crossing the mountains by finding that the path was blocked with some felled trees and abattis. Supposing this to be the work of some Bulgarian insurgents, the General ordered forward a battalion of Infantry and a couple of guns, and allowed the column to resume the march. Shortly afterwards some Cossacks who had moved towards Varna rode up to some supposed friends in Russian uniform, were captured, and not allowed to return. No alarm therefore was excited on this side. As, however, the battalion of Infantry moved up to the abattis in order to remove it, they were fired upon by unseen foes, and many of them fell. A brigade was now ordered to advance and clear the ground. As it moved forward within close range of the hills it, too, was received with Infantry fire from unseen foes.

THE BATTLE OF KOSLUJI.

ROUT OF THE RUSSIAN ARMY.

THE dispatch from our Correspondent of June 18th, published last week, stopped abruptly at the moment of describing how the column of Russians was advancing into the ambush cleverly laid for them by Lord Wolseley. In the following dispatch he continues the narrative :—

As yet not a shot had been fired by the artillery or by any of Sir Evelyn Wood's troops, whose position was absolutely unknown. The column was now halted in considerable confusion.

The General commanding the Russian brigade, uncertain as to what he had in front of him, did not like to commit himself to an attack without previous preparation by artillery, and asked to have some artillery sent him. Six batteries were brought out in succession from the column on the road at a gallop, and began to shell the heights.

Uncertain as to what they were firing at, they produced very little effect, and none of the guns on the hills replied to them. Meantime the column on the road was in the greatest confusion. A fresh brigade was, however, gradually formed out of it, and moved up towards the right of the road. A third brigade was to be seen also moving up in support of the other two. As the right brigade moved up in successive lines towards the heights, its right came within easy range of the position in which, concealed behind a long line of under-feature, Sir Evelyn Wood's advanced division lay. When the rear of the brigade had fairly passed beyond his left, a withering volley, followed by magazine fire, was poured into it from the whole line of the division.

Staggered by the unexpected blow, the brigade fell into confusion. Sir Evelyn, seizing the moment, advanced the whole division, having given orders beforehand that the men should be kept in hand as much as possible; and that instead of a skirmishing attack, which was quite unnecessary under the circumstances, lines at least of companies should be kept together as much as possible.

The Russian brigade, though taken in rear as well as flank, endeavoured for a moment to present a front in the new direction. As they did so the guns from the high ground for the first time opened, tearing through the Russian ranks in all directions. Under the double storm, taken in flank whichever way they turned, the brigade gave way, and was followed closely by the leading division of Sir Evelyn's Corps.

The Russian brigade next on the left began immediately to attempt to dig in order to form a rallying point for the flying brigade, but, overwhelmed by the fugitives, fired into from the heights, and pressed by the pursuing division, they too broke, and carried confusion amongst the guns.

The whole of the troops that had debouched from the road were now little better than a confused mass, unable to act with effect, and suffering appallingly from the cross fire directed upon them by Sir Evelyn's troops and those on the hill, whose fire was now continually increasing in intensity.

The remainder of the Corps, with little space to deploy, and whelmed by the mass of fugitives, was huddled back upon the road. At this moment a pre-concerted signal from Lord Wolseley

THE BATTLE OF KOSLUJI: SIR EVELYN WOOD'S ATTACK ON THE RUSSIAN FORCES.

directed Sir Baker Russell, who with the whole of the cavalry, less Colonel French's regiment which was on the extreme right, had been placed near Varna to the left of Sir Evelyn's force, to charge into the confused mass which now represented the right corps of the Russian Army. Enormous numbers of prisoners were taken, and sent back promptly to Varna to be embarked on

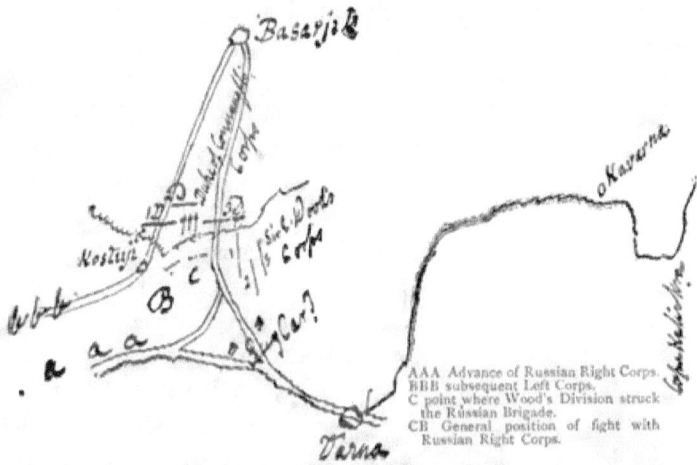

AAA Advance of Russian Right Corps.
BBB subsequent Left Corps.
C point where Wood's Division struck the Russian Brigade.
CB General position of fight with Russian Right Corps.

MAP OF THE FIGHT NEAR VARNA.
Facsimile of Sketch from our War Correspondent.

board ship. Meantime the left Corps of the Russian Army had begun its advance along the other road towards Bazardjik, but before it approached the heights the news of the disaster which had befallen the right corps reached the General. Though at first his intention had been to attempt to out-flank the position opposed to him on the English right, in order to relieve the pressure on his own right, the rapid progress of the disaster of the right made him change his determination. With his intact Corps he took up a position to cover the retreat of the remnants of the broken Corps. Practically only one English division, besides the cavalry, had been seriously engaged. From the nature of the case the losses had been comparatively small. Smokeless powder had told altogether in favour of the English in the action.

Practically the fate of the Russian army was decided. Lord Wolseley was in full communication with the Bulgarian General, who, with a force between forty and fifty thousand strong, had been following close upon the heels of the Russians. There could be no hope that, with their diminished and discouraged troops, the Russians would be able to defeat the English forces, against which with their intact army they had failed on the previous day. Nor could they turn on the Bulgarians without having both armies upon them at once.

To avoid useless slaughter, the Russian General forty-eight hours later agreed to lay down his arms. As soon as the Russian army had given up its guns and was no longer in a position to act effectively, the English army marched back to the coast, and, according to our latest information, a considerable part of it had already embarked and sailed in an unknown direction.

Lord Wolseley, with Admiral Markham and their Staffs, have returned to Constantinople, doubtless in order to be in communication with Ministers at home, the Ambassador, the Sultan, and other sources of information. It is only fair to a gallant enemy to say that the startling success which has attended our arms is, apart from the gallantry of our soldiers and the skill of the General who led them, to be attributed to the enormous advantage which is possessed by the Power that commands the sea.

From the moment that our fleet cut off the communications of the Russian Army, the Russian General was in a position, such as in our time can rarely happen, of being completely deprived of all means of knowing what his enemy was doing, while, on the other hand, our own Commander was able to obtain information far more accurate than is common in war of everything that his opponent did. No other Power in Europe could have reached and destroyed with the same ease and certainty that dangerous Russian force, susceptible of indefinite increase, as long as Russia held the sea. Meantime, speculation is rife as to the direction in which our army is next going to strike.

ENTHUSIASM IN CAIRO.

DEPARTURE OF THE ENGLISH TROOPS.

(*From our Special Correspondent, Mr. Francis Scudamore.*)

CAIRO, *May* 8.

FOR the past two days the entire populace of this city has lived in a state of frenzied excitement, to which the seething clamour of the days immediately following the memorable 15th September 1882 is only faintly comparable. Then it was, with the arrival before the gate of the citadel of Sir Drury Lowe and his cavalry brigade fresh from Tel-el-Kebir, that England's peaceful occupation of Cairo began. There were no Europeans in Cairo at the time, and even the better classes of Egyptians had either fled to distant parts of the country or lay hidden in their spacious houses, closely barred against intrusion by friend or foe. Demonstration of popular feeling was confined to the astounded and panic-ridden natives of the lower orders, whose bewildered minds swung for a week between fearful anticipation of the horrors they had been taught to expect at the hands of the English, and trembling delight that the reign of terror under Arabi and Toulba had at length come to an end. They needed time, these stricken, starving people, to discover the state of their feelings; to decide whether they were pleased that foreign aid had come to them, or were only glad to know that Arabi had fled, and would soon be in prison; and in their indecision, for two whole days and nights dense crowds of wandering Arabs, Fellaheen, street merchants, clerks, donkey-boys, and small officials, thronged the European quarters of the town, ceaselessly jostling each other through the streets, and murmuring repeatedly, 'The English have come. The Effendina is coming.'

That was ten years ago. During those ten years the English soldiers and the Cairenes, both natives and foreigners, have learned so well to know and appreciate each other, that when it leaked out (who shall say how) on Sunday evening that orders had been received for the immediate embarkation of all the British troops in garrison here, the announcement clanged like a tocsin through the startled town.

Once again the Frank quarter was filled with an anxious wondering mob, formed not of Arabs only, but of all the varied nationalities that make up Cairo's thriving population, who roamed the broad streets round the Esbekeeyeh Gardens, silent, orderly, and sad, or gathered in tight-packed masses in front of Shepheard's and the New Hotel, and the Sporting Club, and lingered for hours in slowly changing thousands in the great square facing the Abdeen barracks.

It was near midnight, and the moon was high, when the news became generally known. The band of the Alexandria Regiment had for some time ceased playing in the Esbekeeyeh Gardens, and nearly all English soldiers were back in barracks. Some few men, however, who had twelve o'clock leave, were still abroad, and as, on their way home, they shouldered through the throng—wondering, no doubt, what could be the matter—they were instantly seized upon by scores of eager well-wishers, delighted to find an outlet for some portion of the cordial enthusiasm pent up within them. Of one of these spontaneous outbursts of affection towards 'Thomas Atkins' I was myself a witness. I was standing with other Englishmen and ladies on Shepheard's balcony watching the shifting masses of the crowd below, when suddenly there arose, some way up the street—beyond the British Consulate—a wild confused noise of cheering. It was a queer kind of cheer, such as could probably be heard nowhere else in the world—a strange blending of the Zughareet of Arab women—the guttural Fellah Hâgh, the Italian Viva, and the Greek Huzzah, with a leavening of Levantine squeal; but the outcome of the mixture was sufficiently startling to make us turn—for a moment anxiously —in the direction of the sound. Then the crowd before us took up the cry, and quickly pressing back on either side of the way, left room for the passage of the most extraordinary procession it has yet fallen to my lot to behold.

SCENE OUTSIDE SHEPHEARD'S HOTEL, CAIRO: TOMMY ATKINS ABOUT TO QUIT EGYPT.

First, leaping in a frantic dance such as one sees here at weddings and religious festivals, came some score of sayces, their lawn sleeves flaunting as they waved their arms, and their gold-broidered waistcoats gleaming bravely in the moonlight. Their usual cry of '*Shmarlek, Gemeelek*,' was interrupted now by hoarse shouts of 'Inglis, Inglis, long live the Inglis!'—shouts which the crowd readily took up. Immediately behind them paced a tall, half-naked negro, who—such is the length to which enthusiasm will carry these fanatics—held outstretched before him (a sacrifice to friendship), his brawny right arm transfixed by a long knife, from whose blade his blood dripped freely to the ground. A carriage followed—an ordinary hack victoria, captured, doubtless, close by—round which a frenzied mob surged, yelling and gesticulating madly. There was no driver on the carriage. The box-seat was occupied by a mandolin player and a harpist, whose fingers were very busy, though of their music not one note could be heard. In the victoria were the objects of the demonstration, two English soldiers, one of whom, while preserving his good temper, was struggling manfully though vainly against a dozen pair of hands that held him in his place, and loudly declaring in words as unavailing as they were forcible that he was due in barracks at midnight and could not 'stay fooling' any later. His protest was disregarded, and his comrade, who had apparently succumbed to the hospitality of a burly Greek who faced the pair, on the Strapontin, nursing a huge demijohn of some pernicious liquor, gave him no help, expressing neither approval nor condemnation of the proceedings, and, indeed, but for the tender ministrations of an old äalem in a saffron robe, who stood on the step beside him, he would probably have fallen out into the road.

The motley carnival passed slowly into the night; the shouts softened in the distance and then died away; but the crowd, silent again, remained staring vacantly at the hotel windows. As I turned from the balcony railings a quiet native spectator on the pavement beneath me looked up and spoke in Arabic: 'Ah,

Hawaga,' he said, 'Toufik Pasha has gone; Allah rest him! Now the English are going—evil days are coming.'

Throughout Sunday night and during the whole of yesterday the great crowd filled the streets. Even the announcement made yesterday afternoon that, although the English soldiers were called suddenly away, their Indian brothers-in-arms would replace them, failed to satisfy the public mind, or to remove the painful impression it had received. In some vague way the feeling of the native populace was that, though the Indian troops might be soldiers of England's Queen, they were not the English they had known; the English who wore yellow clothes, and blue goggles, and hats with towels on them, and who paid so well for donkey hire, and bought so freely in the bazaars, and were so easily persuaded to accept bits of imported blue glass as valuable turquoises, 'and wonderfully cheap.'

With very few exceptions all British troops were confined to barracks yesterday—not so much on account of their preparations for departure, for ever since the reinforcement of the garrison the commanders of regiments have been held in readiness to entrain in two hours after receipt of orders—but in order to avoid the repetition, on probably a very large scale, of Sunday night's demonstrations. The natives, therefore, were fain to be content with standing in thousands outside the barrack-yard gates gazing at the busy scene within, while from time to time some English-speaking donkey-boy would accost the impassive sentries on behalf of himself and friends with some such speech as, 'You going, Missa Soja, Arab prenty solly.'

Thanks to the energy and foresight of the Commander-in-Chief in carefully policing the whole length of the canal with troops from Suez to Port Said to prevent any such apt accident as the sinking of a dredger in a narrow part, the transports suffered no delay. Each ship—there were eight (chartered vessels of the P. and O., British India and Orient Lines)—on reaching Suez landed the troops she had brought from Bombay and passed on into the Canal, employing the time of her passage in cleaning up for the reception of the English regiments at Alexandria. The Indian brigades are for the moment encamped on the Sweet Water Canal, pending dispatch to their several stations.

The British troops were entrained to-day at noon. Two Soudanese and one Egyptian regiment lined the entry to the railway station as a guard of honour. The young Khedive himself, accompanied by his brother, Mehemet Ali Bey, and followed by Zulfikar Pasha and many of the court functionaries, drove to the station to bid them farewell, and arriving a few moments before the first of the departing regiments, caused his carriage to be so placed that the men must march past it. As each regiment passed him, His Highness, who had alighted and stood beside the victoria, saluted, and said repeatedly 'Good-bye, gentlemen,' in English. To entrain the troops took, of course, some little time, and the ——— remained a while in the small square outside the station while their comrades were taking their places in the coaches. His Highness, who looked very grave and had spoken but briefly with Sir Evelyn Baring and other English gentlemen present, had entered his carriage, and the sayces had leapt to their places before it, when suddenly a voice shouted, 'Three cheers for Abbas Pasha.' Who the enthusiast was I do not care to guess; but the cry was taken up eagerly. Despite discipline, despite etiquette, against propriety even though it was, a mighty cheer burst from the waiting troops round the royal carriage, and was echoed from within the station with redoubled volume.

The Khedive seemed for a moment overcome. Then he drove quickly away. The farewell of the native populace to the troops as they marched through the streets was pathetic in its earnestness. By a purely spontaneous motion all Cairo had gathered wherever it could to wish the Englishmen 'God go with you.' The passage of the regiments was marked by innumerable incidents showing the affection in which the men were held and the genuine distress of the people at their loss. A typical instance of this native enthusiasm is worth recording. In the ——— regiment—I purposely avoid naming it—for some time quartered in the Citadel, is a turbulent giant known as 'Mad Donald'—a long service man, greatly liked, known for gallantry in the field, and steady enough on parade; but who has twice lost his stripes for drunkenness. For he is not content to be passively drunk, but must also be violent. Under the influence of alcohol destruction becomes his ruling passion. In his periodical outbursts Donald has been a terror to the many street merchants whose displays of fragile wares cumber the Er Rumeyleh Square, at the head of the Mooskee. He has overturned their tables, made wholesale havoc of their goods, and fought the crowd with the trestles of the spoiled. His chief enemy and victim has been an old dealer in gaudy crockery and glass ornaments, whose entire stock he has several times reduced to shivers, and then danced upon the wreck, defying the police. Yet to-day as the —— marched by, with stalwart Donald leading man of his company, this old man dragged his table forward, crying, 'Ya, Donal; ya, Donal; break something for luck' —and was quite distressed at the tall soldier's smiling disregard.

When the last train had steamed out of the station the immense concourse of people who, on either side of the line, had for an hour yelled farewells, fell once more to silently pacing the streets, where they still remain at this late hour. I have been for long among them and am forced to say that what was indicated to me on Sunday night by one man is now the prevailing sentiment of the multitude, 'The English have gone—the Effendina will go soon—evil days are coming.'

ALEXANDRIA, *May 28th*.

You are aware that the English garrison was detained in the neighbourhood of Alexandria, and was largely reinforced by other troops forming part of the Eastern Expedition. Among the exciting events taking place in other parts of the world there has been nothing here of sufficient interest to occupy your columns. The troops have been waiting for orders to embark, which came immediately after our great naval victory.

All the regiments embarked to-day, and five of the transports have already started. Their commanders have sealed orders, but we fancy here they are bound, in the first instance, for Cyprus, and then to take part in a movement against Algiers, unless, indeed, they are bound for the Black Sea. You will probably know their destination sooner than we shall.

FRENCH INTRIGUES IN EGYPT.

RISING OF THE MAHDISTS.

(*From our Special Correspondent, Mr. Francis Scudamore.*)

CAIRO, *June 3rd.*

You have heard from other sources of Sir F. Grenfell's reappointment to the command in Egypt, and of the fact that he had undertaken that, if a certain number of Indian troops were sent to him, he would be responsible for the safety of Egypt, although all the garrison then in occupation was sent to join the Eastern Expedition. My last letter from Alexandria informed you of the departure of these troops. I may add that the Brigade of Indian troops sent to our support had landed two days previously at Suez, and had been moved up to Cairo during my absence. Yesterday they marched past the Khedive in the square of the Abdeen palace. Their splendid appearance recalled the impression which had been produced by the contingent from India which had in the same square marched past the former Khedive after the campaign of 1882.

We have heard of the arrival of the English fleet and part of the expedition at Constantinople, and are anxiously awaiting further news.

We have, however, little time for reading. Our troubles at home give us plenty of occupation. The European population of Cairo is made up mainly of Germans, Italians, Greeks, French, and English. The French, to whose ranks are added Coptic, Armenian, and Levantine *protégés* and sympathisers, greatly outnumber any of the other nationalities, and, with some noteworthy exceptions, are not very estimable representatives of their nation. To preserve peace and order among these excitable peoples, whose countrymen are all cutting one another's throats at home, is no light task, and has, despite the precautions taken, occasionally proved too much for all the powers of diplomacy, even when backed by General Baker Pasha's *gendarmerie*. On the first rumour of war Sir Evelyn Baring and his colleagues, fully appreciating the dangers of the situation, formed themselves, with some leading citizens, into an International Peace Committee, of which the Prime Minister is chairman, and agreed on various measures for the preservation of tranquillity in the community. The first of these measures (and subsequent events have shown its necessity) was the general prohibition to Arabs and Europeans alike, from carrying weapons of any kind (including walking-sticks or umbrellas) in the streets of Cairo or Alexandria. In 1882, between the time (11th June) of the Arab rising and the bombardment (11th July), a like prohibition did good service in Alexandria; but now, despite its rigorous enforcement, there have already been several fierce encounters between the hot-blooded French and Italians. The new French Consul-General, I am forced to say, has given no help to the Peace Committee, and has rather made it his business to frustrate their counsels and mar their plans.

A very clever French journal, *La Dernière Nouvelle*, published since the opening of the war, which daily prints marvellous accounts of British, German, and Italian defeats, is notoriously concocted in its entirety within the four walls of the French Legation. There are, indeed, no Frenchmen in the community outside of these walls capable of producing at once so witty and so scurrilous a sheet, or one so entirely dependent for its news on the imagination of its editors. Their reports are accepted by their own readers. None of the more accurate accounts from other sources are believed. But the arrogance and aggressive attitude of the French colony and Consul-General, the vicious blatherings of *La Dernière Nouvelle*, the nightly chanting by turbulent members of the French community outside Shepheard's Hotel and the British Legation of 'Malbrouque s'enfuit du Caire; On ne l'y verra plus,' and kindred versions of old songs adapted to the requirements of the moment, together with the breaking of some dozens of English and Italian heads in dark by-ways and noisy taverns, are, after all, but minor matters, and very trivial as compared with the rumours of impending trouble that reach us from the southern frontier. Our news from the Nile outposts is grave.

The Khalifa Abdullah Taaishi and the Emir Osman Khalid Zogal, who commands at Dongola, have long been in communication with Cairo. Indeed—since we are at war with France, it may as well be said—for years it has been known in well-informed circles here, that leading members of the French colony were in constant, though, thanks to General Grenfell's vigilance, irregular, correspondence with the Khalifa's officers. Thus there is no doubt that the Khalifa has been informed of the withdrawal of the English troops from Egypt, and of their replacement by Indian regiments. He has probably been assured that, owing to the general conflict in Europe, Egypt can in no event hope for further reinforcements from England. His opinion of the fighting value of Indian soldiers is presumably low. The only operations in which Indian troops have taken part in the Soudan were those near Suakim in March 1885 (McNeil's Zareba and the Battle of Hasheen); and Osman Digna, in his written reports to the Mahdi, claimed these engagements as decided victories for the Ansar. The Khalifa, therefore, with some degree of reason, considers the moment opportune for a descent on Egypt in force, and for this descent he is making preparations on a large scale.

Colonel Wodehouse, who is at Wady Halfa, reports the existence at Ginnis of a new Mahdist camp, formed within the past month, which now numbers from six to seven thousand Tokuls. On the west bank, a smaller camp is being formed at Dal. The Arabs daily scout in numbers right up to Sarras and to the fort at Khor Moussa, on which they fire nightly. Saleh Bey, the Sheikh of the Abadeh tribe, whose duty it is to guard the eastern desert between Korosko and the Wells of Murat, has reported that last week, having news of preparations for a forward movement at Abu Hammid, he occupied Murat with a body of 250 men. He was attacked on the night of May 29th by a large force of horse and camel-men, and after a hot engagement, in which he had 57 men killed and lost 108 camels, he was forced to abandon the Wells to the enemy and retreat to the Bab-el-Korosko. The Murat Wells, he says, will not supply a force of 500 men for more than three days, and he, therefore, fears an advance on Ongat and Haimur. A small body of Kababish tribesmen, the remnant of that once powerful clan who, though for some time with the enemy, are still loyal, have reached Halfa from Dongola, where they say great preparations are being made for an advance. Daily small detachments of Jehadieh and considerable bodies of Ansar arrive at Dongola from Omdurman, and large supplies of provisions are being collected. Three nuggars, laden with dhurra, were wrecked, they say, less than a month ago, on the rocks near Barkhal. A good deal of doubt attaches to this statement, but if it be true, it indicates a very early rise of the Nile, for at this season, as a rule, the whole 140 miles of river from Abu Hammid to Barkhal is a veritable maze of rock-strewn passages, impassable by even the smallest boats. These tribesmen travelled by the west bank, and say that from Dongola to Dal, the route was like that to a fair.

The Sirdar starts for the front to-night, and kindly permits me to accompany him. Colonel Kitchener expresses himself thoroughly confident that his own troops are strong enough to cope with any forces the enemy may bring to meet him; but a feeling of uneasiness in some high quarters here, coupled may be with the fact that troops at Halfa and Korosko have lately suffered severely from influenza, has caused some pressure to be brought on him, with the result that it has been decided that the 17th Bengal Native Infantry and the 29th Beloochees are to act under his orders and co-operate with the Egyptian forces if necessary. They were sent by train to Assiout yesterday afternoon, and have already started for Assouan, Mr. Cook having undertaken their transport in flat-bottomed barges, towed by steamers of four feet draught. My next letter will probably be from Wady Halfa.

FIERCE BATTLE NEAR WADY HALFA.

FULL DESCRIPTION OF THE FIGHT.

WADY HALFA, *June* 14*th*.

THE 17th Bengal Regiment reached here last night in four barges towed by steamers, having made the distance in six days—without accidents—and is encamped on the west bank, opposite Halfa. The Beloochees, one of whose towing steamers ran aground near Derr, occasioning seven hours' delay, will probably be here to-morrow. We are still in uncertainty as to the Arab plan of attack. The state of the river between Sarras and Semneh has prevented the use of the armed pinnace for reconnaissance purposes, and, although the Egyptian Camel Corps has repeatedly pushed forward along the west bank to within a few miles of Dal, their Commander has been able to gain very little insight into the enemy's movements. It seems likely, however, that the Emir's attack will be made on the east bank, but against what point between Sarras and Korosko it will be directed, there is as yet no sufficient indication.

Sheikh Mustapha Gibran, who, with 150 men, occupies the Selima Oasis in the western desert some sixty miles inland from Dal, reports that, with the exception of a party of some fifty camp followers who came out to Selima in the beginning of last week apparently to obtain salt, he has been unmolested. On the east bank an attempt was made three days ago, at a reconnaissance into the Batn-el-Hagar, or 'Belly of Rock,' which borders the river between Sarras and the wells at Ambigol, forming an almost impassable barrier to troops. The enterprise was near resulting in the annihilation of the reconnoitring party; for the rocks were found to be full of Arabs, who sprang up on every side to the attack. Fortunately their dash was made too early, and Captain Beech was able to retire in good order, but with a loss of four men. We expect, however, that a very few days more will discover the tactics of the Emirs.

The Great War of 189—

WADY HALFA, *June 20th*, 6 A.M.

A decisive engagement was fought yesterday near this place, with the result that after five hours of hard—in some cases of desperate—fighting, during the course of which the issue was at times uncertain, this latest tide of invasion has been rolled back once more into the desert. The Arabs have suffered terrible loss. Our own casualties, of which I have not as yet full particulars, are, I regret to say, very considerable. The Arab attack was intended to be a surprise, but this plan was partially defeated by one of those simple accidents which occasionally upset the calculations of commanding officers.

Leaving aside Assouan and Korosko, the defending forces in and around Wady Halfa numbered, with details, medical staff, bearer companies, etc., about 6500 officers and men. This is without counting the navigating crews of the gunboats (armed with Krupp and machine guns), or the Indian regiment still on its way up the Nile.

Early the day before yesterday, Captain Beech, with a company of the Camel Corps, pushed forward on the west bank to within 200 yards of Dal without touching the enemy. He reported Dal abandoned by the fighting men (who had presumably crossed to the east bank), and occupied only by several thousand women and camp followers, who fled on his approach. The same evening the Colonel commanding at Korosko, telegraphed news of an attack in force on the Irregulars at the Bab-el-Korosko, to whose assistance he had sent the 5th Battalion Egyptian Infantry.

Almost coincident with the receipt of this news was the discovery of a large Arab force in the hills east of Halfa. A small body of Cavalry, under Lieutenant Abd-el-Azrak, scouting at the base of the hills, suddenly perceived two mounted men (on camels) appear on a height, while, at the same moment, a shot was fired. This was probably an accident, but it was evidently regarded as a signal, for immediately, with a great shout, men sprang up everywhere among the rocks. A heavy fire was opened upon the

Egyptians, and a body of some hundred Arabs was seen to dash down a small scrub-clad khor towards the plain. Lieutenant Abd-el-Azrak, who, in the first fire, had suffered a loss of two horses killed and one trooper wounded, trotted back to Halfa (he was not pursued), where the noise of firing had already announced his discovery.

The Sirdar at once made arrangements to meet the impending attack. Deberra was advised of the news by telephone. The 7th

SOUDANESE ATTACK UPON A RECONNOITRING PARTY.

Battalion Egyptian Infantry was marched to Dabrosa to reinforce the half-battalion there; Sarras was warned to keep up steam on two engines, and hold the 11th Soudanese in readiness to entrain if required; and, at the same time a pilot engine, accompanied by half a squadron of Cavalry was sent forward to examine the line. The enemy was apparently not ready, and, though he would have had us at a disadvantage, delayed his attack.

All night long we could hear the noggaras beaten in the Arab bivouac, and the air was so still that even the voices of the Fikis and their congregations wailing in prayer were plainly audible.

In the grey of the dawn the Sirdar made a reconnaissance with all mounted troops, and found the base of the first low range of hills immediately opposite Halfa covered for a stretch of over a mile with the enemy, whose irregular lines were sometimes two or three, and sometimes a dozen or more, men deep. Behind them the heights were thickly crowned with *rayas* (banners), which we estimated at near a hundred in number (we afterwards found they were eighty-seven). This implied that we had a force opposed to us of near 10,000 Jehadieh (regulars), and probably at least half as many Ansar.

One of these *rayas* was pointed out by a deserter as the green banner of Ali Wad el Helu, while another was said to be that of the Emir of Emirs, Abd el Maula el Taashi himself. On a height near this banner the enemy had mounted a brass gun.

Everything being reported clear on the west bank, where for miles no trace of an Arab force was to be seen, the Bengal regiment was brought across the river at dawn in native boats, and half-an-hour later the 11th Soudanese arrived from Sarras. With the force thus at his disposal, in all some 4000 men, the Sirdar decided to draw the enemy to an attack.

The hills lie about four and a half miles east of Halfa, extending for some distance in a line parallel with the river bank. For about two miles, however, from the slopes, the ground is irregular, much broken, filled with deep pits and sudden ledges which would be as eminently suitable for the enemy's favourite tactics as it were unfavourable for operations of troops. The Sirdar, from the position he had taken up at the beginning of this broken ground, ordered forward the two guns of the Horse Battery, which opened fire on the enemy's position at 6.30 A.M. This soon had the desired effect; the Arabs—after endeavouring to reply with their gun, whose fire, owing to the long range and their defective ammunition, was quite ineffective—formed into two columns, preceded by a long straggling line of skirmishers, and advanced rapidly. The guns now retired a thousand yards, and the mounted troops having poured (dismounted) a couple of volleys into the advancing spearmen at 400 yards range, slowly retired, still firing, on the artillery. This manœuvre was twice repeated with every success, the well-directed fire of the guns doing considerable execution in the enemy's advancing host, while the galling fire of the mounted troops irritated them to forgetfulness of prudence. The fire of the Arab riflemen posted on the first slopes of the hills and scattered in the broken ground at their base did us less damage than it caused the enemy's advancing lines; but this did not appear to be noticed by the Arab commanders.

When the Horse Artillery had reached a point some 2000 yards from the fort at Halfa, the Sirdar ordered out the 1st Infantry Brigade, consisting of the Indian Regiment, the 12th Soudanese, and the half-battalion 9th Soudanese, together with the 1st and 2d Field Batteries (six guns in all).

The mounted troops were then ordered to make a *détour* to the north to prevent any portion of the enemy avoiding the battle and advancing towards Deberra. At the same time, the 2d Brigade, consisting of the 11th Soudanese, the 7th Egyptian Infantry, and half-battalion of the 1st Egpytian Infantry, were ordered to advance from Dabrosa to check any movement towards the river in that direction. The guns of Halfa Fort were able to do good service in support of the 1st Brigade. Unfortunately the height of the river banks rendered the gunboats useless until the enemy should reach the Nile itself.

The Arabs were fighting for water. Their long *détour* round the Batn-el-Hagar must have tried them severely, for though they had probably found some springs in the hills, these would be altogether insufficient for the wants of so large a force. When they saw the disposition of the Sirdar's troops they did not hesitate for a moment. A force, roughly computed at about six thousand men, of whom some two thousand were riflemen, and the rest spear and swordsmen, dashed forward in a formation something like that of a Zulu impi upon the 1st Brigade, which was at once formed into a square, with the guns about 200 yards to its left rear. The Arabs made three attempts to rush the square; but there was no cover for them in the open plain, and, though in their second charge they succeeded in crushing in for a moment, by sheer weight of numbers, the right front corner, the half-battalion of the 9th Soudanese, which was in reserve, was able to fill the gap and repulse the heavy mass of spearmen. Their signal failure ultimately counselled them prudence. They did not as yet recognise their defeat, but drew off into the broken ground, where they maintained themselves for some time keeping up an incessant galling fire upon our ranks, despite our efforts to dislodge them, and making from time to time dashes in force upon any point in our lines that seemed weak. We had literally to hunt them from cover to cover in this broken ground, and, I fear, suffered severely in the process, as the advantages were with them. At length, however, after three hours' desperate fighting, they drew off to a position behind the first low range of hills, and the brigade advancing poured volley after volley into their retreating numbers; while the artillery shelled their position, with, as we found afterwards, considerable effect. Meanwhile a second body of Arabs in two divisions had made for the river bank, just north of Dabrosa, at a point where, for a distance of some two miles, palm groves and plantations, some hundred yards deep, fringe the bank. While one division of spearmen hurled itself against the 2d Brigade, which had advanced rapidly to meet it, the other gained the plantation, from whose cover a heavy fire was poured both on the 2d Brigade and on Dabrosa village. This success was, however, only temporary. The gunboat *Abu Klea* was able to bring its platform machine gun to bear on the plantation with murderous effect; while, when he had repulsed the division attacking him, which he did with great slaughter, Colonel Wodehouse, commanding the 2d Brigade, detached a regiment to rake the plantation from south to north; before whose fire some thousand Arabs, the remnant of those who had gained this cover, were speedily in hot retreat across the plain. These retreating stragglers the mounted troops now steadily drove southward to the hills.

It was 1 P.M. before the day could be said to be ours. By this time the whole plain was strewn with dead and wounded Arabs, many of them in chain armour, many more in the parti-coloured Mahdi uniform, not a few almost naked. When the Sirdar's forces occupied the first range of hills, we captured no less than thirty-seven standards whose Emirs had presumably perished. All the afternoon deserters came in from the enemy to give themselves up. From some of these men we learned that the force was commanded by Abd-el-Maula himself, and that among the other high commanders were the Emir Ali Wad el Helu, the Emir Kalid Zogal (commandant of Dongola), and Wad Zubehr Rahama, the son of Zubehr, who escaped across the frontier last autumn. Many hundred rifles, swords, spears, and shields still litter the plain, where they are being collected; and in the camp behind the hill were found no fewer than fifty-nine noggaras or war drums.

THE FRANCO-GERMAN CAMPAIGN—RESCUE OF PARIS.

RETREAT OF THE GERMANS.

(From a Correspondent in Paris.)

PARIS, *June* 28.

THE situation is inexplicable. The foe is at the gates. The outposts have been driven in, and it said that two of the forts have been surrendered. All day long a great stream of vehicles, laden with every imaginable article of furniture, and accompanied by crowds of disconsolate citizens, has been pouring into Paris over every available bridge. The Bois de Boulogne is a huge camp, and every tree along the Boulevards serves as shelter to a suburban family. Yet the absence of excitement is extraordinary. There has been a good deal of murmuring at the interference of the Government with the Generals. Divided counsels, it is said, and a refusal to give General de Saussier a free hand, led to the defeats in Belgium. As usual, a mob assembled this morning in front of the Tuileries, crying out for the deposition of the President; and it is reported that a couple of Government clerks were somewhat maltreated. But the demonstration was insignificant, probably the work of German *provocateurs*, and the crowd of roughs and pickpockets dispersed with the utmost rapidity when two squadrons of Gardes Républiques were seen trotting down the Boulevard.

The execution of the seven Anarchist leaders three days ago has had a very salutary effect. I have just had an interview with M. de Freycinet's private secretary. He has become positively bland at the sound of the German cannon, distinctly heard beyond the river. To my reflections on the gravity of the situation he replied, with a smile and a bow, that although New York and Philadelphia were once occupied by the enemy, yet the American Revolution was *un fait accompli*. As we were speaking the President's carriage passed at a trot, and I had a good view of the cool-headed citizen who holds the anxious position of First Magistrate of the Republic. He certainly displayed no symptoms of anxiety, and I fancy the crowd that witnessed his progress found something magnetic in his easy smile. Never in the piping times of peace have I heard such plaudits as followed his equipage.

The same air of quiet confidence characterises all the members of the Government whom I have met to-day. Whether it is justified or not, only the future can reveal; but I may say that, notwithstanding the defeat at Machault, the rapid advance of the Germans on the capital, and the occupation of Rheims, the spirit of the French nation is untamed. My military friends own frankly that at Machault they were fairly beaten by superior numbers. The movement into Belgium, they say, was intended merely as a demonstration, and the commander exceeded his orders in fighting a pitched battle against great odds. As to the capture of Rheims, they preserve a discreet silence; and the report of the annihilation of two divisions near Bar-le-Duc is received with an incredulous smile. Even whilst admitting the fact that many wounded men have been abandoned to the care of the enemy, one of General de Saussier's aides-de-camp shrugged his shoulders, and remarked that they would be none the worse for a short visit to the Rhine. *Nous verrons ce que nous verrons!*

June 29, 6 P.M.

The President's smile seems to have had some reason. The rescue of Paris has been accomplished in as dramatic a fashion as that of Andromeda. General de Negrier is the Perseus. At 2 A.M. the quiet of the summer night was suddenly broken. Above the ceaseless rumble of the carts along the Boulevards were heard the unmistakable sounds of battle, and the eastern horizon was lit up as if by the northern lights. The weird streamers of the electric lanterns in the forts struck quivering through the darkness; and away beyond, the long rattle of musketry rose and fell. Mounting in hot haste, I rode down to the Porte St. Mandé, but could get no further. Very wisely, the road was kept clear for the troops, should they be compelled to retreat, and in any case the long train of ammunition tumbrils and ambulances left but little room for enterprising civilians. The high parapet of the old *enceinte* was thronged with anxious crowds, a black, silent mass, gazing intently into the darkness out beyond. At one time the roar of battle appeared to be coming nearer. It may have been due perhaps to a change in the wind; but the suppressed exclamations and the sudden impulsive movement showed the pent-up excitement of the people. Then there was a lull; and then the muffled roar was heard again, but distinctly further away, and even as we listened, receding in the distance. It was at this moment that a faint echo of trumpets and rolling drums was borne upon the breeze, followed by the far-off sound of a mighty cry, the long shout of triumph of a victorious onset; and a deep sigh of relief burst from the close-packed thousands on the wall. It was not till day had dawned that a staff-officer was seen galloping towards the Porte St. Mandé from the battlefield; and we learned that the garrison of Paris had inflicted a decisive defeat on their over-confident foe, and that last year's experiments in offensive operations by night around the capital had borne their full fruit. As I write, ambulance after ambulance full of wounded, and long columns of German prisoners, dirty, footsore, and begrimed with powder, attest the severity of the fighting and the completeness of the victory.

LATER.

I have had the opportunity of speaking to some of the German prisoners. One of them, a gentleman whom I have often met in Washington and Boston, says the troops were exhausted by the hard work of the previous days, and believing the French were thoroughly cowed, were utterly disconcerted by De Negrier's sudden offensive. He blames the rashness of the leaders in pushing on to Paris with large armies still in the field on either flank of their communications. It appears that before the attack took place news had been received of a great disaster to the covering force of three Corps near Bar-le-Duc, and this was the Medusa's head which paralysed the German power of resistance. 'Oh, for one hour of Von Moltke,' is the universal sentiment amongst the prisoners. Another officer, a Bavarian, was much surprised at the reports of great German successes in the East which have appeared in the English newspapers. He declares that the French movements were merely reconnaissances in force, in two instances pushed too far, and that the Germans suffered very heavily. The number of prisoners taken by the Germans has been very greatly exaggerated; the majority were severely wounded men, and are a great source of trouble to their captors. This officer appears to have little love for the Emperor, scoffs at his 'divine mission,' and hints that Bavaria, at least, is very weary of the Prussian hegemony

. 4 P.M.

The Germans are in full retreat. The force that last night threatened the capital from the west has been heavily defeated by De Negrier. Paris is itself again. A member of the Government tells me that General de Saussier, acting on De Miribel's advice, had resolved from the first to allow the rash offensive of the enemy to have free play; believing that the traditions of 1870 and the terrible strain of a double war on their meagre resources would impel them to make a rush on Paris, in the hope of finishing the war at a single blow. The Emperor seems to have expected much from internal dissensions in France. 'But,' says the Minister, 'when the aristocrats condescended to become Republicans, France became once more a nation. In 1870 we had our Federals and Confederates, our Imperialists and our Radicals. To-day, political differences mean as little as in America.'

ADVANCE OF GENERAL DE GALLIFFET.

SIGHTING THE ENEMY.

(From an American Correspondent with the French Army.)

CHAUMONT, *June* 29, 10 P.M.

AT length the embargo placed on all letters since the 30th of May has been removed, and the correspondents are free to telegraph without restriction as to matter or quantity. Since May the 25th, until ten days ago, General de Galliffet's magnificent army has been quiescent under shelter of the strong camps of Langres, Epinal, and Belfort. Even our cavalry has had little to do beyond sending out numerous officers' patrols, north, east, and west. The General preferred trusting to a strong screen of infantry outposts; and on their side the Germans, though reported to be very strong in the neighbourhood of Bar-le-Duc, have remained inactive

The Great War of 189—

It is surprising with what patience the French soldiery endured this weary time of waiting; but the men have supreme confidence in the hero of Sedan, and their intelligence is of a very high order. However, your Frenchman is a restless being, and discipline was put to a severe test when rumour of a German advance on Paris filtered through the camps. But General de Galliffet, by most judicious orders of the day, exposing the errors of the Germans in advancing without first securing their communications, and enlarging on the strength of the fortifications of the capital, appealed to the soldierly intelligence of the army, and not in vain. Still, the fierce desire of the troops to meet their detested enemies had been curbed almost beyond bounds by the 20th of June, and I scarcely think, strong as the General is, that he would have dared to delay movement for another day.

Long before day had broken on the 20th the march began; and for nine days, over the magnificent roads which run through the rich pastoral country west of the Moselle, the long columns moved past in the blazing summer weather, their faces set northward, and their hearts longing for the battle so long deferred. The splendid marching powers of the French Infantry of to-day, as well as the high-training and experience of the Staff, make the movement of 200,000 men and more than 700 guns a matter of child's play. The marches are long, and the dust stifling; but still order and regularity are the characteristics of the great exodus from the fortresses. The ambulances are empty, and, heavily weighted as they are, the little linesmen in their long blue capotes and wide red trousers swing steadily along, laughing and singing as the sun nears his setting even more cheerily than when the fields on either hand were fresh with the morning dew. Loud are the cheers that greeted the General, active as the youngest subaltern of Hussars in spite of his sixty odd years, as magnificently mounted, he rides slowly past the regiments, with cheery word of greeting and encouragement to his sturdy *fantassins*.

On the morning of yesterday reports came in from the cavalry, riding more than twenty miles to the front, that the Prussians were also advancing; and the same evening came the first presage of the storm: two or three ambulances—full this time—and half-a-dozen captured Uhlans. This sight stilled song and jest: a grim silence fell upon the columns, and an air of fierce determination took the place of the eager excitement which had hitherto lit up those mobile faces. The bivouacs that night were very quiet; the men gathered in little groups round the camp kettles, or sat apart in their shirt-sleeves, assiduously cleaning their rifles.

Late last night, as I was turning into my humble billet, shared by two officers of the Staff, in the Curé's cottage at Maison d'Or, I received a message from the Major commanding a Chasseur battalion, who had for the past three days been moving forward with the cavalry, that he had obtained permission for me to accompany him on the morrow. It was unlikely, so my friends on the Staff informed me, that the armies would come into collision, and if I joined *les petites vitriers* I would have an opportunity of seeing something of the cavalry fighting.

Before daybreak, therefore, I found myself in a tiny village consisting of a church and half-a-dozen farm-houses, with substantial granaries and gardens, and a single cabaret, in company with one of those battalions *d'elité* of the army, the *Chasseurs à pied*, who boast that the cavalry can neither leave them behind nor do without them.

The village stands in the centre of a rolling valley nearly three miles broad, running east and west, with a long ridge to the south and another to the north, dotted with vineyards and potato-patches; but without hedge, or wall, or ditch.

In the tower of the church, where I found a convenient loft and a narrow window, I could see, through the morning mist, little bodies of cavalry well to the front; and behind the village three regiments of Dragoons were standing, dismounted beside their horses. Away to the north one would hear at long intervals a shot or two, and messengers came riding rapidly back to the brigade in rear. One thing struck me as curious; although I was in the midst of the village, scarcely a Chasseur was to be seen; and it was not for some time that I descried blue uniforms lying behind the orchard walls, and now and then a *kepi* was to be seen at the windows looking on to the single broad street.

BRISK CAVALRY ENGAGEMENT.

As the sunbeams gained more power, I saw that the open slopes of the opposite ridge, more than a mile and a half away, were covered with little groups of horsemen, moving steadily forward, and apparently pressing back our scouts. Even the isolated squadrons to the front began to give back at a walk, when by the corner of a wood on the sky-line, a sudden appearance of dark groups of men and horses, with white electric-looking flashes, betokened the advent of a battery. The explosion of the first shells awakes our cavalry brigade to action. A couple of batteries disengage themselves from the mass of horsemen in rear, and from a knoll to the left of the village our guns are soon replying to the enemy's challenge. Shrilly the trumpets sound. The dragoons mount, and with jingling scabbards and tossing plumes trot away to where a deep fold in the ground affords them better cover. This movement is not unobserved by the German scouts; I can see them racing back over the hill, and in a few moments, it seems, a dark mass of horsemen appears against the northern horizon, the serried lances standing out clearly against the cloudless sky. Again the shrill blast of the trumpet, and our eighteen hundred dragoons are moving out to meet the foe. With a rush and rattle the rear regiments take ground to either flank, and the long sabres flash from their scabbards. The hussars are retiring rapidly, away to the left of the guns, and the field is left clear for the shock of the opposing masses. My blood tingles with excitement. The sun glints bravely on the brass helmets of the Frenchmen; the dark blue mass a mile away is gathering pace like the mighty breaker of a stormy sea. The lances drop as if by magic, the long line changes its direction, and then wheels inward. I can see the officers turning in their saddles, far in front of their squadrons, signalling with gleaming swords; a hundred seconds will bring them together, when suddenly, to my horror and disappointment, the French slacken speed, and, before I can realise the fact, have turned rein and are riding past the village as if for their lives. Squadrons to the right, squadrons to the left, and a troop or so clattering madly down the ill-paved street. Far above the crash of iron hoofs and the rush of flying squadrons I can hear the hoarse cry of triumph of the foe. Down they come, heads and lances low, racing in pursuit. A last salvo, which sends a score of horses stumbling in their tracks, breaks for a moment the symmetry of that magnificent line, and hurls an officer helpless beneath the thundering hoofs, and our batteries have limbered up and dash frantically, with gunners plying whip and spur, across the plain.

They are lost, they are lost, so fast follows the foe, riding in furious haste to gather the trophies of the fight. A great cloud of dust rises before them, but I can see the faces of the men as the squadrons diverge to pass the village, and note the laughter and the shouts of those fair-haired troopers with the scales upon their shoulders. Suddenly the leader, riding like Scarlett at Balaclava, twenty lengths in front, leans back in his stirrups, checks his charger in his headlong career, and throws his hand high above his head. The trumpeter beside him raises the trumpet to his lips, but ere the notes ring out they are drowned in a loud roar of musketry. I had forgotten the Chasseurs in the orchards; the Germans had never suspected their presence. The surprise is complete; the disaster overwhelming. Magazine after magazine is unloaded, and thousands of bullets find an easy target in the seething, struggling mass, just now advancing so magnificently in all the pride of order and victory. Round the village the scene is indescribable. The slaughter is terrible, and in a few moments the squadrons that had passed unscathed on either side come flying back in the utmost disorder, pursued on one side by dragoons, on the other by hussars. The valley is covered to right and left with a dense crowd of horsemen, galloping in all the excitement of the flight and the pursuit, whilst the German batteries on the bridge pour shell after shell into the surging crowd, regardless whether their mark is friend or foe. I have little time to reflect on the skill with which the trap had been set and baited. My friend the Commandant calls me from my eyrie, and before I had time even to note the trace of the stirring events I had seen passing before me, the Chasseurs are retreating from the village at a pace which puts my Rosinante to the trot. Very soon we hear the jingle of the cavalry in rear. The dragoons are retiring also, and as I look back across the valley I can see the long screen of scouts falling back slowly across the valley, so still and peaceful but an hour agone, and now strewn with the awful *débris* of the conflict. Such was the first phase of the battle of the 29th of June. '*C'est un apéritif*,' remarks the Commandant.

GREAT VICTORY OF THE FRENCH.

FULL DESCRIPTION OF THE BATTLE.

THE curtain is not long in drawing up for the second act, and on our side at least the actors are ready for their cue. From the crest of the ridge which we have now reached a brilliant scene is visible. A broad expanse of verdant pasture stretches away to the placid river which runs between the willows, past the white houses of the little town. Here and there is a patch of woodland, a few stately poplars, and here and there a vineyard. The white high road, with its leafy avenue of spreading trees, now turned into telegraph poles, runs direct to the bridge. On either side, in squares and oblongs, bright with blue and crimson, with flashing bayonet and brazen helmet, rests an enormous army, and still the never-ending columns of men and guns and waggons are forming up for battle for miles away on every side. On the ridge which hides this huge array from the advancing enemy are three batteries, filling the air with uproar, and attracting volley after volley of Prussian shells. One can hear the shrill whizz of the shrapnel, and turning again to the front, we see that on the slopes below us the cavalry skirmishers, kneeling amongst the climbing vines, are in action all along the line. The Chasseurs have scattered along the crest, but there are no other infantry visible. I cannot believe De Galliffet is napping. Above the town rises a great yellow globe, swaying gracefully with every breath of air, and I know that the General has a penchant for observing his enemy from the vantage-point of the balloon. If he is really poised up there, in the bright morning air, he must see those long sombre lines of skirmishers moving slowly across the plain; those heavier masses doubling rapidly over the opposite crest and moving down the slopes. He must know that there are at least six batteries in action against us, and that there are men bleeding to death beneath the tendrils of the vines.

Still not a sign. A couple of Staff officers stand near those three poplars on the hill; one of our batteries falls back, leaving a gun behind. The cavalry begin to creep further up the hill, but not an infantryman moves. The enemy has halted more than 1200 yards away. They are lying in long rows athwart the valley, and the incessant movement of the rifles, even more than the deafening rattle, tell us that they are pouring in a heavy fusilade. Another battery to the rear, and yet another; horses falling wounded in the traces: and then, as if at a given signal, the long German lines press forward. Their heaviest masses are away over yonder on our left, where that thick wood, with scarped, quarried slopes below, terminates the ridge whereon we stand; and over to the right, where a marshy brook, its stunted willows still shrouded in mist, breaks through the ridge to join the river, we can see shadowy columns moving in the far distance.

Another ten minutes, perhaps five, if the Chasseurs give way, and the enemy will overlook the valley, the town, and the bridges

The Great War of 189—

—the bridges, the most important of all. But even as apprehension gathers it is dispelled. Turn your back for a moment and look to the south. The earth is in motion. Long lines of guns are dashing forward at a gallop, breasting the gentle slope, and driving the dust behind them in swirling clouds.

Long lines of Infantry are already near the crest, and heavy columns are rapidly moving up in rear. The unsuspecting Germans are little more than a thousand paces distant when all along the brow, bare and solitary just now, two hundred field-pieces come into action almost at the same moment.

In a moment more the air is literally shaken by the rush and scream of a hurtling storm of heavy metal; and, lying down in the intervals between the groups of guns, the infantry sweeps the plain with volley after volley. The cavalry has retired behind the hill; the vineyards are no longer tenanted, and the vine leaves, cut by the sheet of bullets, fly in the air as if blown upwards by the wind.

The Prussians stagger beneath the shock. Lines shake and waver; here give back, and there lie still and motionless; columns, though far away, break and dissolve under the shrapnel, and then deploy in haste and confusion; and, above all, the bright sun shines down without a wreath of smoke to sully his radiance, or to hide his target from the rifleman. Vainly the supporting lines of the Prussians are hurried to the front. Impotently the cavalry ride forward. Their guns are already silenced. The squadrons are checked by an inextricable tangle of falling men and horses. The long line of infantry is no longer intact. Men are hastening to the rear, not singly, but in groups. Officers stand out in front for a moment, and then are seen no more save in shapeless huddled forms on the dewy grass. The volleys of the French became more regular and machine-like every moment. A mounted group reaches the hill. It is the General, his Staff beside him, his *fanion* at his side. They are too far off to hear, but I can see De Galliffet pointing to the front, and the infantry are already moving forward, swooping down upon their prey. He must be an

FRENCH CAVALRY CHARGING THE PRUSSIAN INFANTRY.

enemy of more than mortal courage who, decimated and outnumbered, can withstand the swift yet steady onset of these trim, regular lines of blue and red. And look behind—there, in the interval! A long array of tossing heads and nodding plumes. The Cuirassiers of France! Let the infantry shake them; brave horsemen, your time is coming! '*N'oubliez pas Reichshoffen!*' yells a wounded corporal by my side, and the mighty mass breaks into a trot, and across the plain they dash, the horse artillery racing in their wake, whilst *viva* after *viva* speeds their onset. The German cavalry, what is left of it, comes gallantly forward to meet their antagonists, and, if possible, to save their infantry. But it is too late. In a few moments the plain is covered with a broken crowd of soldiers. Groups rallying round their officers are swept away by flying horsemen or serried squadrons; thousands are now struggling for the ridge; in the centre the Cuirassiers are bearing all before them in the frenzy of the charge, and on the flanks the infantry, with rattling volleys, sweep away the *débris* of the battle as leaves before the gale.

Before the French reached the ridge beyond, long after the cavalry had retired to re-form, it appears that they met fresh masses of infantry hurrying forward to the assistance of their comrades; but the impetus of victory was too great to be withstood. The fresh troops became involved in the disaster of their advanced guard, and long ere mid-day De Galliffet was in secure possession of the second ridge, across which at daybreak I had seen the Germans advance.

About the noontide hour both armies seemed, as it were by consent, to allow a breathing space. It was as if some invisible Marshal of the Lists had thrown down his baton. So here, behind the ridge, whilst the blazing sun passed over the meridian, lay the columns of the French. Over against them, in the rolling and open valley, but out of range, were the faint, blue, wavy lines which marked their enemy's position.

It was not till after two o'clock that I saw General de Galliffet —who had been standing alone, looking intently towards the enemy and impatiently beating his foot upon the ground—make a gesture of relief, and turning sharp to his orderly dragoon bid him bring up his horse. At the same moment the German infantry began to move. The artillery had been for some time in action. A perfect hail of shells tore up the level surface of the ridge, and our batteries were one by one retiring. Our present line of infantry is several hundred yards behind the hill, down in the valley, cooking their soup undisturbed by the shrapnel, and only a few are called up now to assist the guns against hostile skirmishers. On come the Prussians, but it is soon evident that the main attack is not against our centre. Away to the left there, where General Jamont, the trusted Commander of the 5th Corps d'Armée, holds watch and ward, the sky is red with dust, and the thunder of the guns and the rattle of musketry is threefold heavier than with us. I can see our troops moving in the valley below, from centre to left, linesmen and guns, hurrying to the point of contact. I am on the point of riding in the same direction, when one of M. de Galliffet's aides-de-camp suggests that I have already a place in the stalls. 'Down below,' he says, pointing to the valley, 'will be played the last agony of Prussia.'

The suspense is terrible. The volleys rise and fall, the roar of the cannon swells and dies way. The minutes drag by on leaden wings. The troops in our front are not advancing, even the Artillery seems lazy this afternoon, and there, even there, where the red dust-clouds hang over a hell of slaughter, the fate of a nation is being decided. It is in vain I endeavour to imitate the imperturbability of the General, our 'lance of iron,' as the soldiers have learned to call him. A messenger or two rides up, and is dismissed. There is not a sign on that impassive countenance. Here is another, galloping at speed, grey with dust, and horse foaming with haste. At last! The General straightens himself up. He raises his hand to his *képi* with the golden leaves, as if he were saluting a superior. Is it France or Fortune!

The Staff, throwing away their cigarettes, are all animation now. Officers and orderlies gallop recklessly down the hill at break-neck speed. There is a stir amongst those sleeping columns below. Men spring to their arms. I can hear the harsh words of command, and note the tricolours with their golden fringes given to the breeze. The long lines ascend the hill. What has happened? The enemy in front is moving to the attack: we shall hold the second ridge as we held the first. But no, it is more than this. This time, as our guns come into action all along the crest, our infantry do not halt beside them. There is no pause now. Straight down the slopes they go, the shells screaming overhead, and the little groups of tirailleurs halting alternately to deliver their biting volleys. Here, sheltered by a friendly poplar, I can look down upon the scene. 'What worthy enemies!' cries a little surgeon who has joined me. 'What a struggle of heroes!' And so it was—while life lasts I shall never forget De Galliffet's charge. Sixty thousand men, line after line, were hurled against the German centre. And how bravely those Germans fought! And now, looking back in cold blood, how needlessly were they butchered! Exactly opposite where I stood, their infantry moved forward with even more than the precision of a parade; in little squads, but shoulder to shoulder, with all the rigidity of a birthday review. I could even see the officers halting and actually correcting the alignment. Needless to say, these living targets were riddled through and through in the very moment of their pedantic folly. In the rear, too, came lines of men, gallantly moving forward to beat of drum, with that extraordinary, high-stepping pace which excites the ridicule of the Transatlantic visitor in Berlin. How the veterans of our Civil War would have scoffed at this slave-driver's discipline! But even the veterans of the Wilderness and Gettysburg would have admired the bravery of those devoted Teutons. At 400 yards from each other the two lines came to a standstill. Very irregular is the front; here the French are giving back, and here the German officers are driving up their stragglers; all are standing, there is no cover on that open plain; the French volleys have dissolved into fierce individual fire, and the masses sway backwards and forwards in that infernal din. Of a sudden, behind me, sounds the blare of trumpets and the roll of many a score of drums. De Galliffet's reserve is coming up to decide the conflict, and as the serried lines crowned the ridge, the Germans, battling fiercely in the valley below, began to break. And then, whilst the setting sun, pouring his red rays athwart the opposing hosts and striking radiance from the golden eagles of the tricolours, sank slowly on that awful Aceldama, the French army moved onward to its triumph. Wild and exulting were the shouts that rent the air; far above the roar of battle and the clang of drum and trumpet pealed the maddening cry for vengeance, and like a tornado—with irresistible strength and order—the young soldiers of the Republic swept down to obliterate the sorrow and the shame of 1870. Not for a moment was the issue in doubt. With all the hereditary courage of their caste, the German officers died in their tracks, disdaining to give back a single foot; but the Cuirassiers were once more let loose, the General himself directing their onslaught, and before darkness fell not a single sound man in the German army but was far upon the road to Metz. Our victory is complete; as I write, the cavalry is still pushing the pursuit.

THE GENERAL SITUATION.

THE LIBERATION OF POLAND.

LONDON.

SINCE the great battles took place which ended in the falling back of the Russian forces, events have followed in that region which have been of the utmost importance, though the mere details from day to day have not been of sufficient interest to chronicle. The Russian army in the field, unable after its severe losses to oppose the far out-numbering forces of its enemies, has adopted its traditional policy. It has retreated into the interior of the country, leaving large garrisons in Warsaw and Ivangorod.

Germany has undertaken the siege of Warsaw, Austria that of Ivangorod. The German and Austrian cavalry, which have now asserted their absolute superiority over the Cossacks, have followed up the retreating Russians far enough to completely separate the Russian forces to the south of the great marsh region which stretches out behind the great fortress of Brest-Litewsk from those in the north. A German army is laying siege to Brest-Litewsk. The single line of railway which connects that fortress across the marsh has been utterly destroyed for an immense distance.

Meantime the two Governments, now in complete command of the open country, have taken a political step which cannot but be received with satisfaction by the civilised world. They have issued a proclamation declaring their intention to erect Poland into a buffer State against the aggressions of Russia, and have pledged themselves not to conclude peace without guaranteeing its independence. The exact borders of the restored kingdom have not been fixed, but it is apparently intended to include Lithuania, and to stretch up to the borders of the marshes.

One important fortress has already fallen. The Germans, taking advantage of the facilities which the rivers and the railways afforded them, have brought up heavy siege artillery, with which they have bombarded the defences of Novo Giorgiewsk. The effect of the cordite shells on parts of the fortifications which had not been adequately prepared to resist them, is described as amazing. These terrible instruments of destruction, now first used in war, are said to have simply swept away the solid defences of the place. The garrison was helpless, and after a most gallant but hopeless resistance surrendered.

It appears to be only a question of time, and not a long time, before the same process is applied to Warsaw. Indeed, the confidence of the Germans in this respect has put an end to what threatened to be an appalling tragedy. On leaving General Hashkoff in command at Warsaw, General Gourko had ordered him to expel the whole civil population of the town. This measure was adopted, not merely because of the notorious sympathies of the inhabitants with the invaders, but because Warsaw has been crowded with such immense numbers of disabled soldiers, and the place had been filled to such an extent by fugitives at the time when it was invested, that it was feared that provisions, on which a large demand had been necessarily made for the army in the field, would not last long. It was a terrible temptation to the Germans to repeat the method of the siege of Metz of 1870, and to throw on the Russians the responsibility for allowing the expelled inhabitants to starve.

Happily, other considerations prevailed. The rapid success at Novo Giorgiewsk, the complete knowledge that the Germans had of the nature of the defences with which they had to deal, the great importance of conciliating the Poles and enlisting them heart and soul in the cause, all contributed to induce the German authorities to receive the fugitives.

But there were forty-eight hours of suspense during which the sufferings of the inhabitants outside the walls, while not yet admitted into the German camp, were terrible, and their agonising fears still worse. The matter had to be referred to the Emperor, now in France. A personal appeal to his humanity by Her Majesty the Queen, most delicately and cautiously worded, but indirectly suggesting how difficult it would be to keep together the great Alliance if anything occurred that outraged the public conscience of Europe and America—and to do him justice, the real humanity of the Emperor himself—finally decided the question.

The wretched inhabitants were not only received, but carefully looked after, and at once dispatched to places safe from the clash of arms. Meantime, enormous numbers of Poles have been enrolled and equipped. Numbers of both officers and men trained in the Russian Army who have surrendered, or made good their escape, together with Polish officers from the Austrian and Prussian Armies serve as an admirable nucleus for enrolment, so that by the time the Russians are ready to attempt any advance against their victorious enemies, a new element of considerable importance will be added to these. A most valuable part of the contingent of trained Polish officers and soldiers was provided by the army which surrendered in Bulgaria. Russia has always pursued the policy of sending her Polish soldiers as far from their homes as possible; the army invading Bulgaria was, therefore, largely made up of these. They have gladly transferred their services on hearing of the coming regeneration of their ancient kingdom.

Meantime, it appears that Russia sees that she has no prospects, for some time to come, of being able to act offensively against the Allied Powers, and that they do not intend to favour her by plunging into Inner-Russia. Stores and transports must be collected in large quantities before the Russians can again advance, and the impoverished condition of the country makes this a very difficult task. As, however, she does not wish to keep her soldiers idle, and is most anxious to score a success somewhere before she asks for peace, which every day is becoming more inevitable for her, she has largely reinforced her army in Asia Minor, which has hitherto been kept inactive by her tremendous necessities in other directions.

Moukhtar Pasha has been falling back slowly and cautiously, as he found the forces increasing in his front. Several English officers are with his army. They speak highly of the efficiency which it has attained, and indignantly deny that any cruelties have been perpetrated by the regular Turkish soldiery, though they speak of the Kurds and Bashi-Bazouks as brutes, whom it is most difficult to keep in any kind of order—men who are as cowardly as they are brutal, and of whom the army would be well rid.

Over the movements of the English Army a dead silence has fallen. All letters whatever, whether of correspondents or others, since the fleet sailed after the Battle of Kosluji, have been stopped.

We have heard, indeed, of some of the fleet, probably cruisers, being off Odessa, and some alarm was recently created at Kertch by what was taken to be a combined expedition against that point. We have, however, as yet heard of no landing. This cannot last for long. We must get some news shortly. We know that immense numbers of vessels with stores, transport, and tools of all sorts have passed Constantinople with sealed orders to be opened only out of sight of land. Ministers are studiously reticent, and appeal to the patriotism of both Houses not to put inconvenient questions. Breathless excitement attends the next move.

Meantime, in France the situation remains nearly as our correspondent left it. The German armies, after their recent disasters, have been falling back and concentrating in the Vosges between the fortresses of Metz and Strasbourg. The French appear to be massing their forces chiefly in the neighbourhood of Belfort, though a large army has approached Metz, which is held by too powerful an army to be ignored. The French are in a state of great exultation and excitement, but considerable disenchantment has taken place as to the Russian alliance. They think that Russia has by no means proved the powerful ally they had expected. It is even no longer treason to say upon the Boulevards that sympathy with Poland was the ancient policy of France. Till the extent of their recent successes began to be popularly realised, it was even suggested that if the Germans would give up Alsace-Lorraine they might have their buffer State against Russian barbarism. Nay, some were not afraid to suggest that Germany might, if she would, create two buffer States on either frontier, a covert hint at the neutralisation of the Reichsland which a few weeks ago was received with silent assent. There can be no doubt also that the German people are becoming very weary of a war which threatens to be of indefinite length on either frontier. The Emperor, too, despite the successes on the Russian side which were not gained under his immediate command, has been not a little disillusioned as to the absolute infallibility of his own military genius.

The Italian forces have been checked by the news of the French successes, and the fear lest the vast forces now available might be turned against them.

Thus everywhere on the Continent it is a moment of temporary lull, though of active preparation for the future.

CAPTURE OF SIERRA LEONE BY THE FRENCH.

THE letter which we publish from our Correspondent who accompanied the troops to India, must be preceded by a few words of explanation as to the circumstances which induced the Government to send a large party of officers and a small reinforcement of men by the Canadian Pacific route. That route for Calcutta is a little longer in point of time than the movement by the Cape. It was recognised from the first that in time of war it would not be desirable to depend upon the Suez Canal route, but it had been fully intended to employ the Cape line. Unfortunately, however, immediately after war was declared by France against us, communication with Sierra Leone was in some way cut. Some time passed before we heard what had happened. Then it appeared that, prior to the declaration of war, the French Governor of Senegal had been warned of the date at which it was intended in France to declare war, and was directed to dispatch from Goree a powerful expedition as quietly and secretly as possible. This, taking advantage of the concentration of the English fleets in the Baltic and Mediterranean, was to sail from Goree with sealed orders to be opened at sea, which directed the commanding Admiral, on a date named, to move straight upon Sierra Leone, and to attack it on the day that the declaration of war was issued in Europe.

It should be noticed, as a question of method and of the facilities presented by steam for such operations, that no great gathering of ships was allowed to attract attention to the preparations in Senegal, and ship after ship arrived, received its equipment, and departed alone, with orders to rendezvous on a given day at a stated point in mid-ocean, fixed by latitude and longitude. In this way, without attracting attention, and without difficulty, the great fleet was collected, and moved off at the time named under the orders of the Admiral and General upon Sierra Leone.

The garrison of Sierra Leone has always been kept at a low

ebb, because of the unhealthiness of the place. It was to have been reinforced in view of war, but this had been postponed. The movement was a complete surprise, and though indignant remonstrances appeared in all the English papers, and in the letter addressed by the Governor of Sierra Leone to the French Commander-in-Chief, the fact remained that Sierra Leone had, for the time being, passed into the hands of the French. Although statements were freely made that such an outrage had never been committed since the beginning of the world, and most English people believed them, there was no difficulty in showing that precedents from the actions of all countries were in favour of the French. However, apart from the merits of that question, the plain fact of the matter was that, with Sierra Leone in the hands of the French, our whole route *viâ* the Cape to India was seriously disturbed.

The French Fleet in Sierra Leone Harbour and based upon it, threatened the whole line between St. Vincent and Ascension, and deprived us of the fortified coaling station which was essential for the supply of steamers along that route. Though no doubt, in the long-run, Sierra Leone must fall to the Power which ultimately secures the command at sea, we could not afford, for some time, to fit out an expedition to retake it. The Government, therefore, wisely decided, after its capture, to employ the Canadian Pacific route for the purposes of communication with India and the East. To Hong-Kong it was already our shortest route. In any case, it was an absolutely safe one. The one great defect in this mode of communication consists in the fact that no first-class steamers at present ply across to Quebec. This, however, was remedied by the Government chartering for the time one of the best Atlantic liners, which easily transported the whole of the force, consisting of about 200 officers and 1000 men, chiefly non-commissioned officers, who were to be sent off to Calcutta.

SIEGE OF HERAT.

EVENTS in India had not developed with any great rapidity—in fact, all those who have studied the question were fully aware that, rapid as has been the approach of Russia towards India, the two Powers are as yet too far distant to be able to come into collision in a single campaign. The first indication of Russian intrigue which reached us was the announcement that the Ameer had been suddenly murdered, and that general anarchy had ensued in Afghanistan. The enormous efforts which Russia is making in other directions appear to have prevented her, so far as we at present know, from attempting several of the routes by which she might cross the mountains into Afghanistan. But an advance was immediately made upon Herat, and the siege of that fortress has been going on for some time. Fortunately two young English officers, Major Craygrove, and Captain Greekill, had been employed on some duty for the Government in the neighbourhood. They immediately threw themselves into Herat, and, inspiring the garrison with the greatest confidence, have been the life and soul of the defence ever since. We hear the most amusing accounts of the mode in which they diversify the rigour of their defence by starting races of all kinds within the place, and by various other forms of sport. On the whole, the Russians seem as yet to have made very little way. The only danger has been lest the English public, excited by the vigour of the defence, should insist upon an expedition being dispatched to Herat. For that we are by no means in a condition as yet. The movement would be a most hazardous one. A force of observation has been assembled at Quetta, and the whole Indian Army is ready to advance at a moment's notice. But it was clearly unadvisable to throw ourselves into the seething cauldron of Afghanistan whilst the tribes were all fighting with one another, and no possible ruler had appeared on whose behalf we could effectually act.

It was under these circumstances that the expedition to

Vladivostock was decided upon, and that the reinforcement of native troops was dispatched to Egypt. It would have been preposterous to make these detachments from the army in India had it not very soon become clear that for the first year of the war, at all events, our position in India must be that of playing a waiting game. We have assured Russia that we shall on no terms make peace as long as she holds a foot of Afghan territory. In view of her failure in Europe, and of the services which we have been able to render to the Central Powers, the zeal of the Russians in the invasion of Afghanistan appears to have materially cooled. They begin to see that whatever successes they may achieve during the course of the campaign, they are likely to have to surrender their conquests at the end of it.

Nevertheless, as the demands of India for reinforcements of officers and non-commissioned officers to fill up the various posts which become necessary when an army is organised for war are very considerable, it has been a great advantage to us to be able to send out these men by the new line. Moreover, it is to a certain extent an experiment which shows how much larger forces could be sent in the event of necessity.

DISPATCH OF TROOPS BY THE CANADIAN PACIFIC RAILWAY TO INDIA.

(From our Special Correspondent.)

S.S. *Teutonic*, QUEBEC, *June* 1.

THIS magnificent steamer has provided us with the most luxurious accommodation, and has landed us here in less than six days since we left England. I am just remaining on board to finish this dispatch to you, and beyond expressing the satisfaction of all on board with the treatment we have received from officers and men, and with the arrangements of the company, I have only one remark of any importance to make. All who have known the inconveniences and delay which have hitherto attended the voyage to Canada agree that it is a disgrace to the Empire that no steamers of the class of the *Teutonic* are available to complete the circle of our connection round the world. I have just been on shore and seen the accommodation which is provided for us by the Canadian Pacific Railway. Nothing can be more perfect than the arrangements for the convenience both of officers and men. If only passengers could start from England and sail here through the splendid scenery of the St. Lawrence up to this

OUR NEW ROUTE TO INDIA: A SLEEPING-CAR ON THE CANADIAN PACIFIC RAILWAY.

quaint old town, and thence pass by this excellent railway, there can be no doubt that travellers, to the East at all events, whether for China, Australia, New Zealand, or even India, would come this way rather than by New York, or any other line. As it is, numbers now cross to New York, join the Canadian Pacific by way of Montreal, and complete their journey in that way to the East. I can only hope, and I express the wishes of all, that no time may be lost in establishing, with the aid of a Government subsidy, a really effective line of steamers from England to Quebec. Here the trains were drawn up by the side of the steamer. The men marched straight into the carriages, the baggage, for the transhipment of which large gangs of men were at hand, was put upon the trains within five hours and fourteen minutes. Precisely at that interval after the steamer had come alongside, the first of the three trains employed steamed out of the station amid the cheers of the crowd which had gathered to see the men off.

It must be remembered that when the party of Marines and Blue-Jackets, who were the pioneers of this line among the military forces, came here in December, they necessarily landed in Halifax. We have, therefore, saved on that expedition three hundred miles of dreary railway travel by the Intercolonial Railway.

VANCOUVER, *June* 5.

We have finished our journey across the continent, and are all as thoroughly content with our railway trip as with our voyage to Quebec. I enclose you several sketches which will show you the accommodation provided for the men, and some of the scenes on the train. What has interested us most, both in what we have seen and what we have heard at the different stations that we have stopped at, is the amazing development which is taking place throughout the whole of this country.

The old Ontario farmers appear to be all on the move farther westwards. Splendid as is that province they appear to prefer to sell off the farms they have made at the best rate they can, and to move on to the rich new lands which are available in the north-west. One hears of men here, who, with their own hands, having three horses with all sorts of improved machinery, but no other assistance, have actually sown a hundred acres of wheat this spring. It is said here that in a very few years this region will be able to supply a surplus grain crop for England equal to the surplus product of the whole of the United States.

The Great War of 189—

We were naturally a good deal interested in making inquiries about the prospects of the great railway itself, which has done so much for Canada and become such an important link between different parts of the Empire. I came over it with the Governor-General's party which went down to British Columbia, soon after the railway was opened. The development of the country itself, of course, is the first thing that strikes me. Green fields of corn and comfortable homesteads as far as the eye can reach, where

TOMMY ATKINS BARGAINING WITH THE INDIANS ON THE CANADIAN PACIFIC RAILWAY.

there was nothing but wild prairie! The trains loaded up with corn of last year's crop are still travelling eastwards to Quebec, because it has not been even yet possible to transport it all, so great is the accumulation. But no less remarkable were the trains travelling westwards which we passed at the several stations in our rapid transit, full of farmers, commercial travellers, and others engaged in the rapidly developing commerce of the country. Great piles of agricultural implements and household stuff going westward showed that even in those parts of the line where the land near the railway has been bought up by speculators, so that cultivation recedes to some distance from it, rapid development is taking place.

The next thing that struck me was the immense improvement that has been steadily effected in the permanent way of the line. Steel bridges substituted for temporary wooden structures, embankments that have taken the place of mere trestles, are visible

OUR NEW ROUTE TO INDIA: RATIONS ON THE CANADIAN PACIFIC RAILWAY.

all along the route; and one sees the work steadily going on. Then gradients have everywhere been eased and curves lessened, so that the traffic facilities have marvellously improved. Of course the improvement is most marked over that part of the line where traffic is heaviest. The great stretch between Ottawa and Port Arthur is now in most excellent condition. The work proceeds steadily westward as the traffic necessities call for it. We are now just about to embark on the *Empress of China*. The

Government had insisted upon two of the Empress steamers being detained at Victoria for fear accommodation should not be sufficient. But, with the adaptations made by the company, the *Empress of China* alone proved ample, and as it was much more convenient to have the whole party together, we are all embarking on her.

CALCUTTA, *June* 29.

We sailed before midnight on the 5th, and have just arrived after a most successful voyage. The only regret of the captain, which was by no means shared by any of us, was that at this time of the year he had no chance of letting us see what a fine seaboat the *Empress of China* is. He boasts that the way she weathered some very bad typhoons last year was splendid. No doubt, from a seaman's point of view, that may be very desirable; but we are quite content to have had a June passage over smooth seas, and with never anything much more than an occasional fresh breeze. The mail is just leaving, and you will know much more than I do of what has been going on out here. I hear the siege of Herat is making little progress, the Russians having had great difficulties in getting up any heavy artillery.

CESSATION OF HOSTILITIES—FRANCE AND GERMANY.

December 31, 1892.

THE Great War has come to an end. The preliminaries of peace have been signed. We have, therefore, now only to record the events in different parts of the world which have brought this about. In the first place, during that lull in the conflict on the Continent which we recorded in our last reports, for many weeks an almost complete silence fell over the centre of Europe. Commercial relations, in their modern sense, were almost entirely suspended.

The German Government, recognising the impossibility of

cutting off the sources of news as long as the telegraphs were used at all, had, for a great emergency, paralysed all the communications of Europe by stopping all telegraphic messages along a broad belt extending from the Vistula to the Rhine, and somewhat beyond those limits. No one knew what was going on; till suddenly the French forces advancing into Alsace-Lorraine became aware that the German Armies in their front had almost doubled their strength.

The Italian Army, warned of the great reinforcement which had taken place, began to show a formidable and renewed activity The English Fleet, completely superior at sea since the victory of Sardinia, vigorously enforced the blockades of the French Ports. The Belgian Government now maintained a rigid line of observation along the whole of its frontier. Similarly Spain exercised a vigilant guardianship over all communications through the Pyrenees. France, isolated, suffering greatly from the enormous disturbance caused by the war, and finding her Generals unable to pursue the successes which had appeared for a moment to attend her arms, was becoming restless and discontented. The statesmen at the head of affairs, by no means anxious to see a successful soldier emerge from the war as their master, far from interfering with the growth of the popular impression that any further success was exceedingly problematical, encouraged it secretly in every way. The Prefects, in fact, had orders to allow no news to circulate which did not tend to discourage further action. Reports of the overwhelming strength with which the Germans had inundated the Reichsland, of the consequent danger of the force at Belfort, were accompanied by suggestions that France had been betrayed by Russia; that the great gathering of German troops against France could not have taken place if Russia had acted with proper vigour on the opposite frontier. It was thrown out, at first covertly, afterwards more and more openly, that the moment was not opportune for France to engage Europe single-handed; that the consequences of any serious disaster might be fatal to France, and that it would be better to be content with the laurels which had already been gained, and which had restored the honour of the French arms. Strasbourg, Metz, and the great fortresses in rear of them, were represented as likely to prove dangerous obstacles to the advance of the French Army. As the Generals were obliged to delay action, this feeling grew, till France on her part was quite in a humour to make peace if it could be concluded on reasonable terms.

The longing for peace in Germany had also become intense. The great increase of the force against France had been secured only by the transfer by rail across Europe of the greater part of the army that had been employed against Russia. For the moment this was a perfectly safe operation; the Russian Army was in no condition to act effectively, and the Austrian Army—with the support of the newly-raised Polish troops, the Roumanian Army, and the Bulgarians, who, having disposed at length of the troubles in Macedonia, were ready to lend effective aid to their allies—was fully competent at least to keep the Russians in check, if and whenever it should again attempt to advance. Nevertheless the consciousness in Germany that virtually her whole forces were engaged against France, and that there was little to spare to resist any movement that might be made by the Russians, kept up a continual feeling of anxiety. There appeared to be every prospect that Russia might be seriously crippled, and prevented from again disturbing the peace of Europe, if peace could now be speedily made. All these considerations were for many months telling upon the two chief opponents in the struggle, during a time when no very exciting events were taking place.

ENGLAND AND RUSSIA.

ADJUSTMENT IN THE EAST.

IN Asia Minor during the same period decisive events had occurred. After all the preparations at Trebizonde and in the neighbourhood were not so purely imaginary as the descent of the English Army on Bulgaria had led us all to suppose. It appears that ever since the beginning of the War a vast number of labourers, under the direction of English engineer officers, had been employed in improving the communications between the neighbourhood of Erzeroum and Trebizonde. Under the protection of Moukhtar Pasha's Army, these preparations had gone on from Erzeroum even during the time when the Black Sea was temporarily abandoned by the English Fleet. As soon as it was possible to do so, landing-stages had been multiplied, and other steps taken to improve the facilities for disembarking at Trebizonde. By the time that the English Army had finished its little campaign in Bulgaria, all these improvements were so far advanced that a light railway had been constructed almost throughout the whole distance, giving the greatest possible facilities for the accumulation of supplies. Huts had been built, and a series of stations arranged for the advance of the English Army in successive bodies as soon as it landed. The landing itself, however, even with all the improvements made, could not be a very rapid operation. Thus it was that, as soon as the surrender of the Russian Army was secured, the portion of the English Army nearest to the coast, and such troops as had arrived from England too late to join in the campaign, were at once dispatched direct to Trebizonde. These were followed by others in regular succession.

The actual disembarkation at Trebizonde occupied about a fortnight, being interrupted for about four days by a very dangerous gale, which obliged the troopers to put to sea. During all that time, however, the movement inland proceeded rapidly, thanks to the arrangements which had been previously made. The English Army advanced by rapid stages towards the neighbourhood of Erzeroum, into a position where it was able to concentrate within half a day's march of the left flank of the position, towards which, in a short time, the Turkish Army slowly and deliberately fell back. The front of the English Army was at right angles to that of the Turkish, and withdrawn from it some four miles, but there was ample telegraphic communication between the two forces. A few Turkish scouts under English officers covered the front of the English. The Russians, in advancing, drove in such of these scouts as they saw. These retired as if upon the Turks. Others, withdrawn behind the features of the ground, were not observed.

The Russians made a mistake not very different from, but much more fatal than, that which they committed in 1877, when they advanced against Moukhtar Pasha, ignoring the force that was threatening the communications of their left wing. In that case Moukhtar had designedly fallen back in order to facilitate the operations against them of the Van force. In the present instance he similarly retired in order to facilitate the aggressive movement of the English Army, of whose presence within the region of operations they were as little aware as they had been in 1877 of the approaching arrival of the Van force. They had much more excuse in the present instance for not knowing of the existence of the English column, both because all its previous doings had been completely concealed from them, while the movements of the Van force in 1877 were known in every intelligence department in Europe, and also because the English Army had only recently and very rapidly arrived at the prepared rendezvous. The Russian Army, therefore, finding Moukhtar Pasha in a position apparently open to attack, and presenting facilities especially for the turning of his left flank, towards which all his dispositions tempted them, committed themselves boldly to a movement in that direction, employing a very large portion of their force in an extended movement round his left. According to an agreement between the Turkish Commander and the English General, the Russian Army was allowed to involve itself for nearly two hours in an apparently very successful attack upon the centre and left of the Turkish position.

All its movements had been well reported, by help of the dirigible balloon which had been captured from the Russians in

Varna. Lord Wolseley was therefore able to determine with some accuracy the right moment for making an attack with his entire strength, first upon the flank and rear of the right wing of the Russians; and when the latter, completely surprised and attacked on all sides, because of the simultaneous advance of the Turks, were broken and thrown into hopeless disorder, he was able by simply advancing his front to drive the fugitives in upon the hitherto untouched centre, which in its turn, assailed in flank by the English Army, and in front by the left wing and centre of the Turkish, was crushed. Thus the left wing was left a helpless prey to the armies which now triumphantly occupied the field.

The English Government, made anxious by the protests which had been directed against a campaign in Asia Minor or the Caucasus, had ordered Lord Wolseley not to remain more than a month on shore unless in the very heat of operations at the time. As the crushing defeat of the Russian Army had left Moukhtar Pasha in absolute command of the whole field of operations as far as Kars, and as it was exceedingly unlikely that, after such a defeat, the Russians would be able, in their exhausted condition, to place another army in the field against him, the Turkish General was well content to carry on the war for himself. The English troops, therefore, were simply placed in healthy quarters until instructions for their future disposition should be received. The immediate object with which England had engaged in the war having been secured by the relief of Bulgaria and the defeat of the Russians in Asia Minor, it was decided to recall the army home. It was considered that a victorious force, easily made up again to 70,000 strong by home reinforcements, might become an important element in assisting the Belgians to bring that additional pressure upon France which might be necessary in order to ensure the acceptance of satisfactory terms of peace.

This further blow in Asia Minor, and the exhausted condition of his country, induced the Czar to make the preliminary proposals for a general peace. It was very soon found, however, that practically Russia was isolated—France was thoroughly disenchanted with the alliance. Russia had attempted too much and too many things at first, and had consequently suffered everywhere. It was evident that, if on the merits of the question either of the two allies was to suffer, it was Russia who would have to pay the piper. The Austrian and German Governments were too deeply pledged to the Poles, and had too much interest in being secure from Russian aggression, not to insist definitely upon the creation of Poland into a buffer State. Though Russia demurred to these terms as long as she could, the unanimity of the allies in insisting upon them, and the secret sympathy with Poland of a large proportion of the French people, obliged her to give way.

THE SERVICES OF ENGLAND.

ENGLAND insisted as a preliminary to all discussion of peace proposals that the Russians should vacate absolutely all the territory of Afghanistan, and retire to the previously deliminated frontier. The services which England had rendered to the Alliance, even as they appear on the surface of the story, were sufficiently considerable. The original purpose of Russia had been to attack Bulgaria. Thanks to the facility with which her fleet had cut the communications of the Russian Army that landed there, and had limited the force which Russia was able to employ, it had fallen to the lot of the English to do what no other army could have done with equal facility, that is, render the necessary assistance to the Bulgarians, occupied as they had been by the Macedonian troubles. The facilities for striking right and left presented by the command of the sea has enabled her to deliver the second deadly blow in combination with the Turkish army in Asia Minor.

But, apart from the enormous general value which England's command of the sea conferred upon the Central Alliance, these were by no means the only or the most important services which

England had directly rendered towards strengthening the land forces of the Continental powers. Up to the time of the battle of Sardinia it would have been impossible for the Italian army to advance against France at all. Her whole coast line, without the defence of the English fleet, would have been at the mercy, not only of the French Fleet, but of an expeditionary force of the French Army; and the Italian Army, in order to be able to meet such an attack wherever it might be made, must be all kept at home. Now, at the critical moment, when Germany was hurrying up every man that she could to the frontier to check the advance of the victorious French, it was precisely the fact that the whole Italian Army was available to join her in moving against France, which created that excess of force that France was not able to resist.

Moreover, it gradually came to be known that, without being aware of it at the time, the English Fleet in the Baltic had conferred another all-important service upon Germany on land as much as at sea. It appeared that the object with which the French and Russian fleets were endeavouring to clear the Baltic of all German men-of-war was twofold. In the first place, if they had succeeded, the Russian Fleet was intended to co-operate with the Russian Army advancing from Kovno in an attack upon the German defences on the Baltic—Memel, Königsberg, and Dantzig. But this was not all. There was a considerable Russian force available at the beginning of the war for which it was impossible to provide transport and supplies towards the German frontier. This had been gathered along the Baltic ports of Russia, with a view to its being transported into Denmark. The Danish Army had been gathered along the fortified frontier of the kingdom, Denmark having declared herself neutral in the struggle. As soon as the Russian force had landed and advanced towards the frontier, the Danish Army would have joined the Russian. At an opportune moment a declaration would have been issued simultaneously by France and Russia, setting forth the wrongs which Germany had inflicted upon Denmark, and declaring that Russia and France were resolved to see justice done her. A French expeditionary force formed of troops which could not, in the blocked condition of the railways (already filled with ample numbers of troops and stores), be transported from west to east of France, had gathered in the western ports. This was to be transported as rapidly as possible to reinforce the Russo-Danish Army. Thus, a large army would have been collected within the frontiers of Denmark, where it would be completely in rear of the general line of German defence along the frontier. It might even threaten, at a time when the German forces were pushed out east and west, to move upon the unguarded capital of Berlin; or at least to break up and destroy railways and telegraphs essential to the forces gathered on the French frontier. All these dangers had been removed by the action of the English Fleet, which, when joining the German in the Baltic, had given command to the Central Allies of the sea communications.

Under these circumstances it was not difficult for the English Government to insist that, as a preliminary to all discussion of peace negotiations, every Russian soldier should evacuate the territories of Afghanistan. If the Indian bazaars had been fluttered by the temporary advance of the Russian Army to Herat, the compensation was ample. The ignominious withdrawal of the Russian Army was not the less effective because it was in exact accordance with the proclamation which had been made at home and in India, at the beginning of the war. Nor did it tell less on the native mind, because two English officers had alone appeared to be directly opposed to the might of Russia; while the whole English Army along the frontier had remained intact, and had not had occasion to put forth its strength.

GENERAL EFFECTS OF THE WAR.

In order to explain our negotiations with France, it is necessary to give an account of the fate of the Australian expedition against New Caledonia. The French, fully aware that the expedition had been tardily sanctioned from home, and forewarned by the noisy preparations which had preceded its departure, had ordered a powerful fleet, gathered from all quarters of the Indian and Pacific Oceans, to rendezvous in the neighbourhood of New Caledonia. The force thus gathered was so superior to any which the colonists could muster that, in order to avoid being simply blown out of the water, the expedition had to beat an ignominious retreat. It was a first point in the negotiations with France for the Home Government to secure arrangements in reference to Caledonia satisfactory to the Australian colonists. Indeed, so far as we were concerned, the restoration of Sierra Leone, and a final and definite settlement of the Newfoundland Question, were all that we had to demand in addition to this settlement of the Colonial question.

In the balanced condition of affairs as between Germany and France, it was obvious that no very material change of frontier was likely to be made. Germany had no disposition to yield any of the Reichsland; France was in no position to demand it. Things on that frontier, therefore, remained very much as they had been, with just this difference, that France, no longer able to count upon the support of a baffled and impoverished Russia, was not likely to become aggressive for many years to come. A general disarmament was discussed, and some steps for reducing the armaments on all sides were actually adopted. But the difficulties in the way of any general agreement were too great to admit of any formal stipulation being recorded in the treaty. The final ratifications have been delayed until quite recently.

Germany has already set to work to put right any weak points in her harness. In England the successes which have attended our arms have glossed over not a few weak points which have been detected in our organisation. The army, it is obvious, will be allowed to lapse again into a condition adapted to mere peace parading, despite the vigorous protests that were addressed by Lord Wolseley at the end of the war to the Government, against the dangers which must attend such a result. The country will continue in the belief that everything is for the best in the best of all possible armies. Prompt reductions in the fleet and army have been insisted on. These steps have prevented the Central Powers from entering into an alliance with us for guaranteeing the peace of Asia and of Europe, for which their experiences of the value of an effective alliance with England had at first made them very anxious. How far the future will justify our omission to secure the peace of the world by taking proper steps to secure it, it is for the experience of future generations to determine. For the moment, England has been once more fortunate in the circumstances under which she entered on the war, in the allies she found in it, and in that increased strength of her navy for which a recent awakening to her dangers had prepared the way. The reserves prepared for her army, despite the most fanatic opposition, have enabled her to place an effective army in the field. Fortunately, the war has not tested her resources beyond that point. One comparatively small, though absolutely great, improvement has been made. Those complaints as to the character of our artillery armament, which were ignored during peace-time, have been enforced by the experience of war. Both the Horse Artillery and Field Artillery are to be armed in accordance with war experience, and not on workshop decisions unconnected with their actual employment and use.

FINIS.

APPENDIX.

SIR CHARLES TUPPER ON IMPERIAL DEFENCE.

IN conversation some months ago with Sir Charles Dilke, he assured me that he considered the suggestion made in the columns of *Black and White* by one of the contributors to the 'Great War of 1892'— that, in the event of an imbroglio with India, we might carry our troops by the American continent—one that was open to much argument. This criticism of Sir Charles Dilke's I mentioned to Sir Charles Tupper.

'Well,' replied this doughty upholder of Imperial Federation, 'let us discuss the whole question, and we will come to Sir Charles's criticism, with which I do not at all agree, later on. I was much impressed by the way in which you fought out your Great War. The case was presented in a very strong light. Should such a contingency ever arise, the Canadian Pacific Railway will furnish a most important service to the Empire in providing a special route to India. As an alternative route to India under the British flag from end to end, and bringing England as it does certainly a fortnight nearer to Yokohama than Suez, it evidently may play a very important part in Imperial policy and defence. As has been stated in your paper, not only does the Canadian Pacific furnish a direct line from Quebec on British territory throughout, but in winter, with the Intercolonial Railway to Quebec, the service is made from ocean to ocean by a complete line. It has already been greatly used by the Admiralty. I do not see any force in Sir Charles Dilke's argument that mercenaries in the States could be engaged to render the line impassable in time of war. Of course we assume we are at peace with the States themselves. We have not only the fact that the line is as capable of being defended against attack as any line here in England would be which might be threatened by dynamiters; but Canada would furnish protection for the line by large bodies of trained militiamen and mounted police in the North-Western Provinces; and there would be the further co-operation of the States in the same direction, just as they came to our aid in the Fenian raids in Canada, when the States heartily seconded

SIR CHARLES TUPPER IN HIS PRIVATE OFFICE IN VICTORIA STREET, WESTMINSTER.

us. England would have the entire force of Canada to help to make the protection of the line as complete as it would be between Liverpool and London. And another point is this: By making a *place d'armes* of Esquimault or Vancouver you could send forward at a few weeks' notice any number of soldiers you required to those two points, and hold them there at a point as near to India as they are now here, *i.e.* within as easy striking distance of India as they are in England going by Suez. And you may always trust to Canadian loyalty in any struggle in which England might be engaged.'

'I am glad to hear that,' said I, 'for when I was in Washington last year I heard much talk of the annexation of Canada by America, and of the pleasure with which the Canadians themselves would receive such a measure.'

Sir Charles shook his head. 'I have said repeatedly,' replied he, 'that there is no annexation party in Canada, and I say so again. I mean that out of the 215 members we send to Parliament not one would be elected if he declared in favour of American annexation. Mr. Goldwin Smith, with all his ability, has laboured for twelve years to convince the people of Canada that it is their inevitable destiny to become part of America. By his pen, with his tongue, and in the press, he has done all he can to bring this to pass; and at his own home, Toronto, a highly respectable and popular man holding Mr. Smith's views was induced to offer himself as a candidate at a local election for the Legislature of Ontario, and out of 9000 votes at the election he only polled 175! No; we are not within even the remotest distance of an American annexation. How mad it would be! You do not know what our connection with England really means to us. Only a short time ago one of the most prominent members of the United States Government said to me, "The confederation of British North America under one Government and the construction of the Canadian Pacific Railway has brought us face to face with a nation."'

'Which leads to another point,' I replied. 'Is there no chance of Canada becoming a nation on her own account?'

'My dear sir,' replied the High Commissioner, 'Canada has *all* to lose and nothing to gain by becoming independent of England. From being a very important part of the mightiest Empire in the world, Canada—or Australia either, for the matter of that—would sink at once, by becoming independent, into a position in which they would become the easy prey of those who desired to subjugate them. I would recommend the strengthening by every practicable means of the bonds that now unite the mother country and the outlying portions of the Empire. I have proposed in a recent article in the *Nineteenth Century* that Australasia and South Africa should be each united under a central Government, as Canada now is, and that these three great British dominions should be represented in London by a leading member of the local Cabinet. You have to take things as they are, not as you might wish them to be. A Parliamentary Federation of the Empire, by forming an Imperial Parliament, in which all these great British possessions should be represented, I regard as utterly impracticable, because it is in antagonism with the constitution of this country, and also with the constitution of all the autonomous Colonies. Therefore I contend that the means of drawing closer the bonds between the Imperial Government and these great possessions must be found in some mode consistent with the constitution of England and the self-government now enjoyed by the Colonies. I come to the conclusion I have suggested, that the representatives of the three great British dependencies, being members of the Local Governments, should be made members of the Imperial Privy Council, and thus be brought into the closest intercourse and communication with Her Majesty's Government here in England, and thus be in a position to give the most hearty and complete co-operation for the defence of the Empire everywhere. Another mode to which I attach great importance, and which is quite practicable, is the adoption of a fiscal policy that would have the effect of placing the Colonies fiscally in a different position as regards their relations to Great Britain from that occupied by foreign countries. Such a policy would lead to the elevation of the Colonies amongst the countries of the world, to their rapid development, and 'to a great expansion of trade between the mother country and them.'

'Ah!' said I, 'doesn't the kernel of the whole question of Imperial Federation lie in this Customs difficulty? If we were entirely a Free Trade empire, there would be little or no difficulty in securing Imperial Federation. The Union of Hearts, it seems to me, must be preceded by a Union of Pockets.'

'Well,' replied Sir Charles, 'there is no reason that I can see why absolute Free Trade should be adopted, and in fact it is impracticable, or any objection taken to the adoption of the same policy pursued by every other country in the world with regard to their Colonies, by which they place their fiscal relations with them on an entirely different basis from that on which their relations with foreign countries stand; thus adding to the strong sentimental tie that binds mother and child, that still stronger tie of mutual self-interest; and the day is not far distant when a very powerful agitation will be promoted by the artisans here in England for **the adoption of the** policy **that** will most expand the trade of England, and promote **the interests of** all who are engaged in the manufactures of this country.'

'Then,' I interjected, 'you thereby make the working-man **the** ultimate Court of Appeal, and he will decide as **to** whether **Imperial Federation** is to become an accomplished fact or **not.'**

Sir Charles said, 'Yes ; **I** believe this policy at no distant day will be **sustained by the operatives.'**

We drifted into other currents of thought, all bearing on the question **how best to** promote **a** true and lasting Federation. I alluded to a remark made to me **some** time since **by a** distinguished Cabinet Minister on the fatal policy, not to say the gross injustice, of pitchforking **any scion** of nobility, **whether** fitted for the post or not, into the vice-regal thrones of the Colonies.

'Well,' replied **Sir Charles,** 'speaking as a Canadian, I can only say we have been **most** fortunate. **The policy which has been pursued** with us of sending out a **Viceroy of Cabinet rank is, I think,** attended with the **greatest** possible **advantages ; first, because it forms a** close connection **between the** Crown **and Canada, and** after the period of service **is over these gentlemen bring their** great **Colonial experience especially to bear here in England in** Parliament, **and at the Council, in a** manner highly conducive **to the** interests **of Canada.** Canada owes much to the high standing and character and the abilities of all her governors since it became a united country.'

'THE GREAT WAR OF 18 —':

AN INTERVIEW WITH THE RIGHT HON. SIR CHARLES DILKE.

BY RAYMOND BLATHWAYT.

No man in England, few even on the Continent, are better qualified than Sir Charles Dilke to judge of the merits or demerits of the other articles which have called forth so much criticism both here and on the Continent. With him these subjects have been a matter of life-long study; to their consideration he has devoted all the energies of a singularly clear and powerful mind. There are **few** men, even in these days when the balance of **education is so much more** even **than it used to** be in the past, who have so thoroughly, and from so scientific a point of view, grasped the great political problems which now confront the thoughtful men in all civilised nations. The splendid potentialities that lie within an energetic and resolute Imperialism; the knitting and welding together of the mother country with her colonies and dependencies, the accurate knowledge and estimation of the means of attack and defence that belong respectively to our own country, and to the great

THE RIGHT HON. SIR CHARLES DILKE.

Continental Powers; these and many other of the great questions, a proper comprehension of which is absolutely essential to every well-trained, well-furnished statesman, have for many years received from Sir Charles Dilke the most careful thought and attention. No English statesmen and few soldiers, even on the Continent, know more of the relative strength and capacity of foreign armies than this quiet student and calm observer in Sloane Street.

Appendix

To no better authority, therefore, could the clever and interesting *brochure* be submitted for judgment and criticism than Sir Charles.

A little older and greyer, a shade more thoughtful and careworn than when I last saw him some few years ago, upon the occasion of some political gathering, when he delivered a speech of much brilliance, and clear, well-defined, consecutive thought, he yet impressed me as he impressed me then, with a sense of wonderful versatility, and a plenitude of knowledge of the subject upon which I had come to talk.

'I feel some little hesitation in replying to your request,' he began, 'but since the Editor is evidently anxious that I should do so, I will endeavour to give you my views as briefly and clearly as I can. Mind you, I don't think it is either an easy or a gracious task to criticise the work of the brilliant staff of experts who have fought this Great War. Any strictures therefore that I may have to offer will deal entirely with generalities, or with political and military considerations; the details of the War seem to me to have been admirably carried out; and nothing else could have been expected, considering who are the men who have had part in it. Then, too, I feel that the Editor was justified, when he wanted to make a war, in making a war which lent itself to literary and dramatic treatment, instead of the war which might be more natural but less picturesque. One of my criticisms also goes to the root of the whole matter, and must necessarily seem a little by the way. It is that we are assured that a Great War 'will probably occur in the immediate future.' I do not think so, and have indeed, during all the alarms of the last seventeen years, been an obstinate believer in the probabilities of peace.'

'In which the writers clearly differ from you, Sir Charles,' I replied; 'I was much struck, however, by the clever manner in which they caused the war to break out in a small, insignificant country like Bulgaria, and then spread like a prairie fire, till the whole world was in a blaze. Do you consider that was a good and probable beginning?'

'Well,' replied Sir Charles, as he leaned forward and began to rapidly sketch out a little map of the Continent, to which he made constant subsequent reference, 'it was, perhaps, more ingenious than either scientific or probable. For my own part, I do not believe that the next great war, when it does come, will arise from events in the Balkan Peninsula. Of course, Russia can cause a war whenever she wishes to do so, but I don't think she does so wish. The writers of this *brochure* state that they have striven to make the imaginary conflict spring from the most likely source of conflicts. They therefore chose Bulgaria, and I think with a good deal of reason from their point of view. But, for all that, Russia has pursued an adventurous and indefensible policy with regard to these States, and however irritating her conduct may have been, she means peace at heart. Therefore it is, I think, they are wrong.'

'It is quite fair then, Sir Charles, that I should ask you where *you* would have applied the match, had you been writing this war?'

'Quite fair,' he replied, with a very genial laugh, as he placed his finger on the Franco-German frontier. 'The most probable cause of a war, which I nevertheless think wholly improbable, will be a frontier incident between Germany and France, exaggerated by the newspapers, and subject to the difficulty, as between two great Powers of equal strength and spirit, of making excuses. It is easy for excuses to be made by one side when there is obvious disparity of strength, and when that side, whether the stronger or the weaker, does not desire to face the risks of war; but, as I have pointed out in an article on the French grand manœuvres of last year, neither side could now make such efforts for peace as were made by the Emperor William I. a few years ago, when frontier incidents of the kind to which I allude occurred.'

'Very good, Sir Charles, your war would obviously have very materially differed from ours; but now, given the causes of ours, what do you think of the strategy supposed?'

'There again,' was the reply of this keen politician, and endeavour as best I might I could not puzzle him for a single moment, 'there again I have a criticism to offer. I cannot see why Russia should attempt a descent near Varna, when a descent near Constantinople would so much better suit her purpose. The garrison of Constantinople is not, numerically speaking, a strong one. It is very deficient in effective field artillery, and its infantry, numbering perhaps 18,000 men, could not make much of a defence, unsupported as they are by a real system of land fortification, against a Russian rush from the Black Sea coast by land, accompanied by another landing on the Asiatic side, and a vigorous naval attack against the Therapia batteries.'

'Talking of Turkey, Sir Charles, should we be certain of her as an ally if France joined Russia, and we supported Germany?'

'By no means,' was his emphatic reply; 'although I grant you that actual temporary circumstances in the Mediterranean would have a great bearing on their attitude, the Turks would look to the possibilities of the moment. If we could terrorise them—yes; if not——' and here my companion smilingly shook his head.

'Was *Black and White* right in sending English troops to Belgium on the outbreak of a Franco-German war?' I next asked.

'I think not,' slowly replied Sir Charles. 'It is not likely that public opinion in England would force the British Government to such a course. And then again,' he continued, 'I think the writers wrong in another important movement. It seems incredible to me that the Russians should expose themselves to the three defeats which they met with in your War. It is much more probable, in my opinion, that when the time comes when they have to fight the battles described, against the Turks near Erzeroum, and against the Austrians on the Galician frontier, they will fight without having the young Emperor William at the same moment in the field against them. They will fight under conditions which will enable them to clear the Black Sea coast of the Turks and the Galician plain of the Austrian forces.'

'And now, Sir Charles, quitting the storied "War of 189—" for a moment, I would like to ask you a question or two as to the character of the warfare of the future, the circumstances under which it will be carried out, the kind of men best suited for it. Smokeless powder will doubtless revolutionise all past methods of attack and defence, don't you think so? Again, who will be the General of the future—the student Moltke or the dashing Skobeleff; the politician, the chemist, or the fighter?'

Sir Charles laughed outright as he replied: 'Rather Moltke than Skobeleff, but not the politician,—and there is no real political soldier in France, for instance,—nor the chemist, nor the man of genius; but the cool-headed man, with plenty of force and of physical strength to stand the five or six days' battles which will be the result of smokeless powder; dash won't go for much. Few realise the changes that will be brought about by this smokeless powder. For instance, the officers will inevitably be picked off. The puzzle to me is how in such cases vast masses of men will be induced to advance without their leaders.'

'And as to the ethical intent of our War?' I queried, mindful of the severe strictures passed by worthy, but ultra-timid old ladies of either sex upon it when its noiseless cannon first disturbed the journalistic peace of Europe.

'Oh,' said Sir Charles, with an easy laugh, 'I cannot see how your articles could do anything but good; certainly they have done no harm—that is, from a moral point of view; but, as regards certain other aspects of their teaching, I am not quite so certain. I am afraid that people will say only, "Here are great experts who give *us* the victory," and will imagine, therefore, whatever you may say, that our state of preparation must be excellent, and our enormous expenditure upon defence not thrown away. It should be borne in mind that you have given us a victory in the Mediterranean by procuring for us an Italian alliance; but that there is, and always must be, a grave risk of our having some day to find ourselves at war with France, or with France and Russia without any European alliance, and on questions which do not interest Continental Powers. Again, the Poland resuscitation is prehistoric. If you leave out the aristocracy and a few townspeople, there is no part of the Russian Empire in which the Russian Government is less unpopular than in Poland, and no Polish force could be collected except one composed of nobles and that small middle-class which really consists of the little nobility. The capture of Sierra Leone by France was capital, for under the present circumstances it would be, of course, inevitable, and it is well that attention has been so ably called to this point, which involves grave risk to the Cape route. I cannot think, however, that the Canadian Pacific route is a very safe one to employ, as our enemies, by spending a little money in sparsely-settled portions of the United States, could easily break up the line by bands of hired raiders. And here my criticisms come to an end. But I would like to say again that in my opinion the War as conceived by your contributors has been admirably carried out. With few exceptions, the consequences flow well and naturally, and in perfect logical sequence from the foundation in facts.'

www.ingramcontent.com/pod-product-compliance
Lightning Source LLC
Chambersburg PA
CBHW030750230426
43667CB00007B/919